AYN RAND
& THE PROPHECY OF ATLAS SHRUGGED

THE COMPLETE DOCUMENTARY INTERVIEWS

Edited with an Introduction
by Director Chris Mortensen

TABLE OF CONTENTS

INTRODUCTION

Like many readers, I discovered Ayn Rand's novels at a young age. In the early 70's, I was living in Chicago, on sabbatical from college, working for a distributor of glass and plastic bottles. The offices and warehouse occupied a converted railroad roundhouse at the end of Canal Street where the Chicago River bends at Wolf Point. Near the opposite bank sat the old Blommer Chocolate factory. In wintertime, at the end of a workday, the delicious aroma of baking chocolate hanging in the chill evening air was nearly enough to make you forget the frigid temperature. It was into this heavy, redolent atmosphere of coal and steel and diesel fuel and chocolate that I commuted each day – on the train, of course. And it was on that train – the Chicago and Northwestern railroad line – that I first read *Atlas Shrugged*.

I had noticed one of the other young guys at the warehouse absolutely glued to a well-thumbed and enormously thick paperback during every coffee and lunch break and asked him about it. Without looking up, he declared it the best book he'd ever read. He was actually reading it for the *second time* – an astonishing revelation, I thought, considering it's size. He promised to loan it to me when he was finished.

It's kind of slow going the first hundred pages or so, he told me as he handed it over. But the story really takes off after 'Wyatt's Torch.'

Yes, it does. Atlas is without doubt a classic page-turner but not in any sense the quickly forgettable 'thrill-ride' that we've come to expect from our novels and movies today. *Atlas Shrugged* offers in abundance what today's literature, film, music and art so often and clearly lack: *resonance.* In his wonderful and insightful book *On Writing*, author Stephen King declares plotting to be hackwork. What he's most after in his story telling is what sticks with the reader afterward – what human truths are uncovered – what Aesop might call the *moral* of the story.

For this nineteen-year-old, reading *Atlas Shrugged* was to slip from a confusing, unjust and contradictory world into an alternative, far simpler, knowable universe where motives were clear, where the dynamic of cause-and-effect was inescapable and where the distinction between heroes and villains was plain.

Like one of the documentary's participants, former CEO of Gillette and Nabisco James Kilts says, "You read a lot of books over the course of a lifetime but you'll never forget you read *Atlas Shrugged.*" Neither have I. Through the course of my life and career in media and entertainment, the truths in *Atlas* stuck with me. The one that has most applied comes from Aristotle by way of Rand: 'A is A' - which to me boils down to: 'if it walks and quacks like a duck, well then...'

But also with time came the understanding that *Atlas* and Rand were not universally admired. That, in fact, when it was first published in 1957, critics and intellectuals almost universally scorned the book, calling its story preposterous and ideas 'simplistic' or even 'fascist.' Through the years - like religion and politics - Rand was a dangerous topic of conversation at social gatherings, merely serving to underscore how fundamental were the issues Rand raised.

When I originally approached the Ayn Rand Institute in 2009, looking for archival support, I told ARI director Yaron Brook I wanted to explore and pursue this line but also in hopes of understanding what was to my mind an even bigger question: Why *is Atlas Shrugged* controversial? Here's a book and a philosophy that celebrate freedom, individualism, achievement, morality, *life itself* and an immigrant author that dared not only articulate but to artfully and painstakingly illustrate the truths that her adopted country's Founding Fathers considered 'self-evident.'

Ayn Rand & the Prophecy of Atlas Shrugged features interviews with educators, journalists, CEO's, authors, biographers, philosophers, Rand associates, et al. Each of them brings deep insight and unique perspective to the subject. The views expressed are entirely their own. They are presented as expressed on camera with little or no editing. In the planning stage I hoped to include others with strong anti-Rand views but ultimately abandoned the idea, as I could see no way to avoid having it devolve into a literary and ideological debate. Even so, I confess to having spent considerable time trying to persuade prominent intellectuals with opposing views to Rand to go on camera and contradict her ideas. Most declined, probably because they were no more interested in appearing in a 'philosophical reality show' than I was in hosting one.

But as I came to understand, they weren't necessary. Because – as the film points out – the *culture* has traditionally provided a formidable antagonist for Rand's ideas. Critics and academics *on all sides of the political spectrum* continue to reject both *Atlas Shrugged* as literature and Rand's ideas as philosophy even as the book continues to sell tens of thousands of copies each year (sales for the last five years approaching three million).

The book's extraordinary and continuing popular success might surprise even Rand. She had come to believe that most people appreciated Atlas and The Fountainhead for the *stories* and failed to fully consider or grasp the philosophical implications they contained. In this way, the author believed she had failed somewhat in completing her mission to change the way America's intellectuals thought.

Through the sixties counter-revolution and the chaotic decades to follow, Rand's ideas found little traction in the mainstream culture. Then came the financial crisis of 2008. In that single year *Atlas Shrugged* sold over two hundred thousand copies – an all time record. The following year over *half a million* books were sold. Perhaps even more surprisingly – you heard the names Ayn Rand and *Atlas Shrugged* popping up in the media and social discourse. It had taken half a century but all of a sudden Rand was news again, talked about, argued about, the subject of Wall Street Journal and NY Times editorials. Finally, thirty years after her death, Rand and her ideas had reached center stage in the public forum.

Why then? Maybe it was the countless new laws and freedoms-limiting regulations Washington churned out in the wake of 9/11. Or maybe because people couldn't see the upside of the foreign conflicts in which their young men and women were sacrificing their futures, bodies and lives. And wasn't it around that time that the government-built Mississippi River Bridge collapsed? Or when Hurricane Katrina destroyed a major American city because incompetent cronies had been left in charge? Or when the housing bubble burst… and the brokerage houses went under….and the banks collapsed….or when the auto industry was nationalized and the stock market crashed and the jobs went away?

Somewhere in there - during that tumultuous first decade of the 21st century - that's when you heard people talking about *Atlas Shrugged.* Because people remembered that events just like these had happened in the book. And how spooky was that?

Ayn Rand said that if you can determine the dominant philosophy of a society you can predict its course. The author conceived Atlas' dire scenario during what most of us consider the most benign and prosperous era in 20th century America: the post war 1940's and 50's. What had she seen back then? How did she imagine where we would be half a century hence? My creative mantra for *Ayn Rand & the Prophecy of Atlas Shrugged* became: 'What did Ayn Rand know and how did she know it?'

I had not considered the prospect of publishing this companion book until filming was complete and I began to read the interview transcripts and recognized an abundance of riches. Virtually every one of the interviews was filled with insight, perspective and personal anecdotes, far more I knew than could ever fit into the finished film. They're assembled here.

Like me, some of the people included here and in the film have had their lives influenced in one way or another by the experience of reading *Atlas Shrugged*. As you'll see, in some cases the novel has inspired entire careers and effected life-changing decisions.

Recent Rand biographers Anne C. Heller and Jennifer Burns, both of whom contributed in such a large part to the documentary are not excerpted here for the sole reason that their perspective and considerable scholarship is represented far more completely in their respective books: Heller's *Ayn Rand & the World She Made* (Anchor Books) and Burns' *Goddess of the Market: Ayn Rand & The American Right* (Oxford University Press). Jeff Britting, archivist at the Ayn Rand Institute, generously lent his time as creative consultant for the documentary. I also encourage you to read Jeff's excellent 2004 biography: *Ayn Rand* (Overlook Press).

From the overwhelmingly positive response to the documentary, it's apparent that there are many, many Atlas-readers out there similarly affected and with their own stories to tell. To all of you, I say: the word is out now. Spread the word.

As for the dire 'prophecy' contained in *Atlas Shrugged*, as prescient as Rand may have been and in spite of increasingly apparent evidence to the contrary, none of our interviewees believes the runaway train is so far down the track that it can't be stopped before it reaches the abyss. But all agree that we need to cut off the fuel now and brake real hard. Because you can definitely see the edge from here.

- Chris Mortensen
  Director/ *Ayn Rand & the Prophecy of Atlas Shrugged*

CHAPTER ONE

CHRISTOPHER CERF

Christopher Cerf is an author, composer-lyricist, voice actor and record and television producer. He is known for his musical contributions to Sesame Street, for co-creating and co-producing the award-winning PBS literacy education television program Between the Lions and for his humorous articles and books. Chris' father, Bennett Cerf was co-founder, publisher and editor at Random House, the publishing house for Atlas Shrugged.

The interview took place in Mr. Cerf's home in Manhattan in the winter of 2010.

How far back do you go with *Atlas Shrugged?*
CHRISTOPHER CERF: Well, really from the beginning, in the late '50s because my dad, Bennet Cerf became Ayn Rand's publisher at Random House.

Did you meet Rand?

CC: Oh yes. She had dinner at our house a few times, even came to stay with us a few times. So it was fun.

Where did you live then?

CC: We lived here in New York City but my dad and mom had a house in Mount Kisco up in Westchester. And so Ayn Rand came and stayed there a weekend or two that I remember very well.

Did you have conversations with her?

CC: Yes. I was just getting ready to go to college at the time and I thought maybe I could have a political argument with her. No way. She would say one of the things that she always said in her book to me. She would just say, young man, examine your premises. (laughs) But she was very, very charming.

Did you find her intimidating?

CC: Oh no, not in appearance. I mean, she could look a little harsh I guess. But she was small. She wasn't a big person. But would sort of glare at you, you know. And she wasn't without humor at all. But she just knew she was right and she knew that she had you. My dad used to say that all the time too, that there was no way he could argue with her. And she would always win. And no matter how prepared he was – because, you know, he wanted to argue against the idea that giving charity to people (laughs) might be one of the most evil ideas of all time. And he would kind of protest that. But she would always have an argument he couldn't answer.

Did he enjoy their association?

CC: He loved her. He, he adored her. And he didn't expect to.

How did your dad come to be associated with Ayn Rand?

CC: An editor named Hiram Haydn brought Ayn Rand to Random House. And my dad at first thought it was an unlikely match because he had published a lot of progressive books. And Ayn Rand was not a progressive. But he thought that it would be cool to publish her, basically. But he didn't think she would pick him. And she grilled him for hours about his politics and everything. But he found that much to his surprise that he liked her tremendously. She was very charming. And when it was all over she picked him and said that he was the only one who gave her honest answers (laughs) among all the publishers. Because he didn't pretend to be more conservative than he was.

Was he actually opposed to the ideas in Atlas?
CC: Actually I think he agreed with a lot of her philosophy and he disagreed violently with other parts of it. The kind of meritocracy part. And I sort of felt the same way politically about it. I don't suffer self-serving bureaucrats very well either. And that's what I've always loved about her philosophy. I think she was a little less generous than I would be (laughs) about helping out people in need. But the part about meritocracy, I think we could all learn from.

I've always heard they had a contentious relationship.
CC: They didn't. They didn't at all. At the end they had an argument that still they were friends after it. But she wrote a book of essays that he didn't want to publish, or he didn't want to publish *one* of the essays. And she wouldn't give in on that. It was an essay in which she tried to compare some of Jack Kennedy's speeches to Hitler's (laughs) speeches. And my father said that he really didn't feel comfortable publishing a comparison of John F. Kennedy and Adolf Hitler (laughs). And she said to him, well you always promised that you wouldn't edit me. And he said, I promised that I wouldn't censor your fiction. But I'm not comfortable publishing this book. And please just take that one essay out. The rest is fine. And she wouldn't do it. But I don't think that they ended up, you know, as anything but friends after that.

3

Was the essay ever published?

CC: Yes. I don't even remember the name, but another publisher published it.

Was it his normal practice to turn down material he disagreed with?

CC: Oh, not at all. I mean, he really believed that publishers should publish good books from any point of view. And I guess on balance he published more liberal books than conservative books. But he published The FBI Story, he published Whittaker Chambers, so he was used to publishing books that he felt were important whether he agreed with them or not.

How did he feel about *Atlas Shrugged*?

CC: He thought that *Atlas Shrugged* was a great story. And he thought before that, that The Fountainhead was a great story. So he looked at her as a novelist as much as a philosopher. And I remember he thought that the speeches in *Atlas Shrugged* slowed it down. He said John Galt says all this stuff 20 times in the book anyway. And it just slows you down. And she wouldn't let him cut a word.

You're talking about John Galt's speech that precedes the book's climax. It runs nearly 60 pages.

CC: Exactly. And he just thought from a novelistic point of view, that it, it wasn't helping the book any. But she wanted to get those speeches in. And he felt people could skip the speeches if they wanted to. I remember when he gave me the book for the first time, he even told me where (laughs) I can skip. But I was a big science fiction fan (laughs) at the time, you know, being in my late teens. And, and the book is kind of science fictiony in a way and I just got completely caught up in the plot.

Can you remember anything about the marketing campaign for Atlas?

CC: My dad had a very imaginative PR campaign for the book. They made little cigarettes with the gold dollar signs on them, like the ones that, that Dagny Taggart and John Galt would pass back and forth. And I thought that was just the neatest thing in the world.

Random House had not published The Fountainhead.

CC: No. I forget who published that. But, but that's what made her famous beforehand. *(Ed. Note: It was Bobbs Merrill in 1943)*

Where was Rand in the writing process when she started shopping for a publisher?

CC: I think she was just finishing it up. But I, I'm not – this is all a long time ago. (laughs) And so, this is 40 years ago or more. So I'm a little vague on some of the details. But as I recall she was just finishing up the final drafts. That's the first I heard of it anyway. And actually there's a funny story that comes out of those early days, though you didn't ask the question. (laughs) When Ayn Rand first came to our house for dinner, I remember my mom was quite nervous about meeting a great intellectual that was known for being confrontational. And she walked in and she said, Phyllis, you don't remember me, but I know you. And my mother said, no, no, that's impossible Ms. Rand. I couldn't possibly have known you, I'd remember.

And Ms. Rand said, oh no, I remember you, but you don't remember. And it turned out my mom was kind of a starlet for a moment when she was in her late teens out in Hollywood. And Ayn Rand was a wardrobe person and actually brought dresses to my mom for some little movie part she had. And somehow she remembered that the whole time. And my mom was astounded that it turned out to be true.

Do you remember your father's expectations for the novel?

CC: Yes, I do. They had high hopes 'cause Fountainhead had been a huge best seller. And they printed 100,000 copies. And at first it got not very good reviews, probably because of the politics of the book as well as its, you know, its readability or whatever else. At first it sold kind of slowly. It did make the bestseller list. But it wasn't selling fast enough to sell out 100,000 copies. And at first my dad was kinda disappointed as I recall. And there was some good natured kidding about that because he had believed in it so firmly when other people didn't think he should publish it. But then over time it began to sell better and better and better and better. And it's still selling today, probably as fast or faster than it ever did. And also of course she's become much more of an icon even than she used to be.

What do you think drove her to write that book at the time she wrote it?

CC: Well, that's a big question. (laughs) Maybe it was the, the cold war to some degree. But, but there had been kind of maybe right before the '40s especially a lot of interest in very far left movements in the country. And then there was McCarthy after that and a huge reaction against it. So that was kind of a polarized time between progressives and I guess conservatives. They probably weren't called that yet. (laughs)

How does that compare to today's political climate?

CC: Now of course I think the dialogue is hugely more polarized than it was then. People – I remember my dad voted for republicans almost as often as he voted for democrats, even though he was a pretty liberal guy. Now it's hard to imagine that would be the case. There's a lot more vehemence on both sides of these issues, I think. But, back then, there was always a lot of talk about whether the unions were destroying business. And the idea that the companies would go on strike is an amazing idea – that the industrialists would go on strike.

She's often described as a radical by politicians on both sides of the aisle.

CC: I'm not an expert on everything she believed. But I completely agree with some of what she says and strongly disagree with other parts. But – take The Fountainhead for instance - if you've worked in TV (laughs) a lot as I have, you can see ideas that you really believe in kind of get watered down and compromised and some of that's fine. But whatever side of me I would call an artist really believes strongly that (laughs) I wanna get my ideas done the way I want them done, especially if I've considered all the other points of view.

Ever think of going on strike to get your point across?

CC: It's pretty extreme. It's pretty extreme. I do believe in compromise. And she obviously doesn't. But I also believe that you shouldn't compromise with idiots (laughs). Or people that are just venally trying to get their own way rather than caring about the project. But obviously the world doesn't completely work with (laughs) with everybody just doing what they think is right.

Did your father Bennett think that way?

CC: My dad agreed with a lot of what she said, certainly with regard to politicians within a company. He didn't have much truck for that. On the other hand he was a very generous guy. He believed in helping people out when they needed help. And he found it unbelievable as I did that there was no place for that in her philosophy at all.

But as a publisher, he regarded Rand as a 'catch'?

CC: Oh, he was thrilled to, to publish it. Her, I mean, he thought she was a great mind - totally brilliant. But also a great storyteller.

That's the part that people forget now because they're so taken, as they should be, with her message. But both The Fountainhead and *Atlas Shrugged* are great, great stories.

Do you think those books have proved 'predictive'?

CC: I do think that there are ways that her philosophy's been borne out, and some other ways where it hasn't been. Take a company like Apple, for example. Would Steve Jobs had been able to do what he's done if everything in that company was a compromise. I don't think so. And that's not the only company I could mention. Bill Gates too. But on the other hand there were excesses too. The bubbles and the greed of Wall Street, or the bank failures were an example. I mean, the bank failures are a perfect example of that philosophy having gone too far.

But then I do a lot of work in education. And some of the fights over the charter schools and how the schools should be run and the teachers unions and seniority and everything, sound like an Ayn Rand novel to me. And boy, I'd take her side mostly on that. Not completely because I think a lot of these schools would take total advantage of teachers if they didn't have some kind of collective bargaining. But the idea that you can't fire a bad teacher in many places is - that's just the kind of problem she was writing about.

Do you remember Rand's reaction to the negative reviews of Atlas?

CC: I remember my father saying, and he's written it too after the fact, that reviewers had it in for her. She wanted my dad to complain to the Times and get another reviewer than the one who did review it. And he said it won't help Ayn, it won't help because they have it in for you for other reasons.

What reasons do you think?

CC: Because her philosophy was so radically to the right of where a lot of academics and reviewers were. Now that shouldn't affect the way you read a novel. I mean, a reviewer shouldn't – they should say, I don't agree with this (laughs) but it's a great book. Whether it's a great book is another matter. I don't remember that her dialogue was the most stunning life like brilliant dialogue that's ever been written. It was a great story, but maybe not a perfectly crafted piece of literary work. But she was hoping that she would sway minds, I guess. And she certainly swayed a lot of them. My dad wrote at the time that he thought that the objectivists were kind of a loony cult. And that she was the powerful leader and they were kind of sycophants. And obviously the movement has become much more potent since then and, and has a lot more credibility than it used to.

What do you think your father's reaction would be to the fact that Atlas today is selling more copies than ever before?

CC: I'll tell you a funny story about that. I was finishing up my senior year at Deerfield Academy up in Massachusetts. And one of my English teachers there was a wonderful guy named, named, Richard Binswanger. He was one of the people who thought my dad was crazy to publish Ayn Rand. And my dad met Richard Binswanger up at Deerfield when he came to visit me. And they started talking about it. And my dad said, I will bet you that it sells 50,000 copies or something by a certain time. And it didn't. So Mr. Binswanger won the bet. And my dad got like 100 copies of *Atlas Shrugged* and he had the middles cut out of them like this. And he put lemons in each one and he sent the whole box up to, to Dick Binswanger as a (laughs) as a joke. I thought it was pretty funny. (laughs) And I kept my copy with a hole in it. But of course in the long run my dad was right.

It was no lemon.

CC: Yeah. That's exactly right. My dad would never have dreamed that 50 years later that it would sell half a million copies a year, which I think it's the number I've heard that it, it's selling now.

That looks like a first edition you're holding.

CC: Well I'm very proud to have this. When the book came out, Ayn Rand inscribed a copy for me and she was rather flattering for someone who had the reputation of being so tough. Let me read it to you. "To Chris Cerf who is one of my best readers and the son of the best publisher in the world. With my sincere appreciation and affection. Ayn Rand. August 27, 1957." So, 53 years ago.

-New York City, February 2011

CHAPTER TWO

REP. JOHN CAMPBELL

John B.T. Campbell III is the U.S. Representative for California's 48th congressional district. Previously he served as a California state senator. An accountant and former auto dealer, Congressman Campbell is a Republican member of the House Budget and Financial Services Committees.

In the fall of 2010, he sat for our interview in his office in the Longworth House Office Building in Washington, D.C.

When did you first read *Atlas Shrugged*?
JOHN CAMPBELL: I read *Atlas Shrugged* and The Fountainhead back in early college which would have been in the early '70s. My mother actually introduced me to Ayn Rand and introduced me

to these books. I was a student at UCLA which even then was not exactly a bastion of conservative or those sorts of ideas or ideals. And it definitely shaped my view of society, of economics, of the world and had an influence on me which persists to this day. I give this book to every intern that works in my office. Since I've been in congress, the gift I've given them is a copy of *Atlas Shrugged.*

Did it clarify anything for you at that age?

JC: One of the things it clarified was the accomplishments of great people, of great inventors. Back on the desk behind me are all kinds of electronic devices. Then there's new medical treatments and drugs and so forth. There's great improvement in automobiles and all kinds of different things. And somebody invented all that stuff. Somebody came up with all those ideas. I didn't do it. I probably couldn't do it. But somebody did. And all those people have made my life better. And they've made everyone's life better. And they've improved our standard of living. And improved our quality of life and extended our lives. And we all actually owe those people.

Not everybody sees it that way.

JC: There are people in society who want to almost condemn those people and say, well they owe us more. They made a lot of money. You know, they're bad people. No, they're not. They made that money by providing a value to society that society appreciated. And why does society appreciate that value? 'Cause it gave us something we didn't have before. That enhanced our lives or our experience.

Do you think people like Rand's heroes exist in the real world?

JC: Absolutely, they exist. (laughs) Absolutely they exist.

Does anyone in particular come to mind?

JC: Yeah. I think people exist out there that are like those characters, but I'd be loathe to pick one or two people in society today and kind of hold them up to that sort of classical standard.

Rand's ideas about individualism, capitalism and freedom are pretty fundamental to America. Why do you think Rand's ideas are considered controversial?

JC: I think that may in part be because she was a controversial person herself. Certainly her manner, her lifestyle – everything she did was not of the mainstream, particularly when you think in the mid 1950s. It wouldn't even be mainstream today for a woman necessarily. But it was really not mainstream in the mid 1950s and prior.

Her ideas were certainly not of the mainstream.

JC: I think sometimes controversy can come when people say things that are known, but no one says them. Something that a lot of people know, but no one before or since has said, that you're kind of afraid to say. And it's just sort of not the right thing to say, but everybody knows it. And it's interesting that we're talking about this book still today, 50 odd years on. And that no one else has done it again. No one else has taken this and done something further with it or expand it in a fictional way, rather than just in a, you know, policy manual, did it in the way of a work of fiction, which I think made it more real.

Do you see it as still controversial?

JC: I've had some of my political opponents write about the fact that I give this book away as to indicate that I'm some kind of, you know, out there person. I'll stand by my (laughs) my understanding and belief in what this book represents. And the truisms that are there. And I will continue to do that because these *are* truisms. This is the way that the world is, the world should be, even if people are loathe to acknowledge it. And I think also whenever something interferes with one's ideology, in a way that is articulate it's sort of like if you can't defeat it on the merits defeat it on some other grounds. And you see that happen in politics. If you can't defeat someone on policy, well then tear them down personally. And that's what you see going on here. Those who believe in the collective, believe in socialism, believe in liberal ideas and don't like what Ayn Rand said, very often attack her. And try and marginalize people who support this.

Do you find that the people who most criticize _Atlas Shrugged_ usually haven't read it?
JC: Oh yeah. No they haven't. (laughs) They haven't read the book. They've just been told, oh, it's a terrible thing that says that, that rich people are great people or something.

What's your take on the 'virtue of selfishness' or with Rand's concept of man as his own moral ideal?
JC: Somewhere in between. I actually often have this argument with people about altruism. One of the places where Ayn Rand and I and many of her other believers step aside is she was an avowed atheist. And I'm not. I am an Evangelical Christian. So that's a place where many of us who are Ayn Rand followers disagree with her personally. But that doesn't change our respect for the ideals presented in the book.

But the concept of altruism is fundamental to Christianity isn't it?
JC: I will often sit down with many of my Christian friends and argue that even someone who does something that appears to be completely selfless, does it because it makes them feel good.

They're doing it by choice, not by obligation.

JC: She said that people do things for themselves always and that may include doing for others because it makes you feel good. I do things for others, and I only do it if it makes me feel good. And I would argue that that's what we do as human beings. The people who want to tear down individualism, objectivism, libertarian, conservative, whatever we wanna call the things that are in this book, will say it is about that selfishness, about greed. And so we have bad words that we can associate with these things. But what they miss is that there's a lot of good in self-interest. Everything from the idea that in society if we first take care of ourselves, then no one else has to take care of us. And that arguably that's our first objective. I want to take care of myself so no one else has to. I'd like to take care of my family so I don't have to impose on others to take care of them, and so they are not a burden on society and others. Is that bad? Is that selfishness? Is that something wrong in society? Not self-interest. But it's actually good for society. That's the message of this book. Don't get trapped in definitions of these terms. Look at how they actually work in society and what they mean. And is it bad that when people go to help others they do it because it makes them feel good? No, what's wrong with that. That's a great motive.

Are you in agreement with those who think we're living in the world of _Atlas Shrugged?_

JC: Socialism, collectivism and dependency tend to grow. I've often said that people who believe in a collective are better at politics than those of us who are individualists. Because they work together as a group by definition. That's what they are. They're together and they believe if we're all this, we must believe this, and therefore we march in this direction. Those of us who are individualists don't do that. So therefore we don't always march in the same direction. So therefore sometimes in political socio-economic contexts we're at a disadvantage to them. And so as those movements begin to get some traction, which one can argue they have in this country in recent time, then this starts to come up.

Do you think that's what Rand was thinking when she began Atlas in the post war years?

JC: Let's think again what the book was about. She was writing when the collectivism started to take over and the dependency started to take over. And so it was prescient in a sense. I don't think she knew when or how. But that the attractiveness of collectivism is out there. You know, from each according to his abilities, to each according to his needs? There is an appeal of that to some people. On a purely kind of intellectual basis there's an appeal there. But the problem is - what Ayn Rand pointed out is that it ignores human psyche. It ignores human nature. It ignores who we are. And therefore it fails in real society. It's wrong and it fails. And so I think she knew somehow that there is that appeal and that at some point it would start to get some traction. And that here was this book to say, don't let it get too much traction, 'cause here's what could happen. And it will hurt the very people who are trying to put the collectivism forward.

How much trouble are we in – ideologically speaking – right now?

JC: Yeah. There's a lot of collectivism out there. There's a lot of statism out there. There's a lot of things that say, if you are a particular ethnic group, if you are from a particular area, if you have a particular religion, if you're a particular whatever, you ought to believe this way and you ought to think this way. And you should do this. There's a lot of dependency culture out there that you are owed this, you are entitled.

Entitlements have become a core issue.

JC: Let's talk about socialized medicine. People say well everyone should have free health care. And I say, okay, how do you do that? Do the doctors do their work for free? Oh, well, no, no, no, you can't do it. Oh, okay, well then who's gonna pay the doctor? Oh, well, you know, whatever. Well, well somebody else should pay the doctor but I shouldn't have to.

This book shows what happens if you go that far. And frankly I think medicine is a perfect example right now of where I think we're in the most trouble going forward. When I was in college, many of the best and brightest people wanted to be doctors. And why do they want to be doctors? They could make a lot of money. And they could play golf on Wednesdays. And, and it was a great deal. And now not so much. And now I know many physicians who have encouraged their children to go into other lines of work. When my kids graduated college, the best and the brightest are in finance they're in entertainment, they're in sports. Not as many going into medicine as did in my day. That's not good for me. I'm 55 years old. (laughs) You know, I need some medical care going forward.

We all do.

JC: That's not good for, for any of us. We need our best and our brightest to go into medicine. But if they don't see the rewards for years of study, for all the risk of malpractice and all that kind of stuff. If they don't see the rewards, they'll go into something else. And that's not good for any of us because we all need good, brilliant, capable, intelligent skilled doctors in the future.

But you have a lot of people saying, if this gets passed in health care, that's – I'm going out of medicine. Or I'm doing this or I'm doing that or whatever. And so that's where the collective is coming in and saying, you all work for us. You all are our slaves. Society's slaves. But what *Atlas Shrugged* is pointing out and Ayn Rand is pointing out, is they don't have to accept that slavery. And if they don't and they won't, we all suffer.

It's amazing how the idea of collectivism as an ideal never seems to go away despite the fact that it's never been shown to work.

JC: There are movements out there and probably will be as long as there is humankind. Dependency sounds attractive and the people who promote it think it's gonna be a wonderful thing. But practice shows it has not been. One of the examples of that was East Germany and West Germany. You know, here were the same people under two completely different forms of government, capitalism and statism. And the East Germans became dependent. And the West Germans prospered. And when Germany was unified and suddenly it was, all right, now you have freedom. Well, but, they always told me what food I was gonna get. They always told me where to live. They always told me this stuff and now I don't know what to do. And they were actually lost for a bit and it's obviously come together quite well, but they were lost for a bit. And I think it shows that, you're not doing those people a favor. You're in fact enslaving them. Dependency is a form of enslaving them.

***Atlas Shrugged* sold half a million copies last year.**

JC: Yeah. You know, when you look at *Atlas Shrugged* and you realize that 50 something years later it's arguably more popular than it was even when it was written, that's simply a testament to the lasting nature of the message. All books are written in a time. And it was. But arguably it was for all time. Because it was about human nature, the human condition and how individuals work, should work, and how society works and should work. And so it lasts. And I think it will be as relevant 50 years from today as it was 50 years ago.

Let's go back to the idea of the book coming true? Do you see that happening?

JC: Those of us who are fans of *Atlas Shrugged* want to keep that from ever happening. (laughs) And that's why the book became so prominent a few years ago again. I can tell you that a lot of what I consider my responsibility as a member of congress is make sure we never do go there. And make sure we never get to the place that the world gets to in *Atlas Shrugged.* So I hope we never do. And I think we won't.

As you know, the politicians in *Atlas Shrugged* were portrayed as villains. Can you pursue a career in public life today and still adhere to Rand's ideals?

JC: Well, remember in *Atlas Shrugged* the reason things go wrong is the politicians are supporting the wrong side of things. So I don't think that there is any contradiction between being in my line of work, between being in politics and the the ideals and principles espoused in the book. I think the politicians in the book went the wrong way but politicians don't have to do that. I can tell you that the power and dignity of the individual and allowing the individual to do what is in their best interest and to keep the fruits of what they have earned it shapes a lot of my thinking.

-Washington, D.C., November 2010

CHAPTER THREE

MICHAEL WALSH

Michael Walsh is an author, media critic and screenwriter. Since 2007, he has written for National Review using the pen name David Kahane as well as another twice-weekly opinion column for the New York Post under his real name. Mr. Walsh's long form work includes novels, espionage thrillers and screenplays and (as David Kahane) the recent biting and often hilarious non-fiction rant: Rules For Radical Conservatives.

The interview was conducted at a Manhattan hotel in the winter of 2011.

As a prolific writer yourself, what is your opinion of Atlas Shrugged as a literary work?

MICHAEL WALSH: I think it's a great philosophical work whether you agree with the philosophy or whether you think the philosophy is hogwash. Is it a great literary work? No. All the criticisms that have been made of it over the years starting when it came out in the '50s, are pretty much true. Their characters are kind of stick figures and, you know, all the princes get to marry the princess and the bad guys are all just irredeemably evil. There's not a lot of character development, in fact, I'd say there's no character development except for Dagny and who she's sleeping with it at any given moment. But the story is, is so big and so cinematic and you remember that Rand was a screenwriter in Hollywood. And while her use of the language isn't particularly adept, she uses it more like a blunt instrument to kind of beat you into submission. All that said, and considering it's over a thousand pages long too, it does hold your attention. And I finished it, which, I think, is always the best thing that one writer can say about another writer's work.

Rand never intended to write such a big novel.

MW: Yeah, it just kept going and Random House published it and they were very excited about it 'cause The Fountainhead had been a kind of surprise break out hit and I don't think they were prepared for the critical reception that it got. But it just slowly did well. And it was a best seller and then it kept building its audience and it's now selling more copies now than it ever sold before. So clearly she was in tune with some part of the national psyche. And sometimes the audience has to come to you and I think that's sort of what happened with *Atlas Shrugged.*

It took half a century for Atlas to see the kind of sales figures it's seeing now.

MW: Yeah, you never know. Mahler once famously said, my time will yet come about his symphonies. And he was right in the sense that it was from the first decade of the 20th century to Leonard Bernstein when the Mahler symphonies really entered the repertoire on a regular basis. I think the audience does have to come to you. You never know when it's gonna happen, and as a writer you hope you find an audience while you're alive. I mean they don't do you much good after you're dead. But it's good for your reputation. Or as somebody once said about Elvis dying, it was a great career move.

Can this current boost in Rand's sales figures be linked to events?

MW: Yes, it's become a big conservative movement book. In fact, I got my copy, at a meeting of Hollywood conservatives. I mean, all three of us each got our, our own souvenir copy. (laughs) Again, it's finding its audience because we're living in a world that in many ways replicates what Rand was writing about. And I think the Tea Party is a good example of that because they're really talking about taxed enough already. And they use words like the looters so some of Rand's vocabulary has now moved into our current political vocabulary.

This is new because through the years neither political side was eager to align itself with Rand. But that's changing, isn't it?

MW: On the left, they generally dismissed Rand. And on the right they sometimes do too rather famously with Whittaker Chambers' review and National Review of this book. But there's a resonance on the right right now that says, society is going out of control. Things seem to be crumbling. We have no money which is indisputable. And that we live in a kind of Randian world of deconstruction and who's going to save us. Now, Rand's theory is sort of the Nietzschean superman comes back in the various guises of Galt and Francisco and Ragnar Danneskjold and the main characters in her book and I think people are kind of looking around to see who's the John Galt. And the whole notion of withdrawing your services as a productive tax-paying member certainly has a fantasy value for people even if it's not entirely realistic. On the other hand, we're looking at places like Illinois that have just raised taxes. And now businesses and people will flee into states that are less taxed, Indiana, Wisconsin, and are in fact making a big pitch. So, a lot of the Randian dialectic is, is going on right now.

We're seeing doctors retiring early as we creep closer to socialized medicine.

MW: Yeah. It's too much for them. I mean we've seen in Britain in the National Health Service, that the notion of the British doctor has practically disappeared so that Britain needs to import its doctors and its nurses from the former colonies. So, Pakistan, India and, and other places that were once part of the British Empire. There's a lot of speculation that that's what will happen here as the native American doctors realize that this isn't worth it - what they've spent, an enormous amount of money to get their education. And now if they're going to be constricted in how much they can make and if the government's telling them that, then they'll withdraw services and do something else. And then we'll have to import doctors. I mean, obviously this is speculation at this point, but we'll have to see how it plays out in the future.

Which way do you think the pendulum is swinging?

MW: Well, I think one thing that's going on is that the Tea Party gets right and which Rand also kind of adumbrates in this book, is the way that our tax structure works. It's not designed to tax wealth, it's designed to tax income. Now this is a progressive era 16th amendment, idea that effectively means that people who already have theirs, don't get taxed on it. So the Kennedys, they already had theirs, they don't get taxed on it. John Kerry married a dead republican senator's widow and took the money, doesn't get taxed on that really, except for what investments cast off. Whereas someone in the lower middle class who strikes it rich, maybe comes up with an invention or writes a best seller or something, is gonna have that money taken away from him immediately by the tax code. So that the tax code effectively functions as a check against the lower orders from migrating up into the upper orders.

It's really quite a vicious thing and I think that's what the Tea Party is reacting to a lot. Perhaps inarticulately and kind of inchoately. But they see that the game is rigged against them. And that accounts for a lot of this anger. And I think vicariously they live through Galt who basically says, okay, the heck with you people, I'm (laughs) gonna go live in this mysterious valley in Colorado with some kind of weird shield over it so you can't see it. And after you've wrecked everything, we'll come back and pick up the pieces.

So the people with 'old money' are in effect pulling the ladder up behind them.

MW: Yeah, well, if it's not a wealth tax, then if you've already got it, you're fine. If you're making it, you're not fine. So that was the structural problem with the tax code during the progressive era, during the Wilson administration. And that's why we have these fair tax, flat tax, national consumption tax, all sorts of ways to ameliorate that. Because right now 50 percent of the people don't pay any income tax at all. And then you're in a kind of de Tocquevillian situation where the party of take becomes bigger than the party of give and that gets us back to Rand, saying the party of take is too big now. And it can't, it's just going to eat itself eventually.

You're talking about Alexis de Tocqueville, the French historian who studied and wrote about America.

MW: Yes. Alexis de Tocqueville.

Ayn Rand said that if you can identify the dominant philosophy of a society you can then predict its future. What do you think is America's dominant philosophy and do you see it changing?

MW: Throughout the 19th century, the dominant philosophy in America was capitalism, unbridled capitalism, robber baron capitalism. As immigrants flooded into the big cities, the disparity of wealth became very obvious. So Jacob Riis wrote the famous book, How the Other Half Lives, meaning the poor half. So he was writing to tell his relatively wealthy New, New York audience what it was like down on the lower east side and other places where the immigrants were coming. The, the progressive era which begins with Woodrow Wilson's election in 1912, begins to kick off an era of social awareness to sort of bring people out of poverty. This became a kind of national obsession. The progressives also were very heavily influenced by the sort of social revolutionary theories coming out of Europe. Marx certainly one of them.

The dominant philosophy which I guess we can characterize as the Protestant ethic, really begins to change. And it changes under two guises. One is the socialistic philosophy that's coming over from Europe. And the other is the dominant American Protestant religious philosophy which says, you know, I am my brother's keeper. We need to do something about the poor and we need *government* to do it. This was the first time that government was looked at as the savior rather than private charities. So, you look at the amendments of the progressive era, very striking. Suddenly we have the income tax, we have the direct election of senators, when instead in the old days they were selected by state legislatures so that they would be effectively representing their states. But then they changed that. The 18th amendment was prohibition of course. And we know how well that worked out. The 19th amendment was women's suffrage. And those were four in a row, bang, bang, bang, that all changed the character of the country and the relationship of the citizen to the state.

So, it's a union of socialist philosophy imported from Europe that has its roots in Protestant Christianity and the Americanized version of the same thing.
MW: So that's all bubbling under the surface. We then have the stock market, you know, the roaring '20s and the stock market

crash and sort of the rise of the great urban gangsters who dominated New York up until about 1935. And then the war. And then during and after the war the Frankfurt School, which was a group of German intellectual neo-Marxists based in Frankfurt, the Institute for Social Research. They came over as refugees and they brought with them their notion that Marxism still can work even though it had never quite got off the ground and the Soviet example was not the best possible example, but on the theoretical level. And they brought that to New York, to Columbia University where the Institute for Social Research sort of started over again.

Ayn Rand had already immigrated by that point, had worked in Hollywood and was now transforming herself into a playwright and novelist.

MW: And Rand coming from Russia, who had seen the Soviet revolution up close - her antenna were very much more sensitive than the average American's, 'cause she had seen what totalitarianism, collectivism, and socialism does to a country and to the soul of the people. So, I think she was way ahead of her time.

So the Progressive Era sees the dominant philosophy switching from capitalism to a social democracy?

MW: Remember, Woodrow Wilson was an intellectual. He was quite a Virginia gentleman. He was sort of the last of the aristocracy. But he clearly wanted to move the country in a different direction. And almost everything the Wilson administration did, certainly speaks to that - taking the Protestant ethic and slightly transforming it.

Moving perceptively to the left.

MW: And the key thing is that it's no longer your personal choice, it's the government's choice. The transition of all these spheres that had been private into public, which begins with Wilson and certainly picks up steam with Roosevelt once he gets to the, the state of the union address in which he talks about the four free-doms that are effectively, an addition to the constitution. It was never adopted of course. But they tell the government what it has to do.

The Constitution didn't do that.

MW: Whereas the *real* constitution tells the government mostly what it *can't* do. And that is really the root of today's political strug-gle. President Obama has said the constitution's a document of negative liberties. That's the way conservatives like it. But the idea that the government must do things, it must give you health care, even though making you buy your own insurance policy. It must do X, Y and Z that's not in the constitution. This is the root of that. And so I think once the Frankfurt School gets here and brings these sort of neo-Marxist ideas and puts them in the academy, by the time I got to college in the '60s, they were well and truly in the academy. Your teachers kind of regurgitated this stuff constantly. And I think the baby boomer generation was raised on this. And it's all now coming to a peak even as we speak.

All right. We've been talking about changes that began near the turn of the century and continued up until and after World War II. Atlas Shrugged was published in 1957, smack in the middle of what many consider a relatively benign and pros-perous era in American history. Do you think that accounts for much of the negative reaction?

MW: We tend to think of the 1950s as sort of Leave It To Beaver, Ozzie and Harriet time, Father Knows Best with a working dad and a stay at home mom and two or three point zero beautiful children. But underneath that in the '50s there's this tremendous bubbling kind of instability that's going on. And it's nowhere more effectively reflected than in Hollywood's B movies from that period. The best movies that came out of Hollywood in the '50s weren't the big A list pictures with the Technicolor and the stars.

It was things like Kiss Me Deadly, the Mickey Spillane novel that was adapted so brilliantly, in 1957, '58. But a whole series of the film noir, all this all starts coming up. It's the dark underbelly of America. Camille Paglia talks about this in Sexual Personae, that when something is suppressed, it goes underground, then it comes up in weird sort of ways.

And when you look at the cinema of the '50s, you can see the destabilizing effects of the philosophical battle that's kind of going on in the country. Remember also the communism party USA was well established in the 1950s. There was a reaction against it, the House Un-American Activities Committee. I remember as a kid, you know, getting the little pamphlets about how evil communism was that they'd hand out in parochial school and we'd all sort of learned about, you know, what a threat to American values of democracy this alien intrusion was. So that's going on. And again, I think that Rand being Russian had seen this movie before, literally. And she was really sending up a warning flag, in her own, you know, kind of prolix and didactic way. That taken to its logical extreme, this is where you could be headed.

Critics weren't exactly receptive to this idea, were they? Even conservatives.

MW: Well, Whittaker Chambers wrote a famous review of *Atlas Shrugged* for National Review for Bill Buckley's magazine in which the most infamous line is 'to a gas chamber go'. Of course, Chambers was a former Communist was involved with the Alger Hiss case. And he felt that Rand had become the thing she loathed. That she was intolerant and, Stalinistic in her approach.

Like the famous scene where the train goes through the tunnel. And then, everything's falling apart and they demand that the train go through the tunnel. And of course it just comes to no good and they asphyxiate everybody and everybody's killed. And she kills off those characters like they all deserved it, you know, to heck with them. So that spirit of intolerance really frosted Whittaker Chambers. And he wrote this famous long essay about what an awful book *Atlas Shrugged* was. And that set off a whole split in the conservatives who kind of liked what Rand was saying about the dangers of totalitarianism. And yet to have the foremost conservative publication in the country in those days, still today, to denounce this book as a kind of moral evil really set off an enormous amount of consternation in the publishing world and in the intellectual world, especially here in New York.

It was certainly a hatchet job, all more scathing perhaps because it was well written.
MW: Well, Whittaker Chambers, who had been involved with calling out Alger Hiss and saying that Hiss was working for the Soviets, later became a senior editor at Time Magazine, where I spent 16 years between 1981 and 1996, '97. And Whittaker Chambers was kind of a legend in Time. He wrote extremely well and I would say having been raised in that tradition near the end of that tradition, that was how you wrote when you wrote for Time. You know, every word had to count 'cause space was always at a premium in the magazine. You looked for metaphor, you looked for the vivid image. And the great Times senior editors, which Chambers was one, all had that ability to bring that out in their writers as well. So Chambers was a very dangerous person to Rand because he, A, had been a communist. And B, could scalpel her to death rather than bludgeon her to death.

That review got a lot of attention and in a way set the tone for the intellectual controversy that would continue to dog the novel.
MW: And it was very interesting that an eleven-hundred page novel and this one review almost began to seem equal adversaries in the field of intellectual combat.

Yet the intellectual brickbats seemed to have little effect on the novel's popularity.

32

MW: Yeah. The split in the reception of *Atlas Shrugged* is very interesting. The intellectuals on both sides of the political divide hated it. The public loved it. And I think it's very interesting that in the '50s people would read a thousand page book, 'cause they didn't have television and they had more free time. And, I think they were probably better educated than the average citizen is today. And they were open to those ideas. Remember this was a time when Time Magazine, where I spent so many happy years, put intellectuals on the cover, put generals on the cover, put captains of industry on the cover. You know, it wasn't all just Britney Spears all the time, the way the magazines have been forced to change now. No, you were expected to be able to read.

And one of the things about Time writing was you were expected to use interesting words that the public would then have to go look up. So Time had a kind of didactic function as well. So you have this split, and Rand's intellectuality appealed to many Americans, in, in addition to the themes of the book. Whereas the intellectual class I think found her a threat again on both sides of the divide. That the left saw her as blowing the whistle on what Stalinism was really like, and what happens to a country when you have a totalitarian system. And the right was threatened by her because it seemed kind of crude and brutal. And in those days especially when Buckley was running National Review, the kind of rapier wit was much more prized than the blunt instrument.

What was Buckley afraid of? Why would he try to destroy her?
MW: National Review in those days as it remains today was largely a Catholic influenced magazine. And Buckley of course was a practicing Roman Catholic. And I think the atheistic undertone which is so pronounced in *Atlas Shrugged* less so in The Fountainhead obviously. But Atlas is really about the rejection of God in favor of the elevation of man to a kind of Nietzschean superman prototype. I think that's really what got Chambers and Buckley angered about this book. That at a time when religion was begin-

ning to start to come under attack, and now it's under attack on all fronts pretty much all the time, especially Christianity. They were very very sensitive to this. And I think that that's one of the reasons why Chambers was sort of unleashed on Rand, to try to – not to stop her, but to really say this is not acceptable philosophy in this part of the conservative movement.

On a strictly literary level, can you put your finger on what made Atlas such a memorable read?

MW: I don't think Rand's book was a challenge to read. I mean, it was a slog in terms of time. But people got it. And clearly it resonated with them. As far as the literary quality, I think The Fountainhead is a much better book. The Ellsworth Toohey character is a greater character than any of them in *Atlas Shrugged*. Howard Roark is a similar John Galt kind of prototype. But it's really not about literary worth. Rand was a screenwriter, so it's about the big scenes, you know, when they discover the magic metal that's gonna conquer the world. And the dinner party scenes, you know, all that wicked banter back and forth. And the train scenes are fantastic. And the view of New York as a kind of crumbling dysfunctional dystopia. These are very vivid things. So that's what we remember about the novel. It's certainly not how she uses the language, 'cause it was a second language and she wasn't a Nabokov who could write in English so beautifully. Or even a Joseph Conrad from the 19th century, again, a writer who had come to English as a second language. But she writes very vivid scenes. And I think that's what draws the reader through the novel. And again, you can criticize for X and Y, but you also have to give it Z in that case, which is she tells a good story, she keeps your attention for 1,100 pages.

The literati certainly did not take her seriously.

MW: I've a couple thoughts about that. There are figures that come throughout history, that are creative artists who gather around them a circle of acolytes. The most prominent example is Wagner in the 19th century in Germany. Wagner was a political revolutionary, was a great lover of other men's wives, was a great moocher who kind of lived off the charity of his rich patrons. And at the same time he's probably one of the two or three greatest geniuses of the 19th century. And he creates a whole new way of looking at – opera is not strong enough a word. He called it the Gesamtkunstwerk, the complete unified work of art. And Wagner left really no significant followers in terms of his influence. You could say Bruckner was perhaps, a follower, although he didn't write vocal music. But Wagner gathered around him a circle of acolytes who referred to him as the master. And it created a kind of quasi-religious cult. Well Rand who comes out of that 19th century romantic tradition just by virtue of when she was born, did exactly the same thing. She had her husband, she had her lover, she had groups of young people who adored her. And I think if she had started out to be a novelist, she turned into a philosopher in part because this circle of acolytes adopted that philosophy. And then they would go out and lecture on objectivity. You know, they took it farther than she did and she kind of became the grand dame of the whole thing. Back in college in the 1960s, Rand was considered more of a philosopher than a literary artist. That objectivism had kind of penetrated. It never quite made it into the academy the way certainly socialism did in the 1960s. But it had a great effect on all of us who were 17, 18, 19. And everyone knew, who is John Galt.

Well, whether she jumped or was pushed into philosophy, it's difficult, in view of current events, to ignore the prescient aspects of Atlas Shrugged or that Rand knew what she was talking about in identifying the 'moochers and looters' in society.

MW: The whole notion of the looters in *Atlas Shrugged* is very interesting. Rand saw two things about communism. One, that it's effectively nihilistic. And two, that it always results in destruction. So in effect the communists get what they want even though that's not what they *say* they want. They're always saying that we're doing this for the people, we're gonna try to make society better. We hear this today with social justice constantly, or economic justice, or X justice, refers to this socialist communism notion of how to reorder society.

I would argue that it masquerades as altruism, although it's altruism forced at the point of a gun. It results in misery. I was lucky to, or perhaps I'm lucky to have spent a good deal of my career behind the iron curtain, starting in 1985 when I went to East Germany for the first time and drove throughout the whole length and breadth of East Germany. I was in the Soviet Union in 1986 when Chernobyl blew up. I was covering Vladimir Horowitz' return to the Soviet Union.

And I've spent a lot of time in the other communist countries. And in fact I left Moscow two weeks before the coup against Gorbachev, which essentially was the end of the Soviet Union. So I got a chance to see the destruction that this philosophy necessarily must wreak when it is put into place. Rand had also seen that. And I think the most effective thing that she does in *Atlas Shrugged* is to point out the looters' crazed passion to destroy. Now, Rand argues that the looters are jealous of the productive class, but that they're inept so that the minute we, the productive class withdraws, the looters move in assuming that everything's gonna continue to run, but it can't run because there's no one that, left to run it. That's a very elitist point of view, and it's considerably out of favor today. But given the track record of the Soviet Union, which I saw many times, and also the ecological destruction in Poland and Czechoslovakia and in East Germany, the grayness of the atmosphere, the misery of the people.

It speaks for itself, doesn't it?

MW: The day that the Austrians and the Hungarians opened the border to the East Germans, I drove down from our home in Munich. We were living in Germany at that time. And I interviewed the people coming over the border in their little tiny Trabants, these horrible cars that the Soviet system produced. And they were crying and they were weeping, they were having a kind of religious experience to be free. I wish that all Americans could have seen that, because that tells you how in a country that's been looted, how their desire for betterment continues to just bubble up inside their breasts. And when they have the opportunity they take advantage of it.

The other thing was the fall of the Berlin wall. I was there for that. I had a sledgehammer in my hand. I knocked out huge chunks of the wall that are now sitting in my study up in rural New England. And to see the holes appear in the wall, and to see the Germans reaching through to touch the VoPos, the Volkspolizei on the other side, to see people getting up on top of the wall and not being afraid of being killed, was an amazing sight. And this would not have happened had those countries not been communist. That communism as Rand points out, cannot succeed. That it must fail because the notion of collectivism is anti-economic. And when that fails, the only way to make it work is to impose it totalitarianism style. And that's what we've seen time and time again. So she's absolutely right about that.

To what do you attribute the current "Rand Renaissance?"
MW: I think because she's resonates for our time. She finally found a time that people can look back at what she wrote and say, oh yes, now I understand what you're talking about. In the 1950s, it really didn't seem like we were being threatened existentially. The country wasn't trillions and trillions of dollars in debt. You didn't have this battle between socialist ideas and hard right ideas. Not to the same extent, certainly in the '50s.

And Rand's vision of a non-functioning dystopia where the unproductive class, as she would have put it, has overtaken the productive class. And the productive class has essentially left the field knowing that destruction will result and then they can come back. That vision doesn't seem as far fetched today as it did in 1957.

Do you think we're living in a 'dystopia?'

MW: Well, dystopia is an interesting concept because at what point do you know that you're in a dystopia. I think every generation says, oh this is the worst it's ever been. And human beings have never faced such turmoil and travail. Kids have never been stupider. You know, we've never seen these rates of illiteracy, blah blah blah. We all like to kind of think that there was a golden age that was just before we were born. And unfortunately we didn't quite get to see it. Therefore, are we in a dystopia now? It's hard to say. I mean, obviously the infrastructure of the United States is not what it was because, you know, for many years we deferred maintenance. New York City went through this in the '70s when deferred maintenance was actually a kind of civic tenet and the city had no money. But if we're seeing New York in the '70s, you know, what I like to call the French Connection New York, writ large across the country, then we're heading towards a dystopia. If we have a budget which we do now in which social services and, and, so called entitlements, take up 40, 50, 60, 70 percent of the budget, which is the way they're heading, that leaves the actual governmental functions almost no money to do what they're supposed to do. And that includes defense. So this battle is raging again intellectually in our time. But if you get the point where all you are doing is keeping everybody alive to do nothing, then I think you've hit the ultimate dystopia. Where you're stealing from one generation to give this generation what. And what do we have to show for it. One of the arguments conservatives make all the time is, yes, the robber barons made a lot of money, yes they did this, let's just stipulate that they were horrendous human beings, which they weren't, but let's stipulate that. They left us railroads, they left us buildings, you know, half of this city, New York, was built by these guys. That money had concrete, reality. And we have something to show for it. The best example of course of the old can do spirit is the Empire State Building. From the time they demolished the Waldorf Astoria which had been on that site, to the time they opened the Empire State Building was something like 16 months. And this was in the depth of the Depression. We now have tied ourselves down with so many regulations, so many lawyers, so many everything, that we can no longer function in a kind of real time way. We got something for our money in the 19th century, however it was made they left behind X. What is the current Wall Street generation, for example, doing? What are they leaving behind? What is the net result of all these transfer payments among generations with social security? Many on the right consider social security a kind of Ponzi scheme, which it is when you actually think about it. Can that continue? If you say it's off the table and it's untouchable and therefore it must continue, what will the end result of that be? That's where a dystopia lies when you can no longer have free will. And I think this ties in with what Rand is saying. If we no longer have the will to stop it, to say we can't go on like this anymore, then we're gonna hit dystopia. And I think that's another reason why *Atlas Shrugged* is so resonant today because the society has lost the will to do anything. It only wants to take.

Who do you hold as more responsible for the brand of 'crony capitalism' we're seeing today – businessmen or politicians? Or does that depend on the side of the aisle you sit on?
MW: One of the cartoons of how government and business, interact on the left is that businessmen are rapacious, soulless republicans who make millions of dollars on the backs of the poor, and don't care about them. That's very well established in popular

imagination. In fact isn't true today. Certainly the Wall Street people tend to vote Democratic, tend to give heavily to democratic and leftist causes.

And this causes a kind of cognitive dysfunction as we look at the relationship between business and government. One of the huge arguments that you always get engaged in when you start to talk about politics, is that on the left national socialism and communism are antithetical. On the right, they're both social-ist movements that fought each other for supremacy and liter-ally fought each other during World War Two. That to those of us on the right, there's nothing conservative about Adolf Hitler and National Socialism which in turn was based on Mussolin-ian fascism. Mussolini came out of the young socialist party in Italy. And he was so radical that they kicked him out of that party and he basically founded his own party - the genius of which was that it brought elements of big business into bed with the gov-ernment. And Rand has contempt for weakling business lead-ers in *Atlas Shrugged.* And I think she might have been think-ing of how it worked both in fascist Italy and national socialist Germany.

The 'aristocracy of pull'?

MW: Business leaders realized that by cozying up to the supreme leader, they would benefit. Now they may have been the ones that the shark ate last. But they could put their competitors out of business if they got into bed with the government. And also put the government into the position of choosing winners and losers. So in Germany for example, Krupp became an ally of the national socialists. I think that kind of is one of the reasons that national socialism and communism, were successfully split by the left because you had all these big businessmen in bed with Hitler and Mussolini.

How did that compare to Russia?

MW: Stalin of course was dealing with a completely different kind of country, it was unindustrialized, it didn't have that business class in it in the first place. They both have the same kind of socialist aims, but they went about it slightly differently. In *Atlas Shrugged*, the weaklings, the people who are the sycophants of Mr. Thompson, the president of the United States are these businessmen. And Rand personalizes them in a way that she does in sort of the unwashed masses. They're all these greedy, grasping, weak men, who just wanna nail their flag to the mast of this good ship government. And they're gonna go down with it in the end. But they don't have the genius or the talent or the drive or the innate decency of her heroes in order to actually serve society properly. But this definitely I think comes from the way that socialism in Western Europe developed in the 1930s and 1940s, and of course came to a smashing end in 1945.

But not before crony capitalism had made inroads into our system.

MW: Remember that Eisenhower in his farewell address warned the country about the military industrial complex. That's really what he was talking about. He was talking about this kind of unholy alliance between two institutions that should be antithetical. If not enemies, they should at least be wary opponents of each other. That the government is there to regulate, not to pick winners and losers. that business is there to compete. Now business actually hates competing, which is why the appeal of fascism and national socialism was so great to those magnates who were on the right side of the issue, however temporarily. Businesses don't like to have to get into the messy business of innovation if they don't have to. So this is a kind of short cut to temporary business success. And that's what Rand is illustrating. And that's what President Eisenhower was warning about when he made that famous remark about the military industrial complex. That you have to watch out when the two things that should be competitive suddenly become one.

Where do you hang the blame for the current economic situation.

MW: Yeah, the financial crisis we're going through today has, been blamed both on the Wall Street aristocracy and the fact that there was too much government regulation. So we get like not enough regulation, too much regulation, too much capitalism, too much socialism. The answer is that it's both. You see in the current administration how many Goldman Sachs figures are in and out of the administration. Wall Street is lampooned as a conservative republican thing. It's anything but. It's, it tends to be much more leftist than we would even suspect. So when they're able to come together as the current administration and Goldman Sachs does, then they have a very effective way of making sure that their profits continue. Remember that when the financial crisis hit, it hit because some of these Wall Street firms were bailed out, and then some of them were allowed to go under. And once they went under, the whole house of cards began to collapse. There's a great anger on the right about the financial crisis because it's felt that it was started by Wall Street and that Wall Street was the only one that survived it. Their profits are great, the Dow's up over 12,000. They haven't really been hurt by it, whereas the Americans whose money was not in the market, but in their houses, have really taken a huge beating. Now, what's interesting to me is that on the left, that's exactly the same way they see it. It's one of the few areas that we are actually in agreement with. I have some very very intelligent liberal friends who blame Wall Street for the crisis. They feel that Wall Street got much too close to the government and was protected by the government and was paid off by the government through the TARP program, and, and these other programs. And that that left us, the citizenry, holding the bag. So it's a very interesting moment in history where the right and the left actually are exactly in the same place with how they feel about it. Now, the right has responded with the Tea Party, let's take the money away from the government. The left has said, you know, there's too much favoritism with Wall Street fat cats. We need it more for the unions and the working people. And funnily they're both kind of saying the same thing. We're just going at it in a different way. The financial crisis seems to be the one thing that's rallied both sides of the political spectrum, the idea that we have a very, very big structural problem and what are we gonna do about it.

So we can postulate that the bigger the government the higher the propensity for corruption?
MW: Right. I think that's the whole point about what Rand's saying - that when the government becomes so powerful, those guys are gonna gravitate to the government to get rid of their adversaries. And they're gonna let the government sort of be the heavy here. It becomes in effect a kind of criminal racket, in which you kick back through legal means and you buy protection. I wrote a novel about the last of the great Irish gangsters in New York, Tammany Hall gangster named Owney Madden. And my researches into the 1920s and 1930s, that's effectively how gangland functioned. And one of the reasons gangland disappeared is that it's kind of moved up, it became legal. You know, all those great sort of street criminals learned how to, behave themselves in a court of law. Their kids became lawyers, and, and their kids became politicians. The Kennedy family are a very good example of this, with old Joe starting out as a bootlegging partner of Owney Madden and then eventually becoming the ambassador to the Court of St. James and his son becoming president of the United States. They were very smart about this and they realized you don't get killed as much and you don't go to jail as much if you moved into the sort of respectable aspect of the rackets.

They graduated to the real big-time.
MW: Well, you're not protecting fruit vendors anymore or newspaper kiosks.

So this is the system that Rand's heroes are struggling against.
MW: Dagny Taggart represents the can-do class. And it's interesting that she's a woman. This is a time when women are not prominent kind of titans of industry in the 1950s. And, I find that very fascinating. She's quite different from Howard Roark in The Fountainhead for example. All she wants to do is keep her railroad running. And one of the through lines of the book is the obstacles that are constantly being put in her way by the government and by other people, to prevent her from getting from A to B. And of course when the bridge gets blown up and the country's been cut in half, you've reached the kind of end game of the transcontinental railroad. Now Rand couldn't foresee the great technological advances that we've had today. And the railroad for her represented sort of the majesty of business, unfettered by government regulation. And again, those robber barons built those railroads without any government regulation. And did they steal the land from the Indians? Yes. And did they run roughshod over people? Yes. And did they do all that? Yes. But you could get from New York to California. And, and in the end, that's kind of what counted at a time when society valued that more than it values sort of snail darters and, and hurt feelings.

Taggart Transcontinental represents America's lifeline.
MW: Well, you can't have a country that's 3,000 miles long and not connect it. One of the reasons the Soviets failed is that you cannot drive from Western Russia to Eastern Russia. There's no road that goes all the way through. Whereas in the United States in the 1950s, Eisenhower built the interstate, highway system, in part to move the military around in case there was an attack on the country.

But also because you have to pull this country together.

So whom do you think Rand would classify as 'moochers' and 'looters' today?

MW: The moochers and the looters in Rand's books are these weak minded, get along, go along people who have lost the capacity for innovation, and who now just *want.* And they'll steal other people's ideas if they can, or even better they'll prevent good ideas from coming to market. I think today, the moochers and looters, as, as Rand would define them, are the people who depend on government for everything. And are not giving, but taking.

And again, she's very much about give and take, and she sees this, the productive class as in the end being forced to give everything to the state. And that's what she saw happen in Russia in her youth. And she didn't want that to happen here. So one of the reasons again that this book has such great resonance for our time, is we're having this very argument at the moment. Is the welfare state too big? Are the people who are totally dependent on government actually helpless? Will they die if we don't give them what they need? That's one thing that the left will say. And the right will say, you don't give a man a fish, you teach a man to fish and then he can get his own fish. So this age-old battle between can and can't, between should and would, is still going on in our country today.

The difficulty of course being, one man's looter is another man's hero?

MW: That's right. However you define looters and moochers, and each side would have its own definition. For the left the looters and moochers would be, you know, the Wall Street tycoons and captains of industry - that's who they define it as.

And the right would define them as trial lawyers and politicians.

MW: As long as this, this fight goes on, the, the, the finger pointing will continue, you know. You're a looter, no, you're a moocher, no, you're – and I think that the genius of *Atlas Shrugged* is in the end the productive class says, well to hell with all you guys, we're gonna go live in Galt's Gulch, and call us when it's over.

-New York City February 2011

CHAPTER FOUR
DR. ANDREW BERNSTEIN

Andrew Bernstein holds a Ph.D. in Philosophy from the Graduate School of the City University of New York. He teaches Philosophy at SUNY Purchase, which selected him "Outstanding Teacher of the Year" in 2004.

He is the author of The Capitalist Manifesto: The Historic, Economic, and Philosophic Case for Laissez-Faire (2005); Objectivism in One Lesson: An Introduction to the Philosophy of Ayn Rand (2008); and Capitalism Unbound: The Incontestable Moral Case for Individual Rights (2010). He has written the Cliffs Notes for three Ayn Rand titles: Anthem, The Fountainhead, and Atlas Shrugged.

Dr. Bernstein's latest book, Capitalist Solutions: A Philosophy of American Moral Dilemmas, is available to pre-order on Amazon.com.

His op-ed essays have been published in The San Francisco Chronicle, The Chicago Tribune, Capitalism Magazine, The Baltimore Sun, The Atlanta Constitution, The Washington Times, The Los Angeles Daily News, The Houston Chronicle and many others.

Regarding his introduction to Ayn Rand, he says: "I was fortunate enough to have a high school teacher who was an Objectivist. He introduced me to her ideas in the spring of 1968. That summer I got all of Ayn Rand's novels and read them. I knew immediately, aged sixteen, that her books and ideas were the most important things in the world. Today, more than 40 years later, I am all the more convinced of it. Her books did not merely change my life–they saved it. "

The interview was conducted in a Manhattan hotel room in the winter of 2011.

Most people think of the post-war era as a relatively booming and prosperous period in American history. Yet those were the years during which Ayn Rand conceived and wrote Atlas Shrugged. And Atlas, we know, depicts a very different view of America – a crumbling nation on the brink of self-destruction. When asked why she offered this dystopian scenario, Rand said: 'to keep it from coming true.' But America - on the surface anyway – seemed a far cry from the world of Atlas Shrugged. What had Rand seen beneath the surface that prompted her dire prediction?

ANDREW BERNSTEIN: What did Ayn Rand see in American culture in the 1950s? Don't forget that she defected from the Soviet Union - she came from this society that was dominated by communists. And she came to the to the United States and found Marxism by the 1950s well entrenched in American universities. It was the dominant philosophy of American universities then, had been since the 1930s, still is today. The 1950s were not quite as blatantly leftist as the New Deal era. But those principles still dominated the democratic party. They were becoming more, increasingly influential in the republican party. So she saw the trend towards statism. She had already seen what, what it did in the Soviet Union and you know, individuals that belonged to the state, millions of people mass murdered. She saw the United States moving in that direction. She was terrified.

How did socialist and communist ideas come to be so entrenched in American universities?

AB: That's a fascinating question of how the evilest people in the world, came to control the American universities. I know that German philosophy dominates modern Western culture. That's Immanuel Kant, George Wilhelm, Frederick Hegel, Karl Marx. And I know that the universities are the conduit of the philosophical ideas to general society. Because everybody who's anybody in a society gets educated in the universities. The politicians, the journalists, the film makers, the book writers, everybody who has, has a cultural voice. Already in the 19th century the leading American families were sending their children to Germany to study, study philosophy and study German culture, which was dominated by the, the, the ideas of Kant, Hegel, Marx.

What were they taught?

AB: The ideas that moral virtue lies in selfless service to others. Politically that means in selfless service to the state. Don't forget communism and national socialism or Nazism were both born in Germany. A lot of American intellectuals went to Germany to study German culture. They came back to the United States, they got university teaching positions, they taught the future teachers. This is late 19th century, turn of the 20th century. By the mid 20th century the students and the children of those American intellectuals who studied in Germany, were dominant in the American universities, were dominant and controlled the public educational system. They controlled most of the private schools. They controlled the democratic party. They controlled Hollywood. They intellectually controlled magazines, newspapers, for the most part with some exceptions. They controlled the intellectual culture. and Ayn Rand saw that very clearly.

Why were westerners so susceptible or ready to accept these ideas?

AB: German philosophy became so dominant in the modern Western world because it's basically just a secularization of Christian ethics and Christianity teaches that virtue lies in selfless service, whether it's to God or other people. They don't mention so much the state, but God or other people. But selfless service, altruism, self-sacrifice, is dominant in religion. And egoism or the pursuit of your own happiness, the pursuit of your own interests, of your own selfish values, is rejected. And so the Germanic philosophy that we're talking about including Marxism basically cashed in on Christianity. It secularized Christianity and now the, the, the dominant being or entity to whom you provide service is no longer God, but now it's the state.

You're saying what we now know as communism or socialism – altruism - has its roots in religion?

AB: Yeah. The modern German philosophy that's so intellectually dominant over the last 200 years is basically a secularization of Christianity. Modern socialism is the direct application of an altruist ethics to political economic questions. 'Cause if you believe that, that virtue or moral goodness lies in selfless service to others - to your family, to friends, to strangers - it has to logically mean at the level of the macrocosm, selfless service to the state. The society as a whole has to be dominant to the individual. The individual provides selfless service to society. And that's the essence of socialism.

But doesn't modern communism preclude religion? Where's the disconnect?

AB: Kant himself was a puritan. Hegel studied for the ministry. He was a Christian, probably a Lutheran, I don't remember for sure. Certainly a Christian. Marx was an atheist. But their intellectual heirs in the 20th and 21st century are overwhelmingly secular, even atheistic. They reject the metaphysics of Christianity. You know, the idea that there's this world and there's a higher spiritual world, higher transcendent world beyond. They reject that world view, that underlying philosophy, but they accept the ethics, the moral code of selfless service. And then the secularists and atheists they simply replace God with the state. And of course that's the essence of communism. They're atheistic.

Why is altruism the dominant philosophy among academics and 'intellectuals'?

AB: Most humanities intellectuals in the United States and, and the western world, are Marxists or socialists. They've simply secularized the religious ethics. They believe that virtue lies in, in selfless service to others. And if you start from that moral premise, and if you're consistent, and most of the intellectuals are gonna be consistent 'cause they're trained, you know, in logic. They're trained to think. So when you start with altruism and you're logically consistent, then socialism is unbeatable as a political economic system.

You can't beat it?

AB: I'm saying logically if you start from altruist premises, and if you're logically consistent, you cannot be led to support capitalism. Logically you must believe in socialism. And here's a, here's a really interesting irony. since they believe in this world. There is no higher world. And since they claim to care about the people and about the poor, you think they, they'd support capitalism. The only system which raises the living standards across the board. And certainly raises the living standards of the poor. And yet they don't. Morality trumps economics.

On their moral code, socialism should work. Even if it doesn't work, it should work. It's good. It's morally good. It's the morally proper system. Even if it doesn't work, people should sacrifice for the state.

What's the saying – the trouble with socialism is that it doesn't work and the problem with capitalism is it does?

AB: Yeah. That's right. But for the common man, it's not a problem. The common man overwhelmingly prefers capitalism because it works. Notice when people get to vote with their feet, when they get to leave these repressive regimes around the world, including Marxist ones, and when they're allowed into the United States - the United States is the overwhelmingly popular destination of immigrants. Whereas the Marxist intellectuals they don't want to live in capitalist America, they want to transform capitalist America into Cuba.

What were Rand's hopes for Atlas Shrugged?

AB: She was hoping to basically bring about cultural renaissance. Ayn Rand wasn't looking to foment political revolution. She wanted to resuscitate American civilization with a new found respect for the mind, this recognition that the mind is the source of all human values. Not manual labor like the Marxists claim. Although manual labor's certainly valuable. But the mind is fundamental. And that the mind requires political economic freedom. And it flourishes under laissez faire capitalism, both logically and historically. And she wanted then as part of the cultural renaissance, as part of the culmination of this cultural renaissance to move the country towards the principle of individual rights and laissez faire capitalism.

What makes Atlas so powerful?

AB: It's the vast integration of literary elements on the, on the grandest possible scale. I mean, it's the story of a man who said he would stop the motor of the world and then he does. He brings the statist socialist regime to its knees. He resuscitates American civilization on, on the basis of a, of a philosophy of reason, egoism, individual rights and capitalism. He transforms the world and he does it while remaining observationally unapparent to the narrators of the story and consequently to the reader. For fully two thirds of the story he's behind the scenes. This is a literary tour de force.

The book is filled with philosophy but it's a page-turner nonetheless, isn't it?

AB: Right. It's not primarily a philosophical manifesto. Ayn Rand was first and foremost a novelist. Her stated goal as a novelist was to project the ideal man. Howard Roark in The Fountainhead, John Galt in *Atlas Shrugged*.

Do you think that's part of the reason that Rand and her philosophy have been disregarded in academia?

AB: Fifty years after publication of *Atlas Shrugged*, almost 30 years after her death, philosophy professors are finally starting to recognize Rand. And they're starting to study objectivism in academic philosophy departments. University of Pittsburgh for example. University of Texas. You know, top 20 philosophy departments. But in the English departments, amongst the English professors and the literary critics, the people who are supposedly expert in the field of literature, they either ignore or revile her. The English professors will literally be the last people to recognize Ayn

Rand's literary genius. That is a sad irony, but it's true. That book sold millions of copies. So the common man tends to love *Atlas Shrugged*. But the English professors pay no attention to Ayn Rand whatever.

Do you think that by traditionally advocating obscure, idiosyncratic or difficult to read literature, that some instructors are engaging in a bit of 'job security'?

AB: Let me give you an example first and then we can see if we can understand it. It was at the turn of the millennium, they did all these, you know, best of the 20th century lists. And it might have been Modern Library - I don't remember - but they did a survey amongst their in house experts, literary critics and English professors of the greatest novels of the 20th century. And they did an online survey amongst, you know, the mass readership. Well, amongst the, the English professors and literary critics James Joyce's *Ulysses* was considered the greatest novel of the 20th century. And *Atlas Shrugged* didn't make the top hundred. Amongst the general readership world wide, *Atlas Shrugged* was considered the great novel of the 20th century, and Joyce's Ulysses didn't make the top hundred. Another example of the vast gulf between the humanities intellectuals and the common man.

That's an awfully wide gulf.

AB: One reason for this is that modern literature has been taken over by the anti-hero mentality. Again, influence of German philosophy, the social determinism of Marx. The idea that the individual is basically a molded plaything of society. Society's all powerful, the individual is helpless. And so when you translate that view into novels and stories about human beings, it has to be a story of anti-heroes, you know, people who are pushed around by their family, they got crazy Jewish mothers, or they're dysfunctional families, or they're victims of the capitalist system.

Ordinary people.

AB: That's Joyce's view of human nature and it makes sense that he would be popular amongst the literary critics and English professors and humanities intellectuals broadly. Whereas Ayn Rand, the hero worshipper resonates with the intelligent layman especially in America which was founded on the principle of individual rights, the efficacy of the individual, the self made man, the self made millionaire, the rags to riches Andrew Carnegie kind of story.

The American Dream alive and well.

AB: Sam Walton did it. Certainly the immigrants to America still have that view. They still love the self made man. They still admire the self made man. Bill Gates drops out of Harvard. Mark Zuckerberg drops out of Harvard. They're self made men. These towering heroes are like Howard Roark who carves out this rational universe in his own life. And John Galt in *Atlas Shrugged* who changes the world. These great stories about great heroes resonate with the intelligent layman.

But the literati tend to write off such characters as 'one-dimensional'

AB: That's right. Ayn Rand's heroes are just alien to the idea that the individual is an efficacious agent – that he can make his own way in the world. It's just foreign to the modern intellectuals. But it goes deeper than that is born in a society, he's raised in a society, he's educated in a society, he's steeped in its mores and its beliefs. Then morally you should serve society. You should serve others. And politically of course that means you should serve the state. So part of the reason the literati hate Ayn Rand is her advocacy of capitalism where they're socialists. But it goes deeper than that - to their view of human nature. This kind of helpless view of the individual as the plaything of the state, as molded by the state, can't make his own way in the world, so socialist welfare state is necessary. Politically he's gotta be taken care of by the state.

Rand takes the opposite view.

AB: In Ayn Rand's view the individual makes his own way. He's morally strong and controls his own life and his own destiny. That idea is just completely alien to the modern intellectuals.

Were Americans naïve or misled as to what was actually going on in Russia in the 30s?

AB: Yeah. They called the 1930s the red decade. You know, FDR's brain trust were basically Marxist. Journalists like Walter Duranty, the New York Times reporter in Moscow. And writers and intellectuals like Lillian Hellman and Dashiell Hammett - and I don't think naive is the word. I don't regard them as naive. I think they were willfully evading the horrific truths of what was happening in, in Stalin's Soviet Union. You know, the purges and the man made famines and the gulags and the 20 million murdered. Walter Duranty we know today who's a Pulitzer Prize winning reporter for the New York Times, he was in the Soviet Union. He saw it. He basically lied in his reporting in the New York Times.

The last I checked, the New York Times, even though he's been exposed as Stalin's boy and a liar for the communists, the New York Times still had him proudly listed on their website as one of their Pulitzer Prize winning reporters.

Was there a concerted effort to bring communism to America?

AB: A lot of the progressive educators for example. John Dewey and George Counts visited the Soviet Union. And they came back wanting to incorporate Soviet – I mean, this would be laughable if it wasn't so evil. They wanted to incorporate Soviet techniques of education, i.e., indoctrination, into the American education system. They wanted to indoctrinate American students with the ethic that you exist for the state. They regarded America as too individualistic. They saw the public schools as encouraging that.

It's interesting and ironic that an immigrant from Soviet Russia winds up perhaps the most uncompromising exponent and champion of America's founding principles.

AB: Yeah. It's interesting. Ayn Rand of course loved the original founding principles of this country. The principle of individual rights, that an individual has a right to his own life and consequently you know, a right to freedom of speech, freedom of religion, and the right to pursue his own happiness and the right to own property. The right of intellectual expression liberates the human mind, which led to all the enormous advances in the United States in science, in the arts, in technology. What a contrast that is with the movement towards Marxism in the 20th and 21st century. That's what Ayn Rand was fighting for and that's what she was fighting against.

And it *is* ironic that the person who saw most clearly the imminent danger was an immigrant to this country. She was not born and, and, and raised here. She didn't grow up in the United States, taking for granted the principle of individual rights and freedoms that most native born Americans do. She was educated under the Soviets. She saw communism first hand. She saw the results of Marxism. And when she came here she saw Marxism dominating the American intellectual culture.

Why do you think Rand's novels have a particular appeal to the young?

AB: Teenagers and college students very often tend to love Ayn Rand's books. I think because when people are young they have hope. They tend to be idealistic that the *good* can and will triumph in the world.

In *Atlas Shrugged*, Ayn Rand shows that the *good* is the *rational* - the free thinking mind. And it's by means of the mind, by means of being good that mankind flourishes. It creates all these values, whether it's growing food or writing novels or curing diseases. And that the evil is the irrational, is the rejection of the mind. And the evil is impotent. If you reject the mind, you're rejecting mankind's survival instrument. It's like birds rejecting its wings. If he rejects his wings, he can't survive, he's gonna die. For mankind to reject the mind, he's gonna die. And so Ayn Rand shows the power of the good, the impotence of the evil, only the good can create flourishing life. All the evil can do is destroy.

That's clearly illustrated in her novels and especially in Atlas Shrugged.

AB: And so to the young who are hopeful and idealistic, they believe, they wanna see the good triumph. Nobody has explained that or validated it the way Ayn Rand has in *Atlas Shrugged*. That's why they tend to love *Atlas Shrugged*.

Atlas Shrugged is about the consequences of rejecting the mind, isn't it?

AB: Well, there's many ways to reject the mind. Religion is one. you know, where you subordinate reason to faith. In the dark ages, the fifth to the ninth centuries where the Catholic church was culturally and politically dominant, they burned heretics at the stake, they burned free thinkers at the stake, they burned the best minds at the stake, and burned books. The, the necessary result was the Dark Age. Now, statism including modern secular statism under the communists for example, that Ayn Rand fled from, they also they suppress the mind.

Because the mind fosters dissent.

AB: Whether it's Stalin in the Soviet Union, or Mao in China, or Pol Pot in Cambodia. They executed the intellectuals, the teachers, the professors, they burnt, they burned books. North Korea, you know, is exhibit A. They're desperately poor. The Soviet Union collapsed despite billions and billions of dollars of aid in various forms from the United States and other capitalist nations.

Where in our culture do you get this rejection of the mind – of rationality?

AB: There's simply what I think of as the Oprah Winfrey school of philosophy. There's the always somebody on one of those daytime TV shows - they'll say, oh, just trust your heart. You know, just follow your heart. As if your emotions were infallibly self certifiably correct in the determining what's right for you or what's true for you. You don't have to think about it. You don't have to examine it.

You don't see objectivism taught in universities. Is it considered a 'real philosophy'?

AB: Absolutely. It's in my judgment the wisdom of the ages that philosophers have searched for, for the last 2,500 years. And although they've ignored Ayn Rand for the most part for 50 years now, they're finally starting to recognize her. There's an Ayn Rand society in the American Philosophical Association, the professional organization of American philosophers.

Objectivism is actually making inroads in academia?

AB: Whether they agree or disagree is irrelevant. They're starting to recognize that objectivism is a systematic body of thought in metaphysics, the theory of reality. In epistemology, the theory of knowledge. In metaphysics, the theory of human nature. In ethics, the theory of right and wrong. In politics, you know, theory of what's a good society is. And in aesthetics, you know, the theory of art. Across the board objectivism is an integrated rational philosophy. It's innovative, it's original, it's revolutionary, it's brilliant. And above all, it's true.

How did Rand's philosophy come to be equated with Nietzsche or even fascism?

AB: To consider Ayn Rand a fascist is ridiculous. A lot of Marxists have, have called her a fascist. And I've heard conservatives label her as a communist. Just at the political level, fascism is a totalitarian state. The individual is nothing, the state is everything, the individual exists to serve the state. It's an intellectual blood brother of communism. Ayn Rand's an unremitting individualist. She's the polar opposite. She's the antithesis of fascism. She stands for the inalienable rights of the individual, laissez faire capitalism. If you want to criticize Ayn Rand, fine, it's a free country. But to label her a fascist or communist, that's intellectually dishonest. They want to disagree with individual rights and laissez faire capitalism, they are free to do so. But attack her for what she stood for, not for something that was polar opposite to what she stood for.

On the other hand, do you see her ideas being appropriated or misrepresented by groups with whom she would not have supported or chosen to associate?
AB: Yeah, some of the libertarian types are anarchists. I mean, they believe in no government. And to Ayn Rand that ridiculous. And she's right. I mean just in the last hundred years the country's been militarily threatened by the Nazis, the Soviets and the Islamists. Now if we don't have a government, how are we gonna defend ourselves against these totalitarians? That's just one proper function of a government.

Rand called Libertarians 'hippies of the right.' You know, that they were hippies who had some understanding of economics. They understood that capitalism worked and that socialism didn't. But basically as a friend of mine once put it, objectivists defend capitalism because they support individual rights. Libertarians defend capitalism 'cause they want to do drugs. There's a certain amount of truth to that. They're subjectivists, they're emotionalists, they go with their feelings, they're not men of the mind.

Why are we seeing a resurgence of interest in Rand now?
AB: Yeah, there is a renaissance in interest but I think we need to see the back story here because Ayn Rand was never unpopular. She was always a popular writer amongst the intelligent laymen.

Her books have always sold well. They've sold millions of copies for years. Remember, in The Fountainhead, Ayn Rand wrote about this underground stream of support for the hero Howard Roark. There was always this underground stream of support, interest in Ayn Rand and objectivism. It's becoming mainstream in the last 20 years.

Do you remember the 1991 readers survey that called Atlas one of the most influential books of all time?

AB: The bible was, was number one. But *Atlas Shrugged* was number two. 1991, that's only 34 years after its publication. It was already, as early as 1991, it was already the second most important second most influential book in the country, second only to the bible, which although a ridiculous book, has had something of a head start on on *Atlas Shrugged*. Like 2,000 years worth. So, so there was already this, this, this interest. Secondly, the Ayn Rand Institute has reached thousands of young people since 1986 with its essay contests on Ayn Rand's novels. On The Fountainhead, on Anthem, on *Atlas Shrugged*. They tend to be the best humanities students in the high schools. And the ARI essay contest over the last 25 years by this time have reached hundreds of thousands of top high school students who have since gone on to leading colleges and universities, graduated, gone out into the culture. Many of them have become professors, some of them become teachers. You know, and and they're influential. And I think a third point here is, um the recent trend towards socialism. In the last five years the government has pushed us remorselessly towards socialism. It's taken over large aspects of the financial sector of the economy, of the automobile industry, of health care. Many of the American people recognize the, the evils of this, they oppose it. They turned to Ayn Rand and *Atlas Shrugged*. And consequently the sales of *Atlas Shrugged* have just leaped ahead in the last three to five years.

Do you agree that the greatest obstacle to mainstream acceptance of objectivism has been Rand's declaration of selfishness as a virtue?

AB: Is, is selfishness a virtue? Yes, of course. What Ayn Rand means to be selfish, is to hold life, support life. She's promoting values. She doesn't mean go after anything you feel like. She does not mean by selfish the conventional view of exploiting others, victimizing others, stepping all over others. Which is not selfish actually. It's not your self interest to do that. Because if you do, you're gonna make enemies. Your life is gonna be filled with anxiety and dread. It's in your self interest to be on, on good terms with other people. If you treat other people respectfully, if you respect their right to pursue their own happiness, then you are on unshakeable logical grounds when you expect and demand them to respect your rights.

What do you believe we owe to our fellow man?

AB: Absolute respect for the rights of each individual to pursue his own happiness. And to expect that from them. Anything else is voluntary, it's by choice. But we absolutely owe to our fellow man, respect for his right to his own life, his right to his own mind, his right to the pursuit of his own happiness.

Are we heading toward the sort of bleak dystopia depicted in Atlas Shrugged?

AB: Well, one of the great elements in *Atlas Shrugged* is its predictive power – its prophetic power. If the basic philosophy of a society is rejection of reason, whether it's for touchy feely emotionalism or for authoritarianism of the state. If it's altruism over egoism, collectivism over individualism, socialism over capitalism. If those are the basic premises of a society, then it's necessarily gonna move toward statism. And then we *are* living in the world of Atlas Shrugged.

So your outlook is pessimistic?

AB: But here's a key difference. In the world of *Atlas Shrugged*, there wasn't a great writer who wrote a novel like *Atlas Shrugged*. In real life, there was this great writer who wrote this novel to educate people to a philosophy of reason, egoism, individualism, capitalism. And those ideas are gaining currency around the world, but especially in America. And I think while I think the near term future is it's gonna get worse - the longer you look into the future for America, the brighter the picture gets.

To the best of my knowledge, in the history of mankind, whenever a culture has started to go down, Greece or Rome or, you know in enlightenment Europe, whenever a culture has started to go down it has never been able to reverse itself. It has slid into the abyss. I think America is gonna be the first great culture in history who started to go down, went a long way down towards the abyss, and then reversed course and went back to greatness, became even greater than it was originally. And that's gonna be because of *Atlas Shrugged*.

-New York City, January 2011

CHAPTER FIVE
DR. AMY PEIKOFF

AMY PEIKOFF earned her BS in math/applied science and her JD at UCLA, where she served as an editor on the UCLA Law Review. After completing her law degree she went to USC, where she earned her PhD in philosophy. She is currently an Associate Professor at the United States Air Force Academy and previously taught at the University of North Carolina and the University of Texas. She has published academic articles on the right to privacy, Searle's theory of rational action, and aspects of the novels of Ayn Rand. She has also published several opinion pieces in leading newspapers. Besides the right to privacy, Peikoff also has research interests in the rules of legal ethics and intellectual property law.

Our interview took place at Chapman University in Orange, California in the fall of 2009.

What's your take on the fact that more people are reading Atlas Shrugged today than ever?

AMY PEIKOFF: There's so much going on these days politically that can just be taken right out of the pages of the book. So people who have read it in the past are remembering that and saying oh gosh it's really happening. And then there are some people who are hearing about it and deciding that they're curious enough to pick it up for the first time.

When the book first came out there was quite a bit of hostility and a lot of negative reviews about it in the press. And then in terms of the general public reading it, it just slowly gained popularity.

Why the hostility?

AP: Atlas is a book ideologically that you either love or hate. Because it is so radical, because it basically challenges two thousand years of philosophy, in that it says that self-interest is good. Self-interest is a moral characteristic.   That really can set some people off.

They hear 'self-interest' and think 'selfish?'

AP: People are very hostile to the idea of self-interest because they look at it as somebody who is willing to climb all over everybody else to get what they want. To basically treat it like a dog-eat-dog world so its either you or me and if I'm gonna get what I want that means that you have to suffer, you have to not get what you want. And Rand didn't mean that at all. Rand thought there was no conflict of interest at all between people who are rationally self-interested.

Self-interest doesn't preclude benevolence.

AP: What I think people don't understand about selfishness is – yeah sure – sometimes giving to charity is consistent with self-interest. I think what they don't like is it's being declared a moral duty. So many people think from their upbringing, from their religious background, what they've been taught in school, whatever, they feel that they have a *moral* duty to give to charity, to go work in a soup kitchen and things like that. And Rand would say no, you don't have a moral duty, you shouldn't pat yourself on the back for all the times you do it necessarily but it is in your self-interest to help out sometimes too.

Rand said it's up to the individual to decide.
AP: There's basically an industry of people who use guilt as some sort of weapon to basically get people who are successful, who have a lot of money, who have succeeded in their chosen profession, to get them to feel guilty about those who haven't or maybe, who are down on their luck and stuff, and they make a whole industry out of taking those people's money and it doesn't really end up in the place that it's supposed to go obviously. There is corruption in the charity industry as there is in parts of government that redistribute wealth as well.

For years it seemed like the surest way to get elected to public office was to run on a 'tax the rich' platform.
AP: There is so much vulnerability in the population that they will vote in the politicians who have poverty as their agenda or need as their agenda. Maybe that's also why there is so much corruption.

Atlas was first published in 1957 and it's interesting that, although it sold tens of thousands of books through the sixties, Rand and her ideas were largely ignored by the so-called counterculture – even though that movement was supposed to be about personal freedom. Why do you suppose her strong views in favor of individual rights never caught on with the 'hippies'?

AP: In the sixties, it was about doing whatever you felt for what-ever reason you felt it or trying to be different – meaning trying to gauge what everyone else is doing and doing something that is different from them deliberately. Which isn't being an individual. You're still being guided by what everybody else is doing. You're just reacting to it in a way that you're setting yourself apart from other people.

A lot of it was very superficial, right? So I'm going to make myself look grungier. I'm going to do different kinds of piercings, gonna do different kinds of tattoos. Make myself look different, color my hair. Mohawk, whatever. I'm gonna make myself look different. I'm gonna do the things that I feel for whatever I feel. I don't want to have reasons constraining me. I don't think that's about individualism.

When you've got everyone walking around with piercings and a neon Mohawk, that's just another form of conformity, isn't it?
AP: Usually if people are doing that they're doing it on a very superficial level having to do with their appearance. Not with any-thing essential in terms of their ideas.

Non-conformity for its own sake?
AP: The reason that that sort of culture would reject Rand is that Rand would say, sure, be an individual, do what you think is right but do it because you think it's right, not because of some fleeting emotion of the moment.

Being an individual has to do with thinking and pursuing the things that are in your rational self interest based on your charac-teristics, your aptitudes, your set of values, and being honest about that. And it's not about looking at what everyone around you is doing and doing something different just for the sake of setting yourself apart from other people.

Today we're seeing some elements of Atlas Shrugged playing out in real life to the extent that comparisons are being made in the media and public discourse. Do you think the novel was being prophetic or are Rand's themes so fundamental as to be inescapable?

AP: I believe that *Atlas Shrugged* would be prescient *because* it's fundamental. A real classic novel is not going to be dated. Now of course Atlas, because it has the railroad in it or talks about typewriters, it's going seem a little bit dated but I think in general it's timeless in the sense that the types of government measures, the types of politicians, the way businessmen are treated and how they see themselves, the basic contempt for the role of the mind in human life. All those ideas are timeless and for that reason you could take a society that was in the place it was in Atlas – it doesn't matter if it's now or centuries from now and you can predict where it's going if it continues in the same direction.

With Atlas Shrugged, Rand presents a different kind of hero than people had become used to. Fifties drama was more often populated with the kind of anti-heroes played on screen by the likes of Brando, Dean, Newman and Clift. Dagny, Rearden and Galt are heroes in a more classical sense in that they are avatars for values.

AP: Rand's goal in her writing was always to create her ideal man and also to create the type of world that she would like to live in. Now it's not that she wants to live in a decaying United States. But she wants to live in a world in which there are heroes like in Atlas Shrugged that can deal with or address the issues in the decaying United States and succeed and manage to forge their own lives.

What to your mind makes Rand so controversial?

AP: I think Ayn Rand is accused of being an elitist a lot and maybe that's what a lot of people don't like about her and you see this in so many realms. Whenever you have somebody like Rand who is a hero worshipper who presents people who have used their mind, who have achieved great values, who have produced and someone who is clearly praising those people, worshipping those people, seeing those people as ideal, that is going to be an affront to some people.

I don't think in all of human history, past, present and future that you're ever going to get away from that, that there is going to be people who react to that positively, who say there's a hero, there's somebody I can admire, I can strive to be as much like that person as possible in my own life. And then there's people who are going to take that as an affront.

In Atlas, the heroes and villains are clearly defined. On one side are the producers or makers and on the other side you've got the takers – Rand calls them moochers and looters. Do you think this black vs. white illustration of society accounts for at least part of the controversy surrounding the novel?

AP: Human life is a process of self-sustaining, self-generating action, right? Each human being needs to produce the values that are required to sustain his life. And if he doesn't, either he's going to die or someone else will have produced the values for him. In that sense, yes, everybody is either a producer or a taker of some kind. She didn't necessarily have contempt for somebody who at some point in their life had to be a taker. Obviously children are takers for quite a long time. Sometimes people when they're older and no longer able to take care of themselves, they're gonna be takers. I think the people that she would have contempt for are the people who would say they have a right to take or they have a right to take from you and give to somebody else. And they say that's actually morally sanctioned. I think that that's what she had contempt for.

Which political party or movement today do you think would most likely endorse Atlas Shrugged as a must-read?

AP: *Atlas Shrugged* is not primarily a political novel. It's primarily a moral philosophical novel. I don't think that any political party today could say 'this is our novel.' I don't think the conservatives could do it because they are in a sense altruistic almost as much as the Democrats, some of them. And they're religious. The Democrats can't do it of course because they're for the redistribution of wealth some of them to a very extreme degree. And I don't think the Libertarians can do it because they don't believe in having a firm moral foundation for their politics. I also don't think the Libertarians believe in a strong [foreign policy of] self-defense as much as Rand would. I don't think any of the political parties today could take *Atlas Shrugged* and say this is our novel.

Philosophy and politics aside for the moment, how would you rate Atlas Shrugged as an intellectual achievement?
AP: First of all a novel of that length that is that well written that is that well crafted in terms of plot that also contains an entire new novel philosophy within it. I mean that's a tremendous achievement. And then if you also look at Rand who, for her, English was a second language, right? And she of course had to come here from Russia and teach herself English. She was poor and she had to support herself. It's tremendous, the discipline too, the amount of hours she spent working. I think it took two years if I'm not mistaken just to write Galt's speech? Definitely. A tremendous achievement.

-Irvine, California, September 2009

THE THEME

"Who is John Galt?"

The light was ebbing, and Eddie Willers could not ⟨see⟩ bum's face. The bum had said it simply, without express⟨ion⟩ the sunset far at the end of the street, yellow glints caugh⟨t⟩ the eyes looked straight at Eddie Willers, mocking and ⟨ ⟩ question had been addressed to the causeless uneasine⟨ss⟩

"Why did you say that?" asked Eddie Willers, his voic⟨e⟩

The bum leaned against the side of the doorway; a w⟨indow⟩ glass behind him reflected the metal yellow of the sky.

"Why does it bother you?" he asked.

"It doesn't," snapped Eddie Willers.

He reached hastily into his pocket. The bum had st⟨opped⟩

CHAPTER SIX

CLIFFORD S. ASNESS, PH.D

Cliff Asness is manager and a founding principle of AQR Capital Man-agement, a multi-billion dollar hedge fund. Prior to co-founding AQR, Cliff was at Goldman, Sachs & Co. where he was a Managing Director and Director of Quantitative Research for the Asset Management Division. Cliff has authored articles on many financial topics including multiple publications in the Journal of Portfolio Management and the Financial Analysts Journal. He has received the best paper award from the Journal of Portfolio Management twice (2001, 2003). From the Financial Analysts Journal he has received the Graham and Dodd Award for the year's best paper (2003), a Graham and Dodd Excellence Award (2000), the award for the best perspectives piece (2004), and the Graham & Dodd Readers' Choice Award (2005). In addition, the CFA Institute has awarded Cliff the James R. Vertin Award which is periodically given to individuals who

have produced a body of research notable for its relevance and enduring value to investment professionals. He is on the editorial board of the Journal of Portfolio Management, the editorial board of the Financial Analysts Journal, the governing board of the Courant Institute of Mathematical Finance at NYU, the Board of the International Rescue Committee, and is a trustee of the Manhattan Institute and the Atlas Society. Cliff received a BS in Economics from the Wharton School and a BS in Engineering from the Moore School of Electrical Engineering, both graduating summa cum laude at the University of Pennsylvania. He received an MBA with high honors and a Ph.D. in Finance from the University of Chicago.

The week we interviewed Cliff at his Connecticut home in the fall of 2010, his photo appeared on the cover of Forbes Magazine.

How old were you when you first read Atlas Shrugged?

CLIFF ASNESS: I came across *Atlas Shrugged* in graduate school. I came as a graduate student to the University of Chicago to study financial economics with almost no – this was embarrassing at that age, but almost no world view, almost no political view. I just had never thought about these things. Chicago is, is very famous and justifiably so for a strong free market school. I don't remember how I got the book, who recommended the book to me. But I read it in my, in my first year as a, as a graduate student in, in financial economics. And it was love at first read. I had a feeling the book was telling me a lot of things I already believed. I just hadn't really thought about.

Could you identify with her characters?

CA: Her heroes to me are certainly ideals. Not that they're all perfect - even in her world some of 'em are further along than others.

How *real* are they?

CA: I think they're extreme versions of human achievement, of human clarity, of human self expression and their ability to put into words what they're doing. Is that achievable? When I look at the real world, I have still open questions about whether anyone quite attains the level of a Randian hero. I'm reasonably convinced people attain the level of a Randian villain. (laughs)

What about the scenario – the idea of the mind on strike?

CA: She's trying to be realistic. This is where she thinks the world's going. I'm pretty sure we haven't had the top thousand minds of the world go on strike and leave. So that part is, is heroic fantasy. But I think she's trying to show us the best that's possible that's currently falling victim to the worst that exists. So I think she's trying to write realistic villains. I don't think it's an accident that I find the villains more realistic, than the heroes. I think that's just a truism of, of the book.

Is there one particular character you identify with?

CA: Most days I want to be Hank Rearden. Some days I think I'm Eddie Willers. And once a year I dress up as Dagny Taggart, but those records are sealed. (laughs) I think someone who doesn't see themselves as the hero of their own life, I don't really understand. It doesn't mean everything you do is perfect but I can't imagine not seeing yourself as that. And not having ideals to strive for. I'm just noticing I didn't mention John Galt, who I guess is the *full* personification. Galt is the ideal of all ideals. No one's close to there yet. So to, to hold up that one will be pretty hard shoes to fill on a daily basis.

What about Rearden?

CA: Rearden is a fascinating one because he's incredible achiever obviously in, in the book. But a lot of the book is the story of his journey from not getting why the world didn't work the way he should, why people, why he felt guilty about things, why he seemed so out of sync with everything going on in the world. That idea of trying to achieve, feeling like you're contributing to the world, feeling like you're achieving, but knowing you're not there yet, knowing there's stuff you don't understand. Maybe that's why Rearden jumped out for me.

Francisco?

CA: Francisco's way too suave and cool for me. I couldn't pull that one off.

Eddie?

CA: Eddie Willers I see as a noble character, a moral character who wasn't quite up to the others in terms of achievement. And anyone who says they don't have days where they feel like an Eddie not a Hank is not telling the truth. By the way, the dressing like Dagny part was a joke, right? (laughs)

Would you have accomplished as much had you not read the book?

CA: It's embarrassing what a poor answer I have after thinking about this. It's about one of the only things I thought about beforehand. I still can't make it concrete. I can't say I definitely made this decision or our firm made this correct investment because of this. It's an incredible motivator and, and energizer. I feel like it's really explained a lot of how the world works and should work. And feeling like you're, you're not constantly adrift in that. Not that you can affect it necessarily, not that you can change it. I have yet to feel I can stop the motor of the world but feeling like you understand it is very empowering.

It's not a tangible thing?

CA: I have found myself going back to it, really just for inspiration, not for a roadmap. Oh, uh, you know, I picked the wrong investments last year, I better go read *Atlas Shrugged* and figure out how to, how to do it better. I don't think it works that way. But when you think you're right, when you think you're doing a good job for your clients, for your customers, and therefore for yourself and your firm - and anyone has crises of confidence. And reading a book like that and, and saying, do I really believe in what I'm doing? The answer is yes. Gives you some courage to continue.

So Rand's work resonates for you?

CA: Oh yeah. I've never found anything that in an intellectual sense resonates with me like *Atlas Shrugged* and the broader set of Rand works. But with *Atlas Shrugged* being by far the strongest example. It's still resonating with me. There are still parts that come back to me at different times.

Do you think her ideas would have found a wide audience if she hadn't used fiction to illustrate them?

CA: Yeah. I think one of Rand's most brilliant choices was to present her philosophy first in this incredibly enticing interesting, mystery fictional environment. Obviously it required a tremendous technical skill. But number one for me when you add up the, the attributes of the book is the philosophy. Her philosophy was quite revolutionary. But I don't think it would have had nearly the impact it has.

Considering the millions of books sold and that we're still talking about it a half-century later, how do you account for the overwhelmingly negative reception Atlas received upon publication?

CA: That's a giant question. It's pretty hard to take a whole bunch of people and say, everything you know is wrong, here read this. If you look at the currents of the world - the intellectual currents - your life's not your own. They don't always call it socialism, but some degree of socialism, some degree of mysticism, they rule the world, they still rule the world. The idea that someone would write even a super clear wonderful explanation on why it's wrong, and everyone else that was gonna abdicate their power overnight is just overoptimistic.

But aside from the philosophy, critics attacked the book for its literary shortcomings.

CA: Critics are intellectuals. And I really wish I could use the word intellectual as a positive. I'd like to think a life of the mind and thinking about things and trying to make things better, would not be a pejorative term. But given the intellectuals we have in the world and have had for hundreds of years, I can't use it as anything other than that. Intellectuals are extremely collectivist, extremely leftist and seem to revel in, in degradation and failure more than success. You win an Oscar by gaining 50 pounds and playing a child molester. You don't win an Oscar by playing a hero without flaws. And maybe it's harder to do one than the other but critics come at things with a world view, with a political view far more often than not.

With Atlas Rand was hoping to change America's philosophical direction.

CA: She cared about convincing the world. But she cared a lot more about being right. The grand comment, you know, selfishness is a virtue. Altruism is evil. If you actually parse into what she said, I don't think the common definitions of that are right at all. When she says, the virtue of selfishness, she doesn't mean selfishness in the conventional sense of being piggish and taking more than you deserve or more than you, have earned. I boil it down to you have a right to your own life and a pursuit of your own happiness. Being benevolent and helping other people - I think she was quite clear she wouldn't object to that at all. I won't put words into her mouth, but my guess is she'd be completely fine with that. And that is at odds with what most people hear when they hear the virtue of selfishness.

Most people are taught that altruism or self-sacrifice is the moral ideal.

CA: Altruism to most people is the finest attainable thing. It's sacrificing yourself for someone else. Rand was asked if you sacrifice yourself for your children is that evil, because altruism is evil. And she responded, no. No. You, you've chosen for whatever reasons you have to value them, incredibly. You can value something more than your own life. You can value your children and an ideal more than your own life. That's not an evil form of altruism.

What to your mind are our obligations to our fellow men?

CA: You have tremendous obligations to your fellows. But they're almost all obligations of things you're *not* allowed to do. You are obligated to tell the truth, particularly in commercial transactions. You can't commit fraud. You are obligated not to initiate violence in any way. You can choose to help because you want to. The only people we can have obligations to are our fellow people. You cannot have an obligation to rocks and plants. I believe life is mankind and the idea that you have an obligation to something other than mankind is crazy. Now, this does not rule out environmentalism. If I produce a factory belching smoke onto your land, society has to sort out how it's gonna deal with that. That's an externality, I don't necessarily have a right to do all that. There are things held in common. The air we breathe is held in common. But it's still about your fellow man. It's not about the rocks and the plants. And it's still about not harming them unfairly, not an obligation they get to impose on you.

Do you think the attack on altruism as a virtue is the main source of the controversy surrounding Rand?

CA: Well we have a world that the two biggest things that run our lives are collectivist socialism and collectivist mysticism. It's 99 percent of the world. If you write a book saying those two things are wrong, it should not be a shock that this is gonna be contro-versial.

Rand's fictional heroes are often compared to Nietzschean supermen. That has sometimes led to the author being labeled 'elitist' and objectivism regarded as an intellectual form of fascism.

CA: Fascism is an epitaph they'll hurl at Objectivists as a great insult and think they got you. I don't even know what it means. Fascism is giant government. Fascism is a tremendously collective enterprise where the volk, the people and the nation, are all that matters not the individual. And individual rights go away under fascism. Objectivism which says, leave us alone, let's have liberty, let's have free enterprise and free commerce and free everything else is the *opposite* end of the world from fascism.

For many people that's a hard sell when you consider Rand's unequivocal endorsement of selfishness as a virtue. For them, selfishness is the dark side of individualism. At least that's what they've been taught.

CA: Selfishness in the Objectivist sense is better described as 'self - interest' – *rational* self-interest. It doesn't mean you can't be benevolent. Doesn't mean you can't help if you want to help. But says it's not an obligation. And they go, oh my God, if it's not an obligation you are sentencing the rest of the world to doom and you're a fascist. It makes no logical sense. It doesn't even connect. But that is hurled at us, and it's just almost exactly backwards. If you are a socialist, if you're a believer in big government, if you are even what we'll call progressive these days, you are far closer to a fascist than an objectivist has ever approached.

Do you find it curious that Rand conceived this dystopian sce-nario in the post war era, during what is often perceived as

one of the most benign and prosperous periods in American history?

CA: The timing of *Atlas Shrugged* is fascinating 'cause it was a prosperous time. Most people's welfare was improving. You don't think of it as a revolutionary time, a time that people would be clamoring for new ideas. Having said that, I think that philosophical concepts precede actions by long periods. And she saw the intellectual underpinnings of some very bad things that were occurring in prosperous times that had nothing to do with current prosperity, but a tremendous amount to do with prosperity 50 years on.

Rand said that if you can determine the dominant philosophy of a nation you can predict its course. Does America have a dominant philosophy?

CA: I think we do have a dominant philosophy and Rand identified it. And it extends across all varieties, whether it's socialism, mysticism. The dominant philosophy is your life is not all your own. Your life is owned by the group. And almost every society has this. And the prediction is decay. Moral decay, intellectual decay, and eventual economic decay.

So in your view America's future is bleak.

CA: I think most of civil society still works. You don't see riots in the streets everywhere. And most of that is not that people are being scared that they're about to be beaten with nightsticks. I'm more positive and more optimistic on that. I think most people are still good in their heart and still have a sense of justice and what's right and wrong. And this is why society to me is still savable. I don't think we're all doomed. I still am fundamentally an optimist. I still think people get right and wrong. And that holds society together, even against some forces that to my view are somewhat disastrous.

Atlas doesn't portray government as the sole or prime offender, does it? Rand blames crony capitalists equally. Is that any less true today – in the post-mortem analysis of the financial crisis?

CA: I would not claim people on Wall Street or individual investors or homeowners acted well by any means. They acted quite poorly. But what I see as fundamentally a crisis caused by government, has brought these things to the forefront. In *Atlas Shrugged* the government through its insane laws, immoral and practically moronic laws, ruined things and then came in and said, well, we have to fix 'em by passing even bigger laws. If you, if you just take a broad lens and look at the last anywhere from two to 20 years, that has played out consistently. When Rahm Emmanuel said never let a crisis go to waste, neither did Wesley Mouch and neither did Orren Boyle and neither did Jim Taggart. Every time things got worse in *Atlas Shrugged*, they said, well we need a new rule, we need a new directive. It's like reading the book.

What about the rest of the world? In Atlas, Rand dismissed most other countries as lost 'people's states.' Do you find it significant or even ironic that communist China has the fastest growing economy today?

CA: China always comes up as a place that's outgrowing the heck out of every place else. And they're communist. And which again, by the way, communism gets very confused. All that means is they're totalitarian. I don't see a whole lot of communism going on in China. I see a whole lot of autocracy going on in China. But what China has done in the last 10 to 20 years has been great. The level of freedom is still disastrous. But the change has been in the *direction* of capitalism and freedom. They're growing faster 'cause they changed their rules to look at little bit more like the best parts of us. And if you take a place that's dirt poor and you give 'em a little freedom, they grow faster. When they have a totalitarian country that is far far richer than us per person, I still won't change my beliefs. I'd rather live poor and free. But I will be shaken. I will say, I really didn't forecast that. That's not gonna happen. I'll go out on a limb and say they either won't be richer than us, or they won't be totalitarian.

You don't see Atlas, then, as necessarily a window into America's future?

CA: I think *Atlas Shrugged* has predicted a lot of America's future. I think things can take a lot longer to fall apart. There's a basic productivity to people. People work, people achieve, that still happens and even in a bad system. Technology still marches on. You can keep things going for a long time but if you look at simply the size of government and the growth of government and the intrusion of government, particularly in our economic life the government is far more dictatorial, is far larger, is far more intrusive. The federal registry of bills, with names shockingly similar to the names people thought were childish when Ayn Rand wrote about 'em, has just grown and grown and grown.

In Atlas Shrugged, the producers, the builders and creators are persuaded by John Galt to go on strike against the regulators and exploiters – Rand called them the moochers and looters. Today Tea Partiers call that 'going Galt.' Do you see anything like that happening in society or business today – that kind of passive revolt?

CA: I think the way real people go Galt, the way real people withdraw their services, is they work less hard, less well, and less independently. I don't think many people are in actually just a physical position to, to fully, you know it's not so realistic depending on your money in the bank and depending on the state of society to go, well I'm doing nothing anymore, I'm on strike. Most people won't starve for this principle. But people will pull back. They don't step up. They hide. They take jobs that are beneath them. It's a lot more how I think the world looks to a small extent now. And if it goes on, how it will look going forward. I find that to be a very realistic sad version of the, the future. But explicit strikes of the mind - I think that was great science fiction but I still think that's science fiction.

How did we get to a place – in this cradle, if you will, of individual freedom – where the concepts of capitalism and free enterprise have fallen under such a shadow of negativity?

CA: Show me a drama where the businessman is the hero. The standard story my kids read, the standard story, is there's a wonderful grove of trees where an evil businessman wants to knock down and they have to be stopped by two heroic moppets and their animated sidekicks. I find that stuff light hearted and I actually enjoy it. But a lot of the more serious messages we have out there, be it in dramas, and particularly in kids books and kids shows, there I think we have a real problem with how businessmen are portrayed. And, and a real problem with how anyone who opposes businessmen are portrayed.

They're almost never seen as heroes.

CA: I think a businessman, broadly speaking, I don't mean Wall Street people particularly, I mean business people who build this world, give more to the world than they take every time. You can look at Bill Gates and say would the world have been better off with or without him. And that's an extreme example. I think it's the case all the way down the line. It's way better off with these people. But yet they're the villains every time.

They're portrayed as selfish, out for themselves. Working against the common good.

CA: I personally think there's no such concept of the common good. If you protect individual rights, what people often refer to as the common good, is incredibly protected. The common is just a sum of the bunch of us. If you define the common good as we can rape and pillage this individual's rights 'cause they're 49 percent of the people in favor of the 51 percent of the people. If you call that the common good, I, see you as a criminal.

You see the community as a collection of individuals as opposed to a crowd.

CA: I think if we protect individual rights, the common good follows. In a moral sense, and also as a practical consequence - a material sense dramatically on its heels. But I think it's a straw man setup to fool you into thinking that there is a conflict between these two.

What about when the individuals are united in a common purpose – special interests?

CA: There's nothing wrong with special interests. There's something wrong with special interests having access and ability to get an unfair advantage. People confuse capitalism with crony capitalism. Advocates of small government, libertarians, objectivists, are dramatically against any concept of crony capitalism. Ayn Rand could not have made that clearer in *Atlas Shrugged* when she showed how a business that works through prerogative, through pull, through influence, not through making a better product, not through making a better product at a lower cost.

That was the devil to her. People hear the word capitalist and they think some guy in a top hat bribing a congressman to get special favors. To someone who really believes in capitalism, that's as disgusting as it is to anyone else.

But doesn't capitalism need some government regulation to keep the playing field honest? How much is too much?

CA: I think capitalism cannot become evil if it's real capitalism. When you hear people talk about socialism or communism, they often say, well the real problem in the world is we've never seen real socialism or real communism. I think they have that exactly backwards. My view is that socialism and communism don't work precisely 'cause the real version is evil.

And real capitalism?

CA: The real version of capitalism - there almost shouldn't be a word for it. It's simple freedom and liberty applied to the economic sphere, applied to enterprise, applied to how we all make our bread and our shelter and the things we want in our life.

And that idea can never be evil. Can people be evil within a capitalist system? Yes. And I think it really comes from crony capitalism, the politics of pull. When people try to cheat, to defraud, to gain advantage they could not get in an open marketplace, through government favor, then hell yeah it's evil.

At what point does capitalism – to use the well-worn expression - 'run amok'?

CA: If capitalism means to everyone what it means to me, which is just freedom applied to economics and enterprise, and how we transact with each other, and how we build and make the things we need. Then I don't think it can ever run amok. But when capitalism fuses with the state it can run amok when favors are dispensed by pull and by graft. And certainly within any system, there will be good and bad people.

Bernie Madoff?

CA: Bernie Madoff, I promise you, was a criminal and a fraud. And if he lived in a socialist country, he would've figured out how to be a criminal and a fraud in that country. Bernie Madoff by no means is a capitalist problem. And it's funny when it comes to should we have had more regulation, should we have caught Bernie Madoff. People don't even realize this, Bernie Madoff was registered with the Securities and Exchange Commission. A lot of so-called hedge funds aren't. He was registered, he was regulated, he was part of the security exchanges, he was part of the system. That was a great place for him to hide. The government is often a stamp of approval that can cause people to turn their brains off and to stop thinking. Madoff was a horror show. Does he deserve about 100 life sentences in prison? Absolutely. But does he mean we have to restrict liberty when it comes to commerce? No.

How much regulation does commerce need?

CA: Commerce needs almost no regulation to me. Commerce needs a lot of enforcement of rights. So I'm a big believer in courts. You need to make sure there are rules of the road. But capitalism is tremendously self-policing. We have removed a lot of this, particularly in the last 20 years and in the last two years. The idea of too big to fail is the ultimate taking away of the policing mechanism of capitalism. So if you try real hard to ruin capitalism, you can succeed. Failure in capitalism is as important, arguably more important than success. Capitalism punishes those who do poorly. And by the way, it doesn't execute them. They go find something else to do that's more productive. They move their resources to something else. Creative destruction. But if we stop that, then capitalism ceases to be self-policing.

Public displeasure with the 'too big to fail' concept has been directed primarily at the recipients of government bailouts. Is that fair?

CA: Well, Goldman Sachs – for example - has definitely become the poster child for people who don't like capitalism and don't like Wall Street. I think Goldman's unfairly singled out. There's not a truly large corporation in this country, and maybe that's an exaggeration, but I don't know of one, that doesn't have to play the system to some extent. That doesn't have to know what the rules are gonna be, know how they're gonna be affected, try to get ahead of that curve. Goldman Sachs has simply been better at it than other people in, in their field. I will argue again, if government wasn't so all intrusive, if they weren't setting arbitrary rules, if they weren't trying to get the whole country into a house they can't afford, there would not be a profit to be made by trading securities in houses people could not afford.

The original sin to most of this is government. And one thing that cracks me up, uh, we look at the financial crisis. And we look at a Bear Stearns or a Lehman. And they are castigated by the world for failing so horribly. We look at a Goldman Sachs and they are castigated by the world for succeeding so well for accurately predicting and changing their own positions to at least a minor extent. I don't think they made money from the crisis. I think they lost less than other people. But to have any foresight as to the crisis, they're attacked for that. What was the exact proper thing for a bank to do? What level of profit and loss would have made progressives and the left really happy with the bank through the financial crisis? So I think most of the dislike of Goldman Sachs is jealousy.

And I think whatever dislike that I would share is not targeted to Goldman Sachs. It's targeted to a system where whoever is better at understanding the levers and pulleys that Rand called the aristocracy of pull is more rewarded.

Remember in Atlas Shrugged, even Henry Rearden had to have a man in Washington.
CA: Yes, Henry Rearden had a man in Washington. It was Wesley Mouch. Wesley did not do a particularly good job for Henry. Goldman Sachs has managed its affairs better than Wesley. But when we have this horrible system of pull, of crony capitalism, you're crazy to run a big company if you don't understand that.

Do you see cause for optimism in the fact that Ayn Rand's books are selling at an all-time high?

CA: The fact that sales are through the roof of *Atlas Shrugged* gotta make someone incredibly optimistic who shares my world view. I'm cautiously optimistic. These are the right ideas and exposure's gotta be a wonderful thing. So when these sell half a million a year, and if half the people read it, and if half the people love it, that's a dramatic difference in the world.

Do you think Rand's ideas will ever be accepted in the mainstream?

CA: I think *Atlas Shrugged* is right now and will come to be even more so looked on as the most significant book ever written. Ayn Rand wasn't a God but I can't think of anyone else who took the world from here to here in terms of understanding. Her achievement was the equivalent of Einstein's in 1905. It was a miracle and I think it's the most significant book ever written.

-Greenwich, Connecticut November 2010

CHAPTER SEVEN
ED SNIDER

Ed Snider is chairman of Comcast Spectacor, a Philadelphia-based sports and entertainment company that owns the Philadelphia Flyers of the NHL, the Wells Fargo Center, the Spectrum, and the regional sports network Comcast SportsNet among other interests. In a 1999 Philadelphia Daily News poll, Mr. Snider was selected as the city's greatest sports mover and shaker beating out such legends as Connie Mack and Roger Penske. Mr. Snider was one of the founding contributors of the Ayn Rand Institute, established by the philosopher Leonard Peikoff to promote the advancement of Objectisim.

It was in the fall of 2010 that Mr. Snider sat down for our interview in his Spectrum office.

When did you first read Atlas Shrugged?

ED SNIDER: Well, I read *Atlas Shrugged* in the '70s. A very dear friend of mine pointed it out to me because I was frustrated because I felt that various owners and presidents of teams were voting against their own self-interest. And I expressed that frustration to a fellow owner and he wrote down on a piece of paper, read this book *Atlas Shrugged.* And I wasn't much of a reader at the time. I was very busy working but because I respected him so much, I read the book and it blew me away.

What aspect of Atlas appealed to you the most?

ES: Well, the whole philosophy of objectivism just appealed to me. I realized that it was more or less the way I've always thought, but it was out of the mainstream of many of my friends and they used to criticize me, you know, you want to be the richest guy in the graveyard, you know, with you everything's always black or white. And I didn't have answers. The book gave me the answers and made me realize what I was all about and the more I learned and the more I studied Ayn Rand and the more I studied objectivism the more I realized how much I loved it.

Any 'answers' you can share?

ES: It explained that money wasn't the reason, it was the reward.

Did reading the book change your direction in any way?

ES: I don't think it changed my course. But it gave me a foundation for what I was about. And I also wrote Ayn Rand a letter - I had never written a letter to an author in my life - telling her that I wanted to get the philosophy of objectivism in every college and (laughs) university in the United States of America. And she wrote me back. And she said she'd like to meet me.

ES: My two sons were in college at the time, getting a dose of socialism and communism. And I said, I wanted to bring them up when I came to meet her. And I took my two college age sons up to meet her and had a wonderful meeting with her and established a relationship at that time with Ayn Rand.

What was she like?

ES: She was intimidating. I mean, she was so brilliant but so on target all the time that if you said something that was a little off as far as she was concerned, in other words not on point she let you have it. But I loved it. I mean, I've never been, as a grown man intimidated by anyone like I was you know, by her.

This is coming from a guy who has spent his career surrounded by hockey players!

ES: (laughs) Yeah, exactly. And then this little woman was just, you know, scary. She was so, so bright, so intelligent.

Do you think it's better to read Atlas when you're young?

ES: That's a very, very good question. You have to understand, I'm 77 years old. I don't know how old I'll be when you finish this thing (laughs). But when it was published in 1957, you know, that was a great era in, in history and also in my life. I mean, the '50s, you know, before the crazy '60s, everybody was celebrating. It was prosperous, the war was over, and the recovery was complete. People were having a good time. Personally I don't think I'm smart enough to have read it then and have been influenced by it in 1957. Because I would've said I don't know what she's talking about. I might have understood the objectivist part of the thing as far as, you know, money and things of that nature. But as far as what was going to happen in this country and what's happening right now, I would've thought it was ridiculous.

What do you think she saw back then?

ES: Well, that's her brilliance. And it's also her experience in the Soviet Union, understanding where altruism leads and the nature of man. I remember once asking her, how do you know what goes on in a boardroom? You know, when I read the book. And she said, I don't know what goes on in a boardroom. I just know the nature of man. And I mean it was astounding to me. She just understood way ahead of her time in my mind, you know, what it was all gonna lead to.

Many people were stunned when Rand labeled altruism – concern for others - evil. Jennifer Burns, a Rand biographer, said it was as if she were attacking 'goodness itself.'

ES: People have the right to do whatever they want to do with whatever wealth they've created and whatever they have in life or whatever they want to volunteer for. I mean that's not altruism that's just something that people want to do. I mean, I think that I'm a very charitable person. But I'm deciding what I want to help and what I want to do with the money that I've earned. I don't want the government to decide for me.

Rand wasn't attacking the idea of charity or benevolence. She had a problem with the idea that everybody is more impor-tant than you.

ES: Where others want to tell you what you should be doing. You know what I mean. It's not where you can make up your own mind. It's like the church and the schools and parents telling children what they have to do and how they're supposed to act, rather than allow the person to do what they believe is correct. You know, it's this, you know, everybody's born evil or whatever it's called, you know.

The idea of Original Sin?

ES: Yes. I don't believe in that.

Do you believe Randian heroes like Dagny or Rearden exist in real life?

ES: Yeah, I believe these people exist. There are people out there fighting the good battle, trying hard to do the right thing. Sometimes they're beaten down, you know, by government or regulations or what have you. But there's a lot of good solid people out there that have done great things for this country.

What do you make of the almost universally negative reception to Atlas when it first came out?

ES: It's very understandable in light of today's world. I mean, all of the press almost, the mainstream press is liberal and still hates Ayn Rand and her books.

But even the conservatives came out against it – even William Buckley's National Review condemned the book.

ES: Now when you talk about conservatives, I believe it has to do with Ayn Rand's atheism. And the funny thing she never mentions is I don't think she ever mentions God in *Atlas Shrugged.* She just talks about mysticism. And basically she rejected mysticism and that led to her atheism. But she wasn't preaching atheism. In fact it was a devout Catholic that recommended *Atlas Shrugged* to me.

How successful were you in getting Rand's philosophy of objectivism into college curriculums?

ES: My first experiment was at the University of Pennsylvania. And they said, you can have a lecture there and we'll see how it goes. And the philosophy department will help you present it. To make a long story short, she couldn't come down, Leonard Peikoff did and gave a lecture on the virtue of selfishness. And the kids at the college went crazy over it. And they mobbed him after the speech.

What about the faculty?

The philosophy department gave a party afterward and this professor comes up to me and he says you know, do you believe in this stuff? And I said well, do you? And he said, no it's ridiculous. I said, why? He says, well, she believes that somebody invents a cure for cancer that, you know, they don't have to give it to the world. And I said, no, she doesn't really believe that. She believes that people can't take it from that person. That person invented it. It belongs to him. And any rational person would want to benefit from whatever it was that he accomplished in his lifetime. And he said, well if you feel that way, you know, why don't you endow a chair for her, you know with a million dollars or, or something. And I said I got a better idea, why don't we just replace you and put in a professor (laughs) that teaches objectivism. The guy almost swallowed his pipe. (laughs). But, you know the people who don't believe in objectivism - have absolutely opposite beliefs - obviously are threatened by *Atlas Shrugged.* That's why they hate it so much.

Rand talked about wanting to change America's 'dominant philosophy.' Do you think it's finally starting to happen?

ES: I don't think the majority of people in America really think in those terms. But we've had creeping little socialism going on for you know, most of my lifetime, starting with Roosevelt for that matter. But it's been slow and, you know, not that apparent. And I read a column somewhere where they said the greatest thing that ever happened to America was Obama getting elected. And the reasoning was that he put it right out there. Everyone knows exactly what his thinking is, where he wants to go with this country, going around apologizing for America, you know, internationally, socialized medicine. Trying to almost nationalize corporations if he could get away with it. And I think it was just an eye opening experience. And, and look what happened. Look at, you know the Tea Party movements and the type of people that have been elected. Hopefully we can turn it around and get back on track to what America is supposed to be. I mean, it's a difficult task, but certainly something that's very welcome right now.

Have we come to the point in this country where we're afraid of ideas?

ES: No. I don't think we're afraid of ideas. This is the greatest country in the world and I think the people are still the greatest people. I think we love ideas.

Is it possible to believe in God and Rand and to be an objectivist?

ES: That's a tough question. I don't really know the answer. I know that when people I love are dying, I pray to God and hope that they get better.

Who in our society today compares in your mind to the 'moochers and looters' in Atlas Shrugged?

ES: Well the government is the big moocher and looter. You know, the government with taxes and regulations and hidden taxes. I mean, if you add up all the taxes that we pay, not only directly out of our own pockets, but all indirectly with everything we buy, everything we do, everything that's constructed, every piece of construction material. I mean, when you add it all up, I mean, we're taxed and taxed and taxed. And the government takes this money and does what it wants to do with it. And most of the time whatever it wants to do is wrong.

Do you see America heading for the same disastrous outcome as depicted in Atlas Shrugged?

ES: Obviously what's happening to us now is a combination of things that are in the book and things that are much worse than I think she even could anticipate. The whole terrorist threat to the whole world. And the way we're dealing with it. And the fact that, you know, we can't really just go in and wipe out the terrorists because we might kill some civilians. I mean, if we couldn't kill civilians, we'd still be fighting the Second World War. And believe me, I'm not advocating killing civilians. And as a civilian, I don't want to be killed. But war is hell and we're fighting terrorism and the only way to fight terrorism with our strength and our armies and our abilities, is to just go wipe 'em out. And we can't do it. So in the meantime we take all these hits all around the world, so the world is in trouble if we don't decide that we're going to do something about it.

What about the idea of the 'men of the mind' going on strike. Do you think that's happening?

ES: I know of many doctors who have dropped out. You know, with all the problems that have been created for doctors that want to do their job. They have to go through Medicare and a thousand forms and mostly they're bookkeepers. And they're not allowed to spend an hour with their patient like they used to in the good old days. You know, they can only spend five minutes and charge for this thing. I know many doctors that have just said, the heck with it and dropped out. Many men that retire early are just fed up with a lot of things that go on and just said, you know, the heck with it, I got enough money and I just don't want to do this anymore, in various industries. And, you know, so it's, it's happening, but it's obviously it's not happening in the way it happens in the book.

How do you account for the recent upsurge in Rand's popularity?

ES: I think mostly the remarkable increase in sales in *Atlas Shrugged* are due to people that have read it and remember it, some of which maybe didn't even agree with it. And now realize that there was more in there than they thought. Also, people who read it and did agree with it, but just put it on the shelf, now are buying the book and giving it to friends, family, children, and saying you've gotta read this and you'll understand what's going on in the world today.

Do you think that might eventually result in a new appreciation of capitalism?

ES: I think people that criticize capitalism don't even understand what capitalism is. They've heard that capitalism is a dirty word and that capitalists take advantage of the poor or the this or that. You know, they don't understand capitalism. Ayn Rand is the only person that ever lived that actually gave a moral defense of capitalism. And those people that read it and understand what she wrote, would realize that it's the greatest system man ever developed in economics.

-Philadelphia, November 2010

CHAPTER EIGHT

ALBERT S. RUDDY

After a half-century as a highly successful Hollywood producer, highlighted by Best Picture Oscar wins for The Godfather and Million Dollar Baby, Al Ruddy has many stories to tell. Few of them are as fascinating or revealing as his encounters in 1973 with author Ayn Rand in pursuit of the film rights to Atlas Shrugged.

We interviewed Mr. Ruddy in his Beverly Hills office in the winter of 2011.

After the success of The Godfather, why were you eager to make Atlas Shrugged your next film project?

AL RUDDY: I was no different than millions of people who read the book who always loved it. As a producer, after The Godfather, I got Academy Award, it was the most important novel still not filmed, the most important novel of the 20th century that had never been done. And I figure, I'm the guy to do it right? So I call up Curtis Brown, I tell what I'd like to do. And he said, Al, no, everyone in the world has been through this office to do that project. Now, I could get Ayn Rand to meet you because she loves The Godfather, just out of respect for you. But I can tell you, you're not gonna get it. I said, just get me in a room with her, that's all I'm asking.

So now, a few days later I go to the Curtis Brown office, which is half a floor overlooking Madison Avenue. Huge room. Brown's back is to Madison Avenue. And the center of this huge room there's like 20 chairs, is a little love seat in front of his desk. And sitting in this small love seat is this diminutive woman, Ayn Rand. [laughs) So I walked in, I was such an asshole. I walked in. I squeeze into the love seat next to her. [laughs)I put my arm around her. She says, "Darling, what books do you read?"

I said, "I don't read a lot of novels Ayn, but I've read yours twice."

"Oh fantastic."

I said, "But look, I'm not interested in this book as a political missive or a diatribe of any sort. I'm not a Libertarian, I'm none of that. I'm into it 'cause it's a great love story, it may be the greatest part ever written for a woman."

"Darling, I wrote this before the movement. I'm so glad you see it that way. It is a great love story." I said,"The Hank Rearden, Dagny Taggart relationship is astounding."

And she said, "That's what it always was. I like what you're saying." In short order, have a big press conference at 21. I'm announced as the producer of *Atlas Shrugged*.

Who was going to finance it?

AR: I got calls from all over the world from the most mysterious, I'm sure gun runner and dope dealers, any guy that had over a billion dollars in the bank, all wanted to finance this movie, literally.

Whom did you envision playing the novel's characters?

AR: I was gonna do it with Clint to play Hank Rearden, Bob Red-ford to play Galt,, Faye Dunaway to play Dagny Taggart, and Alain Delon to play Francisco. I mean, I literally had these people in my hand. And we're all going along swimmingly with the contract. Except, as we got closer to the end, Ayn Rand started coming up with certain demands [laugh] that I had never heard before from anybody.

What kind of demands?

AR: Darling, again, I must in my contract that I have a private jet to fly to California. Because if the Russians find out, I'm on flying commercial, they'll hijack the plane. Okay. Private jet. Now we get to the last point and she says, I must have script approval. I can't do that. I said, all due respect to you Ayn, John Galt says goodbye to America 60 pages into your book.

That's not cinematic economy. I can't get any major director on that basis. She says, you don't understand. I'm worried the Russians will buy Paramount Pictures. I swear to God. I said, the Russians may be smart, they're not that fucking dumb. No Russian is buying Paramount Pictures from Charlie Bluhdorn, forget it. And so we locked horns, literally. And she wouldn't give in.

Curtis Brown said, "Look, Al, this is the most important thing this woman has owned in her whole life. Once she sells it, what is she – especially if it turns out badly. Especially if it turns out badly. So why does she have to run the risk?" She didn't need the money. She lived simply, a little apartment on 34th Street. Smoked like a chimney. So we're back and forth. I told her that I, I'll make this movie right. I'll get this to 100 million people that have never really heard of your book or had any interest in reading it. That's what was in it for her. I said, I will expand the readership past what anything else could do. And I say, you know, let's bring this to a head. Her cat had died. So I called Ayn and said, "I have a little present for you." I had a little baby Siamese cat. Gave her the cat.

And now we start, and we're going back and forth on this, why I'm trying to explain to her why I can't give her script approval. And she started explaining to me how she trusts me, but she's afraid of the Russians that she can't – so now I'm missing every flight. I said, "Ayn, let me be as blunt as I can be so I know how you like to deal, so I'm gonna deal with you the same way.

"I will never give you script approval because I can't get the movie made. However, if I have to wait 'til you fucking drop dead, I will, to get the book, to do it the right way." She said, "Darling, I (will) put it in my will the one person can't get it is you." I said, I'm a producer. I'll have someone else get it and give it to me. So the answer is no. If you can't agree to it now, I'm out of here. And I walked out.

And that was it?
AR: Dissolve. Five or six years, or whatever years later, I got a call from this woman who's working for John, the guy who owned the book in New Jersey.
(Ed. Note: John Aglialoro, eventual producer of Atlas Shrugged – Part One, the movie, had purchased the film option rights to the novel in the early 90's from the estate of Ayn Rand)

An interesting proposal was put on the table. Would I be interested in doing it as a mini-series. I said, that's interesting. Because the book as you know, like 1,000 pages. The idea of doing it in long form was a dream to me. So we made a deal at TNT. And this is where you have to have an ego to be a producer. At a certain point in thinking it through, 'cause you always have to say, when you, when you're developing anything for the screen, or you're writing a book or anything, you always say, who's this movie for? What is this movie about? And why make it? And this is why I really walked away. The whole thing in *Atlas Shrugged* are the guys, they take – Hank blows his factory up, Antonio (sic) sinks the boats, (laughs) she blows up the railroad. I said this movie's lost its moment. Do

I think America wants to watch a movie (laughs) where these guys are blowing up America.

You're talking about post 9/11?

AR: Remember the whole thing in *Atlas Shrugged* is it's all blown up. And at the end there's one light comes back on to start all over again. In truth of fact, it was Eisenhower years before her, said that we have to watch out for the industrial military complex. That was before *Atlas Shrugged*. The forewarning, the foreshadowing what she was trying to say. But in my mind, I said, no. I really think it lost its moment. And I'm not interested anymore.

That's when you threw in the towel?

AR: I literally said sayonara, walked away.

But John Aglialoro resolved to go ahead with the project.

AR: I warned John Aglialoro, when you could do *Atlas Shrugged* that's almost like getting the bible. There's a certain obligation, a certain inference that you better do a good job. This is not another book. Oops, we did The Great Gatsby, it didn't work, okay, who cares. This book is a foundation of a whole philosophy. You know, this must be done extremely carefully.

You have to satisfy millions of readers with high expectations.

AR: You must deliver. Or you will destroy something that's of great value, and you will have God knows how many people hate you forever. I always (had) great respect dealing with that material. Because I love the book, I love the Dagny, Rearden relationship. I mean, when she gets (laughs) his wife the bracelet, the alloy. And going over that bridge with the two of them. I could see the shot. Her with the hair ruffling blowing in the wind. And him and this – give me a break, it's paradise.

Would you have staged the film in the present?

AR: You're unaware of the time in the book. But unfortunately in film you have to make a decision. (laughs) The reason the book still lives is the body politic in Washington hasn't changed, of the looters hasn't changed, of the corruption in politics. I mean, it's still as current as it was then. The conclusion may be different. But the inference is still there. It's still the same. So could you do *Atlas Shrugged?* Of course. You can't do the hideout and all that stuff. Today they laugh at you. You got satellites, you know, they can find out who's scratching his ass in, in Albuquerque right now. So there were certain changes that had to be made.

The conventional wisdom in Hollywood has always held that Atlas Shrugged is tough to adapt for the screen.
AR: The narrative's easy. Keeping the characters alive and integrating the story, moving it ahead with a certain dispatch. She portrays her characters, so big and so pure and has such a big attack in their drive on life, and what their need is and what the obstacle is. The book is very heroic. It's a very theatrical piece.

The characters are written like movie stars.
AR: Exactly.

But there's a lot of story. The novel's action spans a dozen or so years.
AR: When you look at 1,000 pages, the embarrassment of riches... I mean, I thought the Godfather was tough at 600 pages. This is 1,000 pages. So what you have to do is you just have to keep boiling it down in your mind. What is it about, what is it about? I mean, if you, can you get to that point, that purity of thought. And then hopefully you've made the right assumption.

Did you get there?
AR: I think I did when I was gonna do the three hour. Yeah, I did.

What did you see as the essence?

AR: You must understand the, the, the – the reason these characters are heroic characters, is they forsake their own treasure and their own creations because it's become polluted and corrupted in this society. And they can no longer – you know what *Atlas Shrugged* means, they've been holding the world up on their shoulders. And now they want to start all over and get rid of the looters. Well the purity of thought that's - you know what, fuck 'em. I'm tired of kissing everyone's ass to run that railroad and seeing all the money going to the looters. People running the railroad, when I'm the guy that built it. I want it to be a certain way. I own it.

That's the basic conflict?

AR: Make it white, make it black, don't be gray. And she was, Ayn Rand was never gray. She made a certain point and she drove it home. The looters are taking over the world. The socialists are taking over the world. We're shutting everything down. The heroes, the guys who did it, they're stopping the wheels of the world. They're gonna get rid of the looters and start all over. So it's a very big concept. But along the way, it's a great relationship between Hank Rearden and Dagny Taggart – I mean, the narrative drive doesn't mean a God damn thing in a movie if you don't care about those people. We love Dagny Taggart. The way she dealt with her brother the wimp. And, and everyone else around her and just wanted to keep it all going and selling out. Hank Rearden had to fight everyone to get his alloy made. Even the, the union guys wouldn't build the fucking bridge.

Everyone stopped 'em. So against all odds, what do you do at that point?

You don't find these kind of heroes in literature or even in movies anymore.

AR: Hey - her characters are so big and so heroic. They're glamorous, in giant scale. When I saw The Fountainhead, I swear to God,

Gary Cooper, with his rock. Dominique on the horse. I mean, come on. I'm talking about big time real concepts here. I'm talking about someone who, who writes with a certain boldness. And very sexy. She's a very sexual woman. But that's the way she wrote. And I knew, why do you think I squeezed into that seat?

The book became very popular and has never been out of print. But it was critically lambasted and ultimately Atlas and Rand herself became lightning rods for political controversy.
AR: Well don't forget that a certain point she became emblematic of the ultra right in people's minds. Of the right wing lunatics in America. Oh, she's a Nazi. She's a right winger. In an era when, you know, when Vietnam and all the liberal stuff was going on in the United States. To say (laugh) you're an aficionado of Ayn Rand is like saying, I love Adolf Hitler. It wasn't too popular.

It's ironic considering she was championing individual rights and a philosophy that amounts to the polar opposite of fascism.
AR: She was against the grain. And a lot of people wouldn't get near that book, who should have incidentally, but never would. It was deemed to be ultra right wing.

It's also been criticized on literary grounds. Much of it centers around John Galt's speech.
AR: I mean, you could throw half the pages out. John Galt's 60 pages says au revoir at the end of the book. But that's okay, look (laughs) she's a lovely writer and it's great to read. Whether you have to indulge her, you know, Dostoevsky, Tolstoy, these guys write forever. And she was trying to make her point over and over again in the book. Enough already, I got it.

Yet Atlas Shrugged is among the most successful publications in history.

AR: The book has been published every year for the last 50, 60 year. It's always available. And people are always reading it. So you could be a fluke and say, why are people reading this – not after 50, 60 years. There's a reason that people are reading it. They're responding to a theatricality, and characters who are willing to sacrifice. Who can dedicate, who are protective of their art and, and, and creativity. Her three guys and the girl are very attractive characters. We all would like to think (laughs) that those people are around today. You'd have to look hard to find 'em if they are.

How disappointed were you not to get a chance to bring Atlas to the screen?
AR: I really, I wanted to do *Atlas Shrugged*. But I'm smart enough to know that if you can't do it a certain way, I'd just be wasting another year. I've wasted another year of doing the script. And she says, darling, this doesn't work.

Did you have separation pangs?
AR: No. No. The only way you can survive in this business anyhow, is you have to have a number of projects you're doing. 'Cause you don't know which one will collapse. And I love everything I do, (laughs) even the bad ones, you know. You can't tell which ones are bad. So, when I left at that point, I went in business with, uh, Raymond Chow. I did a film with Lee Marvin and Charlie Bronson. I did High Road to China with Tom Selleck. And I did the Cannonball Run movies with Burt Reynolds, did two of those. And blah blah blah, then went down the road with, uh, Ladybugs, Million Dollar Baby. Million Dollar Baby took me three years to get made. Three years of spending time and money.

Ayn Rand died in 1982. Nearly 4 million copies of Atlas have sold since then.
AR: *Atlas Shrugged* has sold more hardback copies than the, any book in the world outside the bible. You know. Only book that's

topped *Atlas Shrugged* in hardback (laughs) is the fucking bible. That's how important the book is. It's the last major novel of the 20th century that has never been filmed. That's what hooked me and will always hook people. It's theatrical, it's grand scale. It's an amazing piece of work. And, and remember this – what woman wouldn't wanna do a movie while she's having an affair with the three greatest guys that ever lived. That's true. That's what it's about. Three guys who were the three greatest guys that ever lived. And everyone jumping on Dagny Taggart.

-Beverly Hills February 2011

CHAPTER NINE
JAMES M. KILTS

Jim Kilts is known worldwide as a world-class business leader. Dubbed a 'brand mechanic' by the Wall Street Journal and lauded in print by such notable observers as Warren Buffett, Mr. Kilts is credited as responsible for 'turning around' established companies like Nabisco and Gillette. As CEO of the latter company, he negotiated its sale to Procter & Gamble for $57 billion.

Mr. Kilts' impressive resume also includes tenures as the former president of the Phillip Morris Companies Food Operations and president of Kraft General Foods. He is the coauthor of 'Doing What Matters: The Revolutionary Old School Approach to Business Success and Why it Works.' He holds an MBA degree from the University of Chicago Booth School of Business and is currently a partner at Centerview Partners, an investment banking and private equity firm based in New York City.

It was February 2011, just a day after an epic snowstorm when Mr. Kilts sat down for our interview in the board room of Centerview Partners in mid-town Manhattan.

What was your first exposure to Atlas Shrugged?
JAMES KILTS: It was in college. I happened to read *Anthem*. And then *We The Living*. And I really enjoyed the books and all of a sudden I became an Ayn Rand addict and read all her books. (laughs)

Had someone recommended Rand to you?
JK: Somebody told me about the ideas of individualism and the resistance to people telling you what to do and how to do it and when to do it. I was kind of a libertarian when I was in college. And Ayn Rand seemed like a very interesting person to read. And then I also noticed that Alan Greenspan was one of her collaborators. I was interested in a few of his articles that I had read.

Where did you go to college?
JK: I went to a small liberal arts school called Knox College in Galesburg, Illinois. It's where the Lincoln Douglas debates were in the front of, Old Main of Knox College.

What effect did Rand's books and ideas have on you?
JK: It helped clarify some ideas that I already had. During the late '60s when I was in college, there was very much a collectivist orientation - you know, the whole idea that you should live for others. And that the idea of creation of wealth and enjoying the fruits of your labor is something that was evil. And increased taxes, redistribution were things that were good. And that didn't ring true with me from a gut level. She helped me think through and understand better why I was so uncomfortable with those as concepts.

There was a lot of that kind of thinking going around in those days.

JK: And there still is. It's even worse today. (laughs) I never thought the '60s would come back, but I think many of the people who grew up in the '60s are important to today's thinking and leadership at both in politics and in the press. And I think that's reflective of the attitude that redistribution and increased taxes is great. While the creation of jobs, creation of wealth is evil and self-aggrandizing.

And your thinking was at odds with that.

JK: I guess I became a life-long libertarian. (laughs). You know, not necessarily an objectivist. But Rand really reinforced and cemented my ideas on individual freedom, individual accountability, and the danger of the tyranny of the majority - the ability of the majority to force the minority to do things that are inconsistent with their fundamental beliefs and values.

So you never bought into the 'hippie culture?'

JK: No, I didn't. My idea of doing my own thing was very different than what their idea of doing their own thing was. Mine was about work, accountability, achievement and the idea that ideas are important. And that I wanted to have ideas that would create value and wealth.

What aspect of Atlas Shrugged most resonated with you?

JK: Oh, I think that government is something that you have to be very suspect of. They might have good intentions but the unintended consequences of those intentions can be very damaging to individual freedom and the ability to live one's own life how they want to live it.

Were you able to particularly identify with any of Atlas' characters?

JK: Well, you know I have to go back 'cause it's been a long time since I re-read it... but Rearden, I think. He's the character that was searching for John Galt. He was troubled that people weren't thinking correctly. But he really couldn't define it as well as he wanted to define it. The other thing that I found really inspiring in the book was the world as it should be rather than as it was. You knew that what those characters represented - the heroes of the book - were what an ideal character would be. Someone who's clear thinking, respectful of other people's ideas, respectful of how they want to live, respectful of the notion of individual accountability.

There is not much cynicism in the novel.
JK: No. I'm not a literary critic but I'm guided by the idea that what you want to do is live your life doing the very best you can and being very respectful of other people. But also respectful of what you want to do. And trying to balance the fact that you don't want government or collectives telling you how to live, how to think, and how to act.

In that way, Rand's ideas parallel what the framers of the Constitution had in mind.
JK: I'm a big fan of Thomas Jefferson. Jefferson always talked about how bad it was for government to take people's wealth under the guise of wanting to help other people and take care of them. And Jefferson was very skeptical of that. He had a very clear view of the role of government and the potential evils of too much government - people trying to tell you how to live and what is right in your life.

But they weren't against government. They were designing one.
JK: The beauty of the constitution was *limited* government. You needed a framework, you needed a national defense, you needed

a framework of laws and, and rights. But you didn't want government to be intrusive into people's lives and tell them what is right, what is wrong.

What undercurrents in society do you think Rand was reacting to when she wrote Atlas?

JK: You had fascism in Europe in the 1930s, 1940s. You had government intrusion into life under the New Deal and many government programs where government taxed and then decided how to spend the money for, quote, the good of the people. And I think she saw all that as intrusions into personal freedom. And that philosophy developed over time. So I think the ideas really came out of that.

What aspect of Rand's philosophy most resonated with you?

JK: What most appeals to me is the idea that you should live your life for yourself rather than to be a slave to others. And you can decide as an individual what you want to do in relationship to others. And you should not be made to feel guilty or remorseful that you have created wealth or something that is productive in today's society.

How were you able to apply this to your life?

JK: It made me realize that you wanted to live your life as best as you could, that you wanted to maintain a set of principles and beliefs, and figure out what those principles and beliefs are, and try to live your life based on those principles and beliefs. And that's to do the best you possibly can with what you have. If everybody would do that, I think, the world would be a good place, a better place.

Which Rand book most appeals to you?

JK: You gotta say *Atlas Shrugged*. That's the longest but the one that you could re-read and think about the characters. The people who criticized it at the time said it's over the top, it's so unbelievable. And then you look at today and you see the take-over of General Motors, advocacy of redistribution, the idea that government is better at taking care of us than we are of taking care of ourselves. All those ideas that she had, those fears of what government could potentially do are occurring today. And as you sit here today, so much of it has happened. It seems like you're replaying *Atlas Shrugged* as you're reading the newspaper.

Atlas is selling more today than ever.
JK: I know, I bought my daughter and my son a copy myself. (laughs)

Many people describe their first reading of Atlas as almost an emotional experience. What was that experience like for you?
JK: It was a little turgid sometimes, hard to read, but at other times so exciting that you didn't want to put it down. It was a book that made an impact, a book that you'd never forget. And, you know, I've read a lot of books and I forget 'em, I couldn't tell you. But you'll never forget you read *Atlas Shrugged*. You will never forget it.

And I'm amazed at how many times I've been in a cocktail party or at a business meeting, and for some reason the, the idea of Ayn Rand will come up. And four or five people will come around and say, man that book made a real difference to how I thought about life and the world and what I want to do as an individual.

In the past people weren't so forthcoming about admitting they admired Rand.
JK: I'll never forget, I was in a college course and my professor was very left wing. And I brought up the fact that I thought Ayn Rand had some interesting ideas. And I was young, you know and innocent. And boy oh boy, he went on about what an idiot I was and

what a terrible novelist she was, and how her ideas were so evil, self serving, materialistic, that I should be ashamed of myself for even bringing it up in class.

I walked out of class kind of humbled. And then I got mad. I said, you know, a lot of these ideas make a lot of sense. I mean all of them might not be right but they certainly got me thinking about the experience of the individual versus the collective. And it made me very suspect over time of the tyranny of the majority.

Why do you think people are more receptive to Rand's ideas today?

JK: Well, I don't know if I agree with your premise. I think you would still get attacked in many quarters for saying you like Ayn Rand. Maybe one thing that has changed is the expansiveness of government and the failure of so many programs that basically redistribute wealth and create more problems. I think the people recognize that the government isn't the best way to take care of individuals. Individual accountability and individual initiative are so important to the success of our free society and how that works in the context of the world. And when you start, start thinking about the government as the answer to the problems and the collective as the answer to the problems, you really abrogate your responsibility for leadership and individual initiative and the creation of value in the society.

Maybe people are wising up?

JK: Yeah. I think people have experienced the idea of big brother. And they don't necessarily like it. I moved to Connecticut not too long ago. And I had to take a whole day off and sat in the lines to get a driver's license, that I should have been able to get in 10 minutes by turning in my New York license. But instead I had to go through a whole process. Now that's totally unproductive. And just indicative of the waste and the idea that bureaucracies can manage people's lives better than people can manage their own lives.

How close in reality are we from an economic system based on influence and pull like the one in Atlas Shrugged?

JK: Clearly companies today are getting all kinds of benefits from government. Whether they're well intentioned or not is arguable. But the consequences of that from the market standpoint is that some people are advantaged. What they've done is taken taxpayers' money, redistribute it to their favorites and disadvantaged the competitors to those favorites.

Do you think the government gets too much blame for our economic woes?

JK: Hard to blame an individual in today's society for the problem. Government is the only thing that's big enough to influence an economy like ours in the massive way it has been influenced. It's the rule makers in government who shape the economy.

What is the correct role of government in a free market system?

JK: The government should set the framework for the legal system, and the contract system to make sure contracts are enforceable. And they should make sure that people who break those rules are punished in the appropriate way.

Why are politicians so eager to regulate business?

JK: Politicians meddle in commerce many times because they're well intentioned; they just don't understand economics or the consequences of their actions. I think one of the best quotes I've ever heard was by Milton Friedman who reminds me in many ways of some of the thinking of Ayn Rand. He said, even if angels were in charge in the government, there would be some people who wouldn't agree with what the angels concluded. And I think that's the risk of government, and that is having people tell everybody what they need to do and how to do it. And so that is very unsettling for me because I don't necessarily agree with what they want me to do.

Do you see America slipping as a world leader and economic power?

JK: I look at it in the long term. We've always been competitive we've always been able to recover from a problem. I can remember when the Japanese were doing terrifically in the world economy and we were already written off. And we have the ability because we have free markets to react to competitive challenges. And right now I think what we have is policies and regulations that inhibit the success of our free markets. And an attitude that is anti-business, very populist, and tends to demonize success in the marketplace. I think what you're seeing is some reaction to that now and we will see some mitigation to that. And with that mitigation, I'm very confident that as an economy, and as a culture, we will respond very well to those marketplace challenges because of our system of government.

New York City February, 2010

CHAPTER TEN
JOHN ALLISON

John A. Allison IV intended his job with BB&T Corporation to be a stopgap between earning his bachelor's degree and attending law school. Instead he wound up spending his entire career with BB&T where he ultimately grew the bank from less than $5 billion in assets to $97 billion as of June 2004, making it the ninth-largest bank in the nation. Mergers and acquisitions were a major component of that growth, as was Allison's all-pervasive philosophy. The company's core values were clearly stated on its Web site: honesty, integrity, justice, reason, independent thinking, reality, productivity, teamwork, self-esteem, and pride. "Everything we do is guided by our core values," Allison wrote. "These values not only guide our everyday relationships with our clients, employees, shareholders and the communities we serve, but also provide the foundation for our approach to sound corporate governance."

Mr. Allison calls 'Atlas Shrugged' the best defense of capitalism ever written. Under his guidance, the BB&T Charitable Foundation has provided funding to promote the study of Ayn Rand's work in colleges and universities.

Mr. Allison's interview took place in the University Club library in Washington, D.C. in November of 2010.

What was your first experience with Atlas?

JOHN ALLISON: I stumbled on Ayn Rand in early 1970, in a bookstore in Chapel Hill where I saw *Capitalism: The Unknown Ideal.* I was very impressed with the opening essay on the moral defense of capitalism. I read *Atlas Shrugged* after that and it had a very powerful effect on me. It really explained in an integrated fashion a lot of fundamental ideas, many of which I had agreed with, but I never had been able to put together and see the way Rand presented it.

Where were you in life?

JA: I was a senior in undergraduate school at the University of North Carolina.

Did you believe that Ayn Rand's characters did exist?

JA: I believed that they were stylized heroes and, that they weren't existing in the normal world, but that their attributes were attributes that needed to be admired, and attributes that I could learn a lot from.

Do they seem like real characters?

JA: I think that they had real lessons. I think they were intentionally concentrations of attributes so you could get the message. Rand is not a naturalistic writer. She's a romantic writer. And romantic writers picture people and events in ways that communicate messages.

That they're bigger than life. And that's Ayn Rand's own intent, and I think makes it much more powerful.

Were the critical attacks aimed at the philosophy or the literary style?

JA: I think that it was a very naturalistic environment. And, of course, Rand was challenging a lot of fundamental beliefs, particularly those held by the left, but held by a lot of people. And so, I think a lot of the criticism of her writing style really didn't have anything to do with her writing style. They really didn't like the philosophy, so they criticized the writing style because they really couldn't challenge, I don't think very effectively, a lot of her fundamental ideas.

Is there a particular age someone should read it?

JA: I've heard of people that have read it in their 70s and it had a lot of effect. My own personal experience with people I've known is anywhere from junior in high school through college tends to be the most effective age. I think that's because people at that age are more willing to look at their fundamental beliefs. It seems like you develop your beliefs mostly either when you're young, or when you go to college or you enter those late teenage years where you're making one last reexamination. And, for most people, because Rand's ideas are so different from the conventional wisdom, they have to reexamine their beliefs to really get the message in the book. The whole idea is that teenagers, and I guess into your early 20s, people tend to be more idealistic. A lot of times you hear people that criticize Rand say, well that's a very idealistic view. I think it's a strength. Idealism is right if the ideas are right. It's not being idealistic that's bad. It's being idealistic in terms of having the wrong ideas. And if you had the right ideas. I think in that case a kind of a uncompromising pursuit of certain fundamental beliefs is good. If they're the right beliefs, it's a good thing.

What did you like best about it?

JA: The philosophy had a huge effect on me. The ideas really impacted me. I didn't grasp 'em all, but they were very powerful ideas. And the fact that she was able to express them in concrete characters, made the ideas much more effective to me. I could really both understand the idea conceptually and visualize it in a character in the book.

What did you think of Galt's speech?

JA: Most people complain about the length of John Galt's speech. I never felt that way. I thought it was a very powerful speech and I read it with a lot of intensity. When I started reading it, I read it 'til I finished it because I couldn't put it down. I thought it was a powerful integration of very complex ideas. And even as long as it is, if you think about how much she put in that speech, it is very dense in, I think, a very healthy way.

Were any of them your hero?

JA: Two of them resonated with me, I think, on a personal level. I had a real association with both Hank Rearden and Dagny Taggart. They both had a lot of attributes that I really, really liked. I had a harder time associating with John Galt. He just seemed so amazing, it was hard to visualize somebody that had that many great characteristics.

Why the gulf between critical and popular reception?

JA: I think the critics, almost all of them, are left-ish. And Rand has an uncompromising defense of individual rights and free markets. She attacks collectivism in every form, she attacks socialism, she attacks communism. All forms of statism. And the critics are, by definition almost, leftist, statist. And so, she was really challenging their ideas. On the other hand, the average American, maybe they don't totally agree with her ideas, but they get the sense of life. The heroes in *Atlas Shrugged* are unique American heroes. And deeper than the philosophy is a sense of life that Rand's heroes have as they overcame difficult odds. They have a huge sense of purpose. They were self actuated. And I think a lot of people that don't grasp philosophy get energized by the sense of life. It is a uniquely American sense of life.

Objectivism has very liberal views.

JA: Objectivism is really a radical new philosophy. It's not consistent with what's called the traditional conservative right, and it's not consistent with the left either. It's closer to classical liberalism. It's not really far from the ideas the founding fathers had, although they hadn't completed the full integration process. It's a classical liberal philosophy based on the sanctity of the individual, based on the belief that reason is man's means of knowledge. The reality is that we have to begin with the facts. Rand is a very strong advocate of limited government. But it's really a new philosophy. It's different.

What would the founding fathers have thought?

JA: I think the founding fathers would have been very upset about what has happened to our country. I think the founding fathers would have loved Ayn Rand. In fact, I think she would have added a lot of value to their understanding. Now I don't think that they could have understood what Rand understood, because they were before the industrial revolution. And one thing she points out is you have to see the industrial revolution to grasp the role of productivity, the role of the human mind, in raising our standard of living. So anybody that was before the industrial revolution couldn't quite make that kind of connection. Rand really took the ideas going all the way back to Aristotle, the ideas based on reality and reason, and took the insights from the industrial revolution and the great progress in human will being that the human mind was able to create. To me, she's a modern Aristotle. Her ideas are based on Aristotle, but she had information that Aristotle simply didn't have.

How is this controversial?

JA: I think the reason it's controversial is first, she is not an advocate of religion. She rejects faith as a means of knowledge. Now interestingly enough, many of the founding fathers also rejected faith as a means of knowledge. A number of the founding fathers were deists, but there was also a religious element in the founding of America. So, I find people that really agree with her values, with her politics, that are extremely uncomfortable with her attack on faith as a means of knowledge. On the other hand, for people from the left, she's an uncompromising defender of capitalism and individual rights. And they hate capitalism. And they're collectivists instead of supporters of individual rights. So she makes them uncomfortable. And the irony is, most people in the middle have muddled philosophies. They haven't really thought through issues. So the very fact that she's a logical thinker and has a fully integrated philosophy, often makes people in the middle a little uneasy, because they have a hodge podge of beliefs and she's challenging pieces of their beliefs.

Why is selfishness a virtue and altruism is malevolent?

JA: A lot of people don't understand the definition of altruism. Altruism really says otherism. It says, by definition, everybody's more important than you. That's what altruism means. So a lot of times when people talk about altruism, they're just talking about benevolence. Rand wasn't attacking benevolence. But she was attacking self sacrifice. On the other hand she was an advocate that we should act in our rational self interest, what I call properly understood. And that means not taking advantage of other people. In fact, taking advantage of other people is not selfish. Because first, people aren't gonna trust you. You can fool Tom and Jane. But pretty soon they're gonna tell Dick and Harry and nobody's gonna trust you. Secondly, it's psychologically damaging.

But she also said, we shouldn't self sacrifice, that you have just as much right to your life as anybody else. And why would you believe anything different than that?

She's an advocate of what I think is a very powerful idea called the trader principle. The concept of the trader principle is that life is about creating beneficial relationships. It's about getting better together. In our business we help our clients achieve economic success and financial security and they let us make a profit doing it. In fact, there are only two stable relationship conditions, win/win and lose/lose. Whenever we get greedy and we set up a win/lose, our partner's gonna get bitter. We see that in spousal relationships, we end up with a lose/lose. Whenever we set up a lose/win, we get bitter and we end up with a lose/lose relationship. So Rand was talking about really creating win/win relationships, not taking advantage of other people, nor self sacrificing. And in that context we should act in our rational self interest.

What is the dominant philosophy is our society?

JA: Well, today I'd say the dominant philosophy is a combination of altruism, skepticism and pragmatism. Altruism based on self sacrifice. Skepticism, which is very dominant in the universities, is there is no truth. In fact, there is no reality is their argument. And then pragmatism, which is the default position of most business people, because you can't really be an altruist and stay in business. And if you're too skeptical, you can't stay in business. So business people become pragmatists, which means they do what works. Now the problem is that some things work in the short term that are very destructive in the long term. And that's why you see so much unethical behavior in business, because people aren't principle driven. And that concoction of philosophy ultimately will have a very negative effect on the economic well-being of the United States.

And the flip side is?

JA: Rand is fundamentally an advocate that people should act in their rational self-interest. That they should use reason as a means of knowledge. As human beings, we have the capacity to think and solve problems. We're not omniscient, but we have a clear means of knowledge. And that we should act on principle. That we need fundamental philosophical beliefs to guide our actions. We need to be purpose-driven people. We need to accept reality as a given. We need to use reason as a means of knowledge. We need to be independent thinkers, to be honest, to have integrity, to be just in in our relationships, to earn pride in how we live our lives, earn a high level of self esteem. So she had a very clear sense of values. She's one of the strongest advocates of values ever. This is an interesting thing because most people associate values with religion. Rand rejected religion because it was based on faith. But she is on the other hand an uncompromising advocate of a clear set of values.

What about natural law and Darwin?

JA: Rand is not a Darwinian in the sense that it's the brutal survival of the fittest. I'm not saying she rejected Darwin's argument. I would guess she would agree that evolution is likely to be true. But, she views man as different than animals in that we can think. And because we can think, we don't have to eat each other, right. We can develop peaceful means to improve our wellbeing.

So it's not a survival of the fittest. In fact, most human progress is based on mutual beneficial relationship. That's what really businesses are mostly about, by the way. We see businesses as mostly competition, and competition is a discipline. But most business activity is people working together. In a large business, it's thousands of people working together to accomplish their end. So she wasn't a Darwinian in the sense of natural survival of the fittest. But that man had a special means to survival, success and happiness, which was the capacity to think. And when used properly, that normally led to healthy, mutually beneficial relationships.

Some sort of innate spirit.

JA: Rand was a humankind worshipper. People don't get that. And she certainly didn't disparage animals. But she said there was a difference in kind. That when we became conscious, when we became fully self-aware, that was a spiritual kind of thing. But spiritual in the sense that we were more than just a bunch of atoms added together, a bunch of mechanical parts. We had something that was unique and that it was a step ladder level advance. It wasn't just a little bit different from the next species.

Does a society need a philosophy?

JA: I think a society has to have a dominant philosophy. It can't avoid having a dominant philosophy. Individuals can't avoid having philosophies. In fact, it's funny the people that reject philosophy have a philosophy. One of the philosophies is to reject philosophy, right? So we all have philosophies. The issue is, do our philosophies make any sense? Have we created a set of values that will lead to our success and our happiness. Or are we just operating on automatic with a hodge podge of ideas. Which collectively you turn into a philosophy, but they don't lead to the outcome we want.

Eternity is now.

JA: Rand didn't believe in an afterlife. And she felt like a lot of people wasted a lot of their life worrying about their afterlife. Her whole belief was that when you died, you just weren't there. Just like you weren't there before you were born. And that there's no point in worrying about death because you will not suffer any pain or have any happiness after you're gone. You're just gone. And I think that's a very good way to live your life. I think a lot of people live their lives preparing to die. And they miss a lot of what life is about.

What would happen if we accepted that?

JA: You know, the argument is because we believe in life after death, we have better behavior. I think that's interesting given how many religious wars there are. I think it's interesting to look at say the Muslim belief that, if you kill a non-believer you get to go to heaven. So, I think in general the belief in an afterlife is a destructive belief. I personally don't believe in an afterlife and yet I am a very strong values person. I'm a very honest person, I have a lot of integrity, because I think those are necessary for my success and my happiness. And I don't view them as duties. I view them as a means to success and happiness. So I think if you develop your values rationally based on mother nature, and the (laws of nature) and human nature, you're more likely to have a more successful and happier life. You don't have to believe in another life to have values or to act ethically.

You're making this the afterlife.

JA: Yes we have to plan for the future, and yes we learn from the past. But we only live in the now, right? This is it. And if you're constantly trying to live in the future or constantly living in the past, then you're never really alive. So she was an advocate of living today, in a very thoughtful way.

Is it possible to believe in God and still adhere to Randian principles?

JA: I know a lot of people who claim they're Christian objectivists. They say they agree with Rand's philosophy, but they also have faith and they believe there's a God. The way they do that in my opinion is they selectively read from the bible. This is interesting.

Most of the objectivist beliefs are actually in the bible. The bible has a defense of reason, has a defense of reality, etc. But it also has the opposite beliefs. To me it's analogous to, "eye for an eye and a tooth for a tooth" and "love your enemy." Those are fundamentally contradictory beliefs expressed in the bible. So people select from the bible what they want to believe. And there are Christian objectivists that select from the bible beliefs that are consistent with objectivism. They can't truly be Christians or objectivists, but they can live consistently with Rand's value system because these values are in the bible, but so are the opposite.

In what sense has Atlas Shrugged predicted our future?

JA: When Ayn Rand wrote *Atlas Shrugged,* she said one of the purposes was to make her predictions not come true. Unfortunately, many of her predictions are coming true. And I think that's why the book is being revived. You can read the book and you can see a lot of the bad characters on the front page of the *Wall Street Journal.* I think she had the insight to see things so much further than most people could see. That was one reason that people initially had discomfort with the book because they said, oh this couldn't happen. Well now it is happening. I think it's unfortunate because that's not what she wanted to happen. But she saw the inevitability of certain philosophical trends in the long term.

Were people closet Randians over the years?

JA: It's been interesting to me as a CEO of a large public company, I would say a huge percentage of the CEOs of large public companies have read *Atlas Shrugged* and been influenced by it. Now, I think they often rejected it over religion because many of them are religious and that makes them very uncomfortable. And even though they would recommend *Atlas Shrugged* quietly to people, they're a little afraid to be strong advocates of Rand's ideas because of the issue of religion.

Are we living in a dystopia now?

JA: I think we have unfortunately moved very much in the wrong direction predicted in *Atlas Shrugged*. A society based on collectivism, a society where individual rights are under attack. The redistributive society instead of one based on life, liberty and the pursuit of happiness. I do not think it's inevitable that we have to have a bad outcome. However, I think it's important that we reexamine our fundamental principles. How did we get here? What is the implication of life, liberty and the pursuit of happiness? And that was the idea that made America great. When people hear that idea, most people think about liberty. And liberty's very important. But the world changing idea was the pursuit of happiness. Rand got that. Before Jefferson, before the thinkers in the enlightenment, we always existed for somebody else's good. Good of the king, good of the state, good of the church. Nobody existed for their own good. What Jefferson said is that each one of us has a moral right to our own lives, the moral right to our own happiness. And that's the idea that created the most successful and the most benevolent society in history. What's really under attack, and this is ironic because the left likes to claim they're the, the spiritual people. What's really under attack is the pursuit of happiness. It's saying that nobody has a right to their own life. That everybody is a slave to somebody else. Somebody else's need gives them a right to your life. And that is an attack on the idea that we can pursue our happiness. So what we really have got to do is go back and defend those fundamental principles, which I think Rand was doing in a very sophisticated manner. So I don't think it's hopeless, but I think the battle is philosophical. And I'm encouraged that more and more people are reading *Atlas Shrugged* in that regard.

Who are the moochers and looters?

JA: I think there are moochers and looters everywhere. They're obviously in government. You see people that basically get elected because they promise to steal from Peter and give to Paul. And

Paul votes for 'em. And it's happening on a grand scale. But unfortunately there are a lot of moochers and looters in business now. A capitalist system encourages freedom from the government. But the system can be abused. And there are lots of crony capitalists. And there are people that run businesses that aren't really capitalists.

They are people that go after the government to help them take advantage of other people or take advantage of their competitors. And we've had a huge drift towards crony capitalism. And the reason that's happened is the government's involved in lots of things it shouldn't be involved in. In a way it's not the crony capitalist's fault, but it is their fault in a philosophical way. But it's not their fault in the sense that government shouldn't be able to do it. But if the government can take from you or keep you from being competitive, then that's where the danger lies.

Is capitalism getting a bad rap?

JA: Unfortunately, people are mis-identifying capitalism with crony capitalism. And I think an example might be some of the bailouts. One of the questions that people, had an honest right to ask, is why did Goldman Sachs get bailed out? That's an interesting question. Was it because Paulson, who's Secretary of the Treasury, had worked at Goldman Sachs and had a lot of stock? Or was it because it was economically necessary? And I think people were right to be concerned about those kind of issues. Because in the capitalist system, people get to fail. They get to be very successful, but they also get to fail. And I think at a gut level, the average person realizes it's unfair to allow people to get rich, and then not let them, get the downside of that process. And that's what crony capitalism is.

Is the account overdrawn?

JA: I do a presentation on the financial crisis and talk about our long term future. And here's the unfortunate reality. If we don't change our philosophical beliefs, if we don't move away from altruism and pragmatism, the free lunch mentality we have in the United States, in 20 or 25 years we have some very serious economic problems. We have huge unfunded actuarial liabilities in Social Security, huge unfunded actuarial liabilities in Medicare. The new health care program is a huge unfunded liability. We have unfunded pension plans. The collective unfunded liability on all of those programs is over 75 trillion dollars. It's incredible number, 75 trillion dollars. And then we're running one and a half trillion dollar deficits each year. We have a dysfunctional foreign policy. We have a real problem with the retirement of the baby boomer generation. We got a failed K through 12 education system with 25% of the kids not even getting through high school. If we don't change direction, in 20, 25 years the United States goes bankrupt. Now, it's a mathematical certainty. If you run the numbers, we go bankrupt. Now countries don't go bankrupt the way businesses do. They typically hyperinflate, they print a bunch of meaningless worthless money to pay off their debts. They become third world economies like Argentina. In 1940 Argentina had a better standard of living than the United States. They went in the wrong philosophical, political direction and they've got the negative consequences. However, that outcome is not necessary. It doesn't have to happen. In fact, all we have to do is return to the principles that made America great. Life, liberty and the pursuit of happiness, individual rights, free markets, limited government, less regulation. We have a phenomenally entrepreneurial society. So a negative outcome is not mandatory, but it will happen unless we change direction.

Can you envision a GM type scenario happening to the whole country?

JA: The whole country. The founding fathers talked about the tyranny of the majority. And they were talking about the abuse of individual rights. But they also recognized that when 51 percent of the people figured out they could get a free lunch from 49 percent. Pretty soon it's over because 60 percent want a free lunch from 40 percent. Then 70 percent want a free lunch from 30 percent. And then the 30 percent quit.

More people are reading the book than ever before.

JA: I think the fact that Atlas sales have gone up so dramatically demonstrates that people realize we're facing some deeper issues. And they're looking for deeper solutions. And I think Atlas now has much more credibility because people can look in the real world and see some of Rand's predictions happening. Therefore, I think Rand is being taken far more seriously. She's become very visible in the academic community for the first time after 50 years. And people are taking her ideas in a different light than they did in the past.

Her philosophy was dismissed as derivative.

JA: Rand was initially totally dismissed by academic philosophers. Because she attacked their very fundamental ideas. And their most fundamental idea is that there really isn't a reality. And if there is one, we couldn't know it. And that virtue meant self sacrifice in the extreme. Duty is an end in itself. She attacked all those ideas, obliterated 'em from a logical, rational perspective. But the academic philosophers didn't wanna deal with that. So they basically attacked her over her personality, human relationships she had. Because they really didn't want to seriously take on her ideas.

Were they derivative?

JA: I think Objectivism is largely an original philosophy with its basic beliefs coming from Aristotle. And you can argue there's a school that runs from Aristotle to Thomas Aquinas to John Locke to Thomas Jefferson that are fundamentally defenders of reality and reason as means of knowledge. They reject skepticism and they defend individualism out of that. But objectivism is a very major advance. And that's why it's been challenged, because it's so different. And so, more insightful I think than arguments made in the past.

If I say capitalism, do you think freedom?

JA: Rand's idea, that I have to agree with is this. That there's a series of steps in philosophy. First begins with your view of metaphysics, i.e., the reality. And she's a defender of reality. What is, is. Second is man's means of knowledge, and she's a defender of reason. Third is ethics, and she's a defender of rational self interest, that people should act in their rational self interest, that your own life is your purpose, to promote your own life and ultimately your own happiness. And then she argues that the only society consistent with this concept is a capitalist society. And a capitalist society by definition is a free society. It's where people have the right to do anything they want to do as long as they don't use force or fraud to take advantage of other people. So that given man's nature, the only kind of society consistent with his nature is a free society, i.e. a capitalist society.

Given man's nature.

JA: Given man's nature, the only kind of society consistent with his long term well being is a free society, is a capitalist society. In a certain sense, capitalism and freedom are really different names for the same concept. They're really the same ideas. You can't have a free society except a capitalist society. People have to be free to think their own ideas to be productive.

-Washington, D.C. November 2010

CHAPTER ELEVEN
HARRY BINSWANGER

Harry Binswanger is a member of the Ayn Rand Institute's Board of Directors and a Professor in ARI's Objectivist Academic Center. Dr. Binswanger received his Ph.D. in philosophy from Columbia University in 1973 and has taught philosophy at Hunter College (City University of New York), The New School for Social Research, and the University of Texas, Austin. During the 1980's, he published and edited The Objectivist Forum, a bimonthly journal devoted to Ayn Rand's philosophy, and in Ayn Rand's last years, Dr. Binswanger became her associate and friend.

Dr. Binswanger is also the author of The Biological Basis of Teleological Concepts and editor of The Ayn Rand Lexicon and of the second edition of Ayn Rand's Introduction to Objectivist Epistemology. He is currently completing a book on the theory of knowledge: How We Know.

A frequent speaker on Ayn Rand's philosophy, he has appeared on TV shows hosted by Glenn Beck, Geraldo Rivera, and Judge Anthony Napolitano.

Dr. Binswanger was in Los Angeles on vacation in the winter of 2011 when we caught up with him for this interview.

What caused Ayn Rand to write Atlas Shrugged in the post-war era?

HARRY BINSWANGER: Ayn Rand wrote *Atlas Shrugged* at the time she wrote it because of her own development intellectually, not because of some reaction to the culture. She had written The Fountainhead, she had developed her idea of the ideal man, but she wanted to attack altruism more directly and to present her new moral code of rational selfishness, which The Fountainhead presents more implicitly than explicitly. So, she didn't write it in response to what was going on in the world of the '50s, any more than The Fountainhead was a response to the world of the '40s. She wrote both novels to present her ideas in dramatic form.

What was going on, philosophically and culturally in the United States at that time that had gotten her attention?

HB: Ayn Rand thought that collectivism as an ideal died in World War II. The revelation of the concentration camps, and the horror that was Nazi Germany, was the immortal refutation of the idea that man should live for the state and obey the state, shutting down his own mind. So, she thought collectivism died then.

But it obviously hadn't. Why not?

HB: The reaction among the intellectuals was to give up the intellect. That's what happened after World War II. We entered an age of anti-ideology. People said: "Look what happens when you stick to ideas—Stalin, Hitler, Mussolini—they had big ideas—and what did pursuing them mean? Mass carnage." Their solution: no ideas.

Ayn Rand was profoundly opposed to that. She thought philosophy, which deals with the deepest ideas of all, was the most powerful factor of all. So, she wanted to speak out for the ideas of individualism, freedom, egoism, that she thought are necessary to save the world.

Why has the intellectual establishment remained at odds with Rand's ideas about individualism and capitalism?

HB: Why are they so leftist? They're leftist because of the ideas that have ruled the universities since the mid-19th century. These are ideas coming from Kant and Hegel, German philosophers who taught that the mind can't know reality, that living for yourself is evil, that self-sacrifice is the highest thing there is. Hegel believed that war was a noble activity, and that the man embodying the "world historical spirit" has to "crush many an innocent rose in his path." So, the ideas that we imported from Germany into our universities in the mid-19th century corrupted the academic world, making intellectuals very much against individualism, against reason.

What is accomplished by rejecting reason?

HB: Nothing. It's in service of nothing. That's why philosophy has ended up in "post-modernism," which is the worship of nothing. There is no beneficiary to the sacrifices that Immanuel Kant says you have to make. He says that if there's a beneficiary for a sacrifice, then it's not as noble as when it's sacrifice as an end in itself. So, they advocated living for nothing. They didn't call it that. Hegel called it living for "The Absolute," for the realization of the "Absolute Idea," as it evolves in this triple-somersault, as Ayn Rand called it, of "the dialectic process." They've got all kinds of pretentious verbiage to hide the fact that there's no purpose to life under the Kantian/Hegelian philosophy, but in fact there isn't in that philosophy.

Where can we see examples of that non-thinking today?

HB: The contemporary offshoots of this German philosophy of Kant and Hegel are familiar to people both as Existentialism (life is meaningless, life is absurd, life is nauseating) and French Deconstructionism (texts mean nothing, we have to find the "patriarchical," racist hidden agenda, when we read, say, Shakespeare). And Pragmatism, which rules our American political system: the idea that you shouldn't have any firm principles, you should play it by ear, go with the flow. You know, Nixon and Watergate, "let's stonewall it," don't stand up for anything. Duck and hide. Dissemble. That comes right out of Kant's philosophy—not in those terms, not in those words, but it is the consequence of saying: our ideas cannot grasp reality.

How did these philosophers develop their ideas?

HB: Kant got it from the Christian religion. The Sermon on the Mount. The basic teachings of Christianity and Judaism are obedience, sacrifice. What's the first commandment? "Thou shalt have no other gods before me." In other words, you must serve God, this incomprehensible spirit. You don't live for your own sake, you live to serve, obey, kneel, bow down. Don't think. That's the message of religion. And specifically the morality of "Turn the other cheek," "Give of yourself," "A rich man cannot get into heaven any more than a camel could pass through the eye of a needle." All that stuff, Kant gave a fancy philosophical rationalization for. He wanted to save religion from the threat of reason. He said, "I had to deny reason in order to make room for faith."

Where does the idea of altruism come from?

HB: The stem of altruism is religion. It is in particular the Christian religion (and the Jewish religion before it). The earlier, more primitive, religions stressed obedience to a powerful God who can punish you. What Christianity injected is that it's good to be self-denying for the sake of other people on earth. So, whereas before you bowed down to a God in the sky, the modernization of that, brought on by Christianity, is that you bow down to your neighbors, who are then bowing down to their neighbors, who are then bowing down . . . you see there's no end to it. It makes no sense. But that's where altruism comes from.

Are you saying religion by definition means the rejection of reason?

HB: Here's the big picture. During the Middle Ages and the Dark Ages that preceded it, man's world was constricted by mysticism. Religion dominated everything. Man lived in fear and guilt. Slowly, with the re-introduction of ideas from ancient Greece, particularly Aristotle's, the long night began to lift. People began to rediscover man's mind. People began to rediscover Greek philosophy, a philosophy that celebrated reason. Religion declined. Slowly we entered the Renaissance. Modern science was born when people stopped looking to the authority of scripture and started looking through their own eyes (and the telescopes that they invented).

This trend provoked a reaction eventually: in 1776, Immanuel Kant wrote The Critique of Pure Reason, which is an attack on pure reason. This was his attempt to save religion from the growing secularism, the growing respect for reason and life on this earth that started with the downfall of the Middle Ages, grew in the Renaissance, and culminated in the Age of Reason, the Enlightenment era. What happened was there was a philosophical counterattack by this genius (an evil genius if ever there was one) Immanuel Kant. Kant swept the field and his basic ideas are now established in every intellectual center in the world and are taught to your children in college, in a million different forms, in a million different departments.

It's the same old message: deny yourself, sacrifice yourself, you can't know, don't claim to be certain, don't think there's such a thing as objective proof or objective morality, everything is relative, everything is subjective. That's the philosophy Ayn Rand is fighting.

But isn't the advance of technology during the course of the last century proof that reason is still going strong?

HB: Technology has progressed because it doesn't deal with value-judgments. It's all the fields that deal with man and values that philosophy has corrupted.

We're riding today on the remnants of Aristotle's philosophy, of the same Greek philosophy that brought us to the Renaissance out of the Middle Ages.

The American common man is not Kantian, he's not a follower of this German philosophy. He's pro-commonsense, he's pro-logic. He believes in individual success. He believes in productivity. He may pay lip-service on Sunday to "Give to the poor and sacrifice yourself for another dimension." But most Americans actually live by a code of self-reliance and self-development, individual success. That code is responsible for the success that we've had, particularly in technology in the 20th century. It's the fields that deal with values, it's the cultural fields, that are the worst.

Examples?

HB: Look at modern art. Look at some of the modern literature. Look at the state of education. Educational theory today is horrible. The schools are horrible. It's the fields particularly that deal with values that have succumbed to the German Kantian philosophy. We have more common-sense rationality when it comes to things you can directly see and manipulate like transistors, automobile parts, and so forth.

When did you first come across Rand's work and ideas?

HB: I read *Atlas Shrugged* at age 17. I've re-read it nine times, I believe, since then. And I'm now 66. Every time I re-read it, I get something more out of it. But when I first read it at age 17, it made me experience emotions that I had never experienced before. Exaltation was an emotion that I had never experienced before reading *Atlas Shrugged*. So Atlas is not just an intellectual triumph, an artistic triumph, a commercial success: it reaches into your deepest soul, if you're the kind of person ready to respond to this philosophy. It reaches in and touches something in the core of your being that nothing else can do, that nothing else can touch in that way.

How was Rand affected by the negative reaction to Atlas Shrugged?

HB: The reaction of the critics really disappointed her. She didn't think that it would gather universal agreement, but she thought that there were a number of remaining advocates of reason and individualism who would rally to its cause. She thought that there would be a minority, but a vocal minority, of intellectuals who would recognize what philosophical achievement she had made with *Atlas Shrugged*. But it didn't happen. Virtually no one in the intellectual world came to her side. Meanwhile the American people—who are not intellectual and had not been brainwashed by bad philosophy—loved Atlas, and it went on the bestseller list right away, sold very well. But the critical reaction from the newspapers and the magazines, was almost universally negative.

Rand never wrote another work of fiction. She devoted her post-Atlas career to philosophy.

HB: After *Atlas Shrugged*, she spent some time investigating the state of the universities, of philosophy. She had friends who were graduate students in philosophy and in some of the other, related fields. She went to symposia on philosophy in New York. And she came to realize that philosophy was in worse shape than she had thought when she wrote *Atlas Shrugged*. Worse in the sense that it had abandoned all concern with real life questions and was merely analyzing sentences. It had become scholastic and ivory tower and logic-chopping rather than focusing on real life concerns. It rejected all those questions. It said: well, let's analyze the meaning of the terms we use. For instance, there was a famous article entitled, "About 'About,'" which was on the different meanings of the word "about." Now, you put *Atlas Shrugged* up against "About 'About'" and you can see they're incommensurable. Those two sides can't talk to each other. It's different universes.

"About 'About'" sounds like Bill Clinton trying to dissemble his way out of the Lewinsky affair.
HB: Yes. That's exactly it. It's exactly what Clinton said, it 'depends on what the meaning of the word is is.' That comes right out of the philosophy of Linguistic Analysis.

Why does Atlas Shrugged hold a special appeal for the young?
HB: The young are particularly interested in *Atlas Shrugged* because they're at the stage—and by "the young" I mean people 17 to 23, 24, when they're trying to define who they are, what life has to offer. They haven't necessarily given up yet and sold out. But by the time you get people in their 40s or 50s, many of them have renounced any ambition, any idealism, they've become cynical.

What's wrong, really, with the concept of altruism and self-sacrifice. Isn't it noble to help others?
HB: Altruism is an impossible moral code. You cannot live on the policy of giving everything you have to the poor, sacrificing yourself. Don't eat, because somewhere somebody's hungry. You'd be dead. So everyone who accepts the altruist morality has to compro-

mise. They have to say, "Well, Jesus was a perfect example of altruism. He died for others. But I can't, I'm not about to die, so I make a few compromises, there are no absolutes." And then you're all the way down the road to pragmatism. Then you're down the road to cynicism, to refusal to even look at principles. Because principles are threatening to an altruist. Because in principle, he should immediately give everything he has to those who are less fortunate than him. So altruism demands hypocrisy.

Why don't we see Objectivism being taught in the schools?

HB: It takes a long time to convince people in an entrenched establishment that they have to change their way of thinking. And in the case of arguing with philosophers, we don't even speak the same language. They say we're not a serious philosophy. We say you're not a philosophy at all. You're not talking about actual problems. You're investigating made-up problems and contemplating your navels. So neither side understands the methodology of the other side.

How do 'serious' philosophers see their mission and purpose?

HB: Well, ask them. Ask philosophers what they think their mission and purpose and function is. They'll tell you: intellectual exercise, to clarify questions. Not: to provide any answers. Not: to give a guide to life.

Now, things have improved a little bit. Gradually through the growth of certain movements such as "virtue ethics," as it's called, reality is beginning to penetrate a little bit back into philosophy. Philosophers are just slightly interested now in looking at the real world, looking at daily life, and maybe having something to say about how it ought to be lived.

Have religion and philosophy always been so closely tied?

HB: Well, religion after all is a primitive form of philosophy. Religion offers answers. Wrong answers in my opinion, but it offers answers. When Kant separated reason from reality "as it really is" (as he called it), when he separated the mind, the rational mind from the real world, philosophers who couldn't answer his arguments, chose to side with the mind. That left reality, real concerns of the world, to religion.

What was Rand's take on the social revolution in the 60's?

HB: She said the hippies were the most docile, conformist, obedient products of the preceding generation. What did they say about their elders? "You're hypocrites," they said. "You mouth socialism, you mouth collectivism, but you don't live it. What we're doing is putting into practice the ideals you talk about but compromise on." And that's true. They were accepting all the premises of the older generation while supposedly engaging in a generational revolt. It was a revolt against not living up to the ideals espoused by the previous generation. Those are the ideals that are poison.

They were in effect revolting against pragmatism?

HB: That's right. They were revolting against the pragmatism of the preceding generation. Not against the *ideas* of the preceding generation. Those they accepted whole hog.

Given the dire warning of Atlas Shrugged, what were Rand's expectations for America's immediate future?

HB: I thought America was going to end in a civil war by 1976. In 1968 I didn't see how this country could last until 1976. Ayn Rand was a lot more wise. She said, the student rebellion is just froth on the surface. It's a public relations exercise. It doesn't represent real America. It doesn't have the support. It's going to fizzle away. And sure enough in a few years it was gone. She marked the turning point as being the Kent State shootings. She said now that these little hippies see that somebody could actually get shot, by accident or whatever, they're not going to be so much out demonstrating.

And she was right. That was a big turning point. And then the McGovern defeat in '72 was an enormous slap in the face of the New Left. And that marked the death knell.

So here we are forty odd years later and seeing a new interest in Rand and her ideas. What's your take on this development?

HB: The answer to why the Ayn Rand renaissance is happening now, as opposed to during her lifetime, I think is that the young people who observed her ideas and agreed with them have now come into their maturity and are now in positions of influence. When I was in college, people would tell me, oh yes, I read The Fountainhead when I was young. Now, people tell you, oh yes, I read *Atlas Shrugged* when I was young. I think Atlas has more of an impact, laying there in people's minds. So, I think it takes a long time for people who in their youth accept this philosophy to start translating it into cultural practice. It has to percolate. It's a departure from what they've been taught. They have to see it borne out in real life experience.

The third factor is that the political situation has reached a kind of climax. We're now at the point where we can no longer afford the welfare state. If we don't give up the welfare state, we're going to collapse. As Greece has. As Ireland is on the verge of doing. As many European countries face economic disaster, so are we. That means people start questioning: "What are we going to do? The welfare state is required by altruism. We are our brother's keeper. But we're going to die, we're going to starve. We can't feed our brothers, we don't have anything more to give them. Or soon we won't." And that's the story of *Atlas Shrugged*: what happens when the looting runs dry? That's the situation we're reaching in the United States today.

Atlas Shrugged is often described as a 'dystopian' novel in that it depicts a bleak future. Have we reached that stage? Are we living in a dystopia?

HB: Ayn Rand said that *Atlas Shrugged* was set in the day after tomorrow. And we've reached that day after tomorrow. People are rebelling. People are now feeling the feelings that the good people in *Atlas Shrugged* felt: Enough! Stop the sacrificing, return to freedom, loosen the controls!

You know, people say the economic crisis resulted from not enough regulations. That's what the media is saying. Did you know that 50,000 regulations were added during the Bush administration? *The Bush administration.* 50,000 new regulations in the Federal Register. This is the regulatory state. This is the failure of the regulatory state. And no regulator has said, "Gosh, if I'd had enough power, I could have stopped the collapse of housing." It's not that there weren't enough regulations. It's not that if the bureaucrats had had more sway over housing this would be better. *They* were the ones who created the problem.

Ayn Rand said that the victims of moral crimes were just as culpable as the perpetrators. What did she mean by the term: sanction of the victim?

HB: Ayn Rand thought the strongest power in the world was not the power of guns, but the power of moral sanction. For instance, just to concretize her viewpoint, why did we lose in Vietnam? Why did the United States, the most powerful country in the world, lose to a pipsqueak dictatorship in the jungle? Because we thought or, eventually we were conditioned to think that we had no right to be there. Now, you can criticize our action in Vietnam. Ayn Rand criticized it as altruistic, as selfless. But that's not the point. The point is: in the opposition between military might and guns, and moral sanction, it's moral sanction that wins. So Ayn Rand held this doctrine she called "the sanction of the victim": if you're being persecuted by a moral code, you must above all refuse to endorse that moral code.

Sounds like the basic premise of Atlas Shrugged.

HB: The heroes of her novels learn to stop feeling guilty for what is actually their virtue, to stop feeling guilty for making money, for wanting to make money, and instead to regard that as a virtue. To stop paying extortion for the sin of keeping themselves alive. Life is not guilt. Life is achievement.

Life is not a zero sum game.

HB: No. The whole of human history is the story of movement from the cave to the skyscraper. From smoke signals to satellite transmission of the internet content. So where did these things come from? Where did everything we have in front of us, where did the synthetic fiber clothes on my back come from? All these products were unknown 2,000 years ago, 10,000 years ago. They were all produced. All wealth is created, and there's no limit to how much wealth can be created. The only operative limit is the state of technology, the state of knowledge. That's why if you're a champion of wealth and greed and life on this earth, as Ayn Rand was, you champion technology, science, reason.

You're saying greed is good?

HB: "Greed" is a very slippery term. If it means the desire to honestly earn the most for yourself that you can, it's a virtue. It's one of the highest virtues. It means the commitment to achieving the best for yourself and never being satisfied that now I have enough and I can stop the quest. On the other hand, some people use the term "greed" as a smear to mean irrational desire for the unearned. Not to make more money, but to steal or appropriate more money. And that is a bad thing. But the origin of the term "greed" is from the word "hunger." To be greedy is to be hungry. To be hungry means to want to get values, to want to achieve, to want to live. That's not evil. That's the essence of virtue.

So – in your opinion – has the 'prophecy' of Atlas Shrugged come true? Have we achieved that dystopian future?
HB: We're living in a semi-dystopia. When we're really living in a dystopia, we won't have this documentary. We'll be in jail. Or digging for roots in the forest. That's the real dystopia. That's the end of the road. This today is the halfway house to that.

Los Angeles, February 2011

CHAPTER TWELVE
JOHN MCINTYRE

John W. McIntyre is the co-founder of Health Care Microsystems, Inc. He served as chief executive officer for 12 years until it merged with New York-based Health Management Systems Corporation, and then served on the board of directors of HMS.

Mr. McIntyre is a former associate professor with the University of California, Los Angeles, teaching at the College of Public Health as well as the Anderson Graduate School of Management.

He is also the former chairman of the board and initial director for the Center for Entrepreneurship and Engineering Management at the University of California, Santa Barbara. CEEM is responsible for the development of entrepreneurial skill sets for engineers who wish to commercialize newly developed technologies and initiate viable new businesses.

He received a Bachelor of Science degree in finance and operations and a Master of Business Administration degree from the University of Utah in Salt Lake City. He is a Certified Public Accountant and private investor.

Our interview took place in Marina Del Rey, California in December 2009.

How did you first become acquainted with Atlas Shrugged?

JOHN McINTYRE: I was a junior in college. I was a football player. A good friend and another football player recommended the book to me because he knew I was a business major at the University of Utah. When I started reading it, I wasn't sure about pursuing business. When I finished reading it I was absolutely sure that business was a noble profession and was something I wanted to pursue with a vengeance.

What aspect most resonated with you?

JM: The novel provided a moral justification or reason why businesses were so important especially in America. And maybe the novel was one of the most American novels I'd ever read.

This despite the fact that the author had to first learn English in order to write it.

JM: Ayn Rand was an immigrant to this country from Russia so she knew more than most people what it meant to be an American. She *chose* to be an American.

And she wasn't shy about expressing her views, was she?

JM: She didn't try to be subtle. She pounded her philosophy into the reader. If you read her novel once you heard her philosophy probably ten times. I think what meant the most to me in terms of personalizing it was that it made the individual the core of society. It wasn't a particular group of individuals. It was *the* individual.

Did you identify with any one character?

JM: The character I was drawn to most was Dagny Taggart. I'm in Utah and I'm not a Mormon but here's a woman and she's one of the most powerful individuals I can imagine, powerful in that she knew what she was all about. She created, she produced and that's what she continued to want to do. I thought that was extraordinary. And then Francisco de Anconia – however many long names he ended up with, I thought he was an interesting character.

And then Hank Rearden. Who was also a magnificent producer and Ayn Rand kept pounding into your brain that there were only two ways to accumulate wealth. One was to steal it or loot it and the other was to create it, to innovate it and produce it. And Hank Rearden was the personification or the embodiment of that production capacity. Next to Dagny, he was the guy I admired most.

What about the villains? Aren't they deliciously low?

JM: Yeah the villains, I think her brother, Taggart, was despicable. I mean he was the guy you loved to loathe. And the guys like Mouch and Boyle, the guys from the government who are here to help, it's quite the opposite. It's sort of like today when I think about it. Today those guys aren't here to help. They're here to loot and here to be parasites.

I imagine you'd like to see Atlas on required reading lists in schools?

JM: I think every effort should be made to do so because the kids today don't know what life should or could be like under capitalism. Capitalism turns out to be a bad word for kids today.

You have to use words like freedom – free enterprise seems to be okay – or entrepreneurialism because kids want to be their own boss, they want to call their own shots, they still have a strong desire to be free. But they don't realize that capitalism is the only system, economic system, in the world today that supports and requires individual freedom.

And it's kind of a rebellious novel too which feeds into young people's natural tendency to rebel from authority and society so I think it's a great idea.

Today people point to characters like Bernie Madoff and say 'there's capitalism run amok.' Greed in a nutshell.

JM: Guys like Bernie Madoff are the *antithesis* of capitalism. When we rely on government regulations or promises to make sure no one is a Bernie Madoff, we're going to fail every time because government's not going to do that for us. Although they promise to and they get votes for that purpose, it's the individual that's going to have to look out for their best interests. Think about it. Government collects our taxes and promises to protect our interest against the Bernie Madoffs of the world. When government fails to do this what do we get? We get more government and more taxes. Our personal interest and government interest are not aligned. With Capitalism, private, competitive watch dog groups are more effective and remain more in line with our interests. And they can be fired, government bureaucrats can't.

Still capitalism or 'greed' is most often blamed for our current financial woes.

JM: As for 'greedy capitalists' creating the mess that we're in now, I would beg to differ. One we're not a capitalist society anymore. At best we're a mixed economy. I think Ayn Rand mentioned that. For instance health care has been 40 or 50 percent government oriented for the last fifty years, since 1964. And as for the financial industry, there are so many rules and regulations that it's an opaque maze. The individual has no chance of understanding what's going on and we don't try to because we think the government is somehow protecting us - another false promise and false premise. The myriad regulations prevent new companies from entering the industry. Crony capitalism ain't capitalism.

With the economic crisis used as political fodder and accusations flying left and right in the media it's hard to reach the heart of any issue, isn't it?

JM: Kids today don't understand what true capitalism is. The idea of being greedy and selfish they equate with capitalism but actually being selfish doesn't mean you're just looking after yourself. Self interest includes looking out for your family, your kids, your neighbors, your community, etc. It's a question of logical, long-term interest rather than greedy short-term and short-sighted interest. So I think there is a mistake there propagated by people who would benefit from having you feel guilty about self-interest.

Politicians in general have become expert in playing the guilt card, haven't they?

JM: When somebody puts you in the position of feeling guilty because you're not living your life for somebody else, I think that's a real problem. And I think it's easy to do. People talk about compassion and the idea that you're free because the government provides your freedom when it's quite the opposite actually and Ayn Rand points that out. We institute the government to make sure we are free as individuals and if we do something wrong as individuals, yeah we should feel guilty but we shouldn't feel guilty about not living our lives for somebody else.

When the government steps in and says I claim part of your life for this group or that group, these professional poverty hounds, etc., we should feel guilty only if we bow to that pressure, to that false premise. In fact it will do more harm for us to feel guilty about pursing self-interest. It takes away from our innovation, our creativity, our production so – I think that's despicable. And I think Ayn Rand points that out very clearly in *Atlas Shrugged*, as clearly as anybody's ever pointed that out.

Has your connection with Rand's ideas influenced your success or the way you do business?

JM: For my company, we started out with two people and ended up with 220 highly paid positions. We were in business to help hospitals bring down their costs, understand their costs, etc. And when we became successful, some employees thought about what we could do to help society, what can we do to give back to society. But in my mind we were giving as much as we possibly could to society by earning a profit ourselves and helping each hospital understand and control their costs so they could earn a profit and charge society less for more. I thought that anything that took us away from that focus and that effort would be a problem. It wouldn't help our company and it wouldn't benefit society. Not as much as we already were. I think businesses are giving as much as they possibly can when they do their best to do whatever they do.

So you probably don't consider money to be 'the root of all evil?'

JM: (laughs) I wish I could refer to Ayn Rand's lengthy speech about money being the root of all good - there are only two ways to accumulate wealth. One is to loot it and one is to create it and money represents the medium of exchange for trade. That means that I create something that someone else wants and I want something that somebody else has created, I can use that medium of exchange to satisfy my needs and they can satisfy their needs.

And I don't have to invade his house or take anything by force and thank God nobody's trying to do that to me. And I think money represents that idea, the idea of trade rather than looting or stealing or coercing.

Rand was adamant, wasn't she, that physical force – or the threat of it - should never be initiated except in self-defense.
JM: No one has the right to coerce or to initiate force against anybody else and I think that's absolutely the first commandment. We may not have a God-given right to freedom but no one has the right to enslave.

It's remarkable, isn't it, that Rand who so unequivocally revered and defended the fundamental values of individualism and freedom upon which America is founded, saw her views often misrepresented as 'elitist' or even 'fascist?'
JM: Ayn Rand is the opposite of a fascist. She is the least scary person when it comes to her trying to control your life. She's offering ideas and you can accept them or you can reject them. You may get her scorn but there's nothing else involved. She was not born an American. She is an American by choice. And remember the Founding Fathers were not born Americans either. They *created* this country. They created this country as a haven for individual freedom.

What parallels do you see between the events in Atlas Shrugged and today?
JM: I keep going back to health care because that was my business. I've seen this industry evolve from a relatively free industry to at best a mixed industry – meaning government and a little bit of free enterprise. Government promised to make healthcare cheaper through regulations and tax funding and proceeded to achieve just the opposite. Their solution? More of the same – which will only further exacerbate the problems. Freedom of

choice for healthcare customers and healthcare providers alike is essential for an effective and efficient healthcare industry. Government intervention is preventing that.

You're saying a society's success is in direct proportion to the freedom it's allowed?

JM: In a society where people are actually free. And by free I mean free to exercise their own volition for everything. I mean whatever they earn and produce they have claim to. It can't be a situation where whatever you have the mob or the majority can decide to take away from you. That's what our constitution is all about – protecting the individual from coercion. But in a society where we are free to produce and keep what we produce and trade that for other things that we would like and have other people trade what they produce with us, etc. Those are the societies where the incentives to work hard flourish. Those are the countries that are the most prosperous.

Where the individual has the most chance to improve his life?

JM: It's all about self-interest, it really is. And that's what at the lowest level creates the highest level of prosperity for a group of self-interested individuals.

And that's what creating this country was all about. That's how it was founded. And that's why you can't do things by fiat nearly as well or as efficiently certainly or as effectively as you can do things if you let people follow their own self-interest.

It's Adam Smith writ large. The virtue of capitalism is supporting the individual in their pursuit of long term, logical self-interest. Ours is the only economic system in the history of the world that has supported the individual and his pursuit of self-interest thereby extending the overwhelming benefits of those pursuits to society at large.

Besides the opportunity to make his fortune, what are some other benefits to unrestricted free enterprise?

JM:. Hope - hope for a better life. Not "hope and change". But real hope so that they are gonna be able to keep what they earn so they have an incentive to work hard. And there's also the benefit of wisdom. You've heard of the "Wisdom of Crowds". Well, it's a composite of the wisdom of each individual that makes up the crowd's wisdom. The crowd combines the different expertise of each individual to achieve a wide ranging expertise for the whole. Why do you think America is so advanced? With unrestricted free enterprise we are each compelled to gain and trade and share our individual wisdom. Wisdom is, after all, intelligence combined with experience. And we can pass that on to their own progeny or to our own communities or neighbors, etc. That is how we all prosper. On the other hand with centralized government deciding for all, the natural tendency is toward indolence and the abrogation of desires or the necessities of acquiring individual wisdom. You rely on government to take care of things. That never seems to work out.

How closely is this country aligned with the principle of free enterprise?

JM: Our country was founded on the basis of every man having a right to pursue his own interests, the right to freedom and a right to not be hassled so to speak by the government. And we created a government to make sure we weren't hassled. Ironically it's that same government that's hassling us most at this point in our nation's history. It has grown large and dangerous – a threat to the very rights that we wanted it to establish and protect.

Can you share any of the ways in which reading Atlas Shrugged affected your life or career?

JM: I owe a lot to that book. I owe my sense of identity in a large measure to that book. It provided a complete philosophy that seemed to fit my understanding of human nature. It made me think deeply about the morality of my business objectives and methods. It also provided a template for engaging potential partners and associates. I looked for people who would work hard to create real value for our clients.

I wish I had met Ayn Rand. One of my biggest disappointments I think, was to read back in 1982 that she had died.

Do you think we'll ever see the producers in this country pull back or start to disappear?

JM: I think the idea of going on strike, the idea of the men and women of the mind, at one point just simply refusing to work and stop carrying the moochers on our backs is a valid idea. It is a real idea. You see it happening everyday – every time a person decides not to start a small business or to shut down a profitable small business because they're fed up with the obstacles that our government puts in their way.

You think it could happen?

People need to discover – it's kinda like Ghandi's civil disobedience - the thing we can do is just say no.

We're not going to continue to produce from a sense of guilt or solely for the benefit of specific groups that some politician deems worthy. We're not going to create the rope for moochers to hang us with any longer. I think that's, in a large measure, what the tea parties are about. And they're not just Republicans, they're not just Democrats, they're not just Independents. It's a coalescence of people that have decided that enough is enough. We are going broke. They are spending money that they have never earned. It's our money. We've earned it. And we haven't sanctioned them to spend it in the way they are spending it. It boils down to politicians taking and spending our money for their own re-election campaigns instead of common infrastructures that might have real benefits.

You're talking about the redistribution of wealth?

JM: I'm talking about a government who sees fit in taking money from wherever it's produced, from whomever it's produced and giving it to their constituents under the guise of giving it to poor people or under the guise of giving it to a group that has rights that are not being recognized, etc., etc. Why should we carry a government that's abusing everyone's freedom?

Last question. When you think of John Galt, today, does anyone in particular come to mind?

JM: John Galt. Who is John Galt? John Galt doesn't have to be famous or a big business tycoon. He can just as easily be your local plumber. John Galt'is every person, every man, every woman who produces and who follows his own self-interest for his own benefit and ends up benefiting everybody. That's John Galt. The guy who produces and creates, who innovates - the guy that we're lucky to have in our society – the guy we want, the guy we need to stay motivated.

-Los Angeles, December 2009

Targeting the rich in a time of need

Oregon voters have a long record of killing tax increases. But they may have found some they can live with.

CHAPTER THIRTEEN
KEVIN O'CONNOR

KEVIN O'CONNOR is a Santa Barbara-based entrepreneur specializing in tech startups. Co-founder in 2009 and CEO of FindTheBest.com, Mr. Conner, in 1995, co-founded DoubleClick, an Internet advertisement-technology company which was acquired by Google in April 2007. Before DoubleClick, O'Connor directed research and development for the Inter-computer Communications Corporation, a microcomputer to mainframe inter-connectivity company.

O'Connor is the author of The Map of Innovation: Creating Something Out of Nothing, which was published in 2003.

Our interview took place in Mr. O'Connor's Santa Barbara home in fall 2009.

What was your first connection with Atlas Shrugged?

KEVIN O'CONNOR: Probably twenty five years ago - I was doing my first startup. We were in the early days. And I was kind of an avowed Socialist, the whole Karl Marxism thing, and it all made sense to me coming out of university. And I had my first run in with the government. And the State of Ohio wanted to shut us down because we hadn't paid our unemployment tax. So they were gonna shut down the company and un-employ everybody because we hadn't paid our unemployment tax. And it was just kind of a series of things like that. And my partner, Bill Miller, said: "I've got this book that you would really, really like and it's *Atlas Shrugged*." And I read the book, and it changed my life.

In what way?

KO: It kind of all made sense at that point. I finally realized that, especially as I got out into the world. Universities, you know, are basically petri dishes, not representative of the real world – and you get out there and kind of see how things really operate. And it all made sense. We were doing a start up. We had no money. We were struggling. We were trying to create new products. I was an inventor. So the characters, I could really relate to the characters.

With whom did you most identify?

KO: I think probably early on, I was probably more like Rearden. I could relate to him more. I was just kinda this inventor. Today, I'd probably say, I could relate more to John Galt.

What Rearden characteristics appealed to you?

KO: Rearden was this inventor who was just passionate about inventing. He loved technology, he just loved what technology could do. And it's kinda where I've always been. I was probably thirteen, fourteen years old. I was an inventor. I just loved technology. I would sit for hours, and hours and hours. Here in my business, I didn't start a business to make money. I started a business to really pursue my hobby, my passion. It was technology. And it just… everything about technology just jazzes me.

Does the book still resonate for you today?

KO: When I read Ayn Rand's *Atlas Shrugged*, Ronald Reagan had just come into office, and Ronald Reagan sort of embodied the Rand philosophies. And over the years… I mean, even Clinton, to me, Clinton was a great freedom and liberal thinker. Laissez-faire thinker. But today, for the first time, in my lifetime, we have a real kinda scary society, where the successful, the people that have accomplished things, somehow have to be sorry for what they did. And this whole class warfare - and by the way when I say "class warfare," I'm not even sure that's a good term, because I didn't grow up rich. I struggled for years, and years, and years, starting a company. To me, it's the fight between the makers and the takers. The people that make things, and there's the people that take things. The class action lawyers, the government. So, that's always been around, for the last twenty-five years. But it hasn't been until really the last year where it's a significant threat. Like, people shaking their heads, saying: "I never thought this could happen again, I thought that, you know, all those terrible years that we had were behind us, and that people weren't stupid enough to allow this to happen again, and here we are. This is probably, to me, and most of the folks I know, this is probably some of the most scary times that we've ever faced.

Just talking to people, there's this kind of this feeling like: "You know what? We could always move. You know, if people don't appreciate what we've done, we'll move. Move to Australia. Move to New Zealand. Move out of California. California, you know, last year they imposed a 1% sur-tax on the rich. The millionaire's tax they call it. Well, in the state of California, I don't know, what is it, 70% of the taxes are paid by the top 1%. We're already paying all the taxes. So you know, at some point people just kinda get fed up. And, you know, they could move.

So do you think of places like Australia or New Zealand as Galt's Gulch?

KO: Well, I always try to figure out where is Galt's Gulch? And it seems to be like New Zealand is the place. You know, it's this big, beautiful country. There's not that many people. They're completely independent and isolated from the world. Sure... I love to ski. I love to surf. What better place than New Zealand?

Do you think the book is more relevant now, than at other times in your career?

KO: I think it was around the Carter administration when a lot of the threats that were happening in *Atlas Shrugged* were taking place. And then we had sort of the new regime, the Reagan years, which were really great years of just of individual freedom, and this whole sort of disdain for government. You know, his famous words: "What are the seven or nine most scary words you can hear? 'I'm from the US government and I'm here to help you'."

So by 'class warfare' you're not talking about rich versus poor, are you?

KO: No. For me it's a struggle between the makers and the takers or - as Rand called them - the moochers and the looters. But she celebrated the makers - the engineers, the inventors, people who are making things to make human life more enjoyable, reduce the pain, live longer, just you know, really positive things.

Producers.

KO: You know, ultimately, the only way you become successful as an entrepreneur is you provide products that people benefit from - to help all of us. And then there's, to me, the dark side. The takers. And the people that are trying just to take the fruits of our labor and our brain – take it for themselves. Of course, they never say that they're taking it for themselves, they're taking for "the common man." You would never hear Mel Weiss of Milberg Weiss talk about how he's enriching himself but it's about how he's, you know, "protecting the little guy." When in fact, everything I've ever seen is about enriching themselves.

Who is Mel Weiss?

KO: Mel Weiss is the head of Milberg-Weiss which is one of the most successful trial lawyers. They pioneered the class-action law suit. To me, that's one of the biggest plagues that's really hit this country. There's been this massive redistribution of wealth by these folks that supposedly represent the "common man," that are getting tremendous amounts of money, and then funneling that money into the government, to change laws, to prop up and make their industry even more powerful.

As a successful businessman in the technology and internet sector, have you experienced much 'interference' from politicians?

KO: I have lots of good stories about that. Back in the internet days, I was running Double-Click and I was fairly politically ignorant. And all of a sudden the internet companies became very successful. And we had lots of politicians – it was my first exposure to politicians – and they were sort of lined up at the door. Well first they'd tell us, you know: "I'm in charge of the committee that is setting rules that could, if we make bad rules, destroy your industry. And we'd really like to understand how we can help you, and make good rules." And then, as they're walking out the door, they'd say: "Oh, by the way... how much money do you think you could raise for us?"

And these are some of the top political figures. This is John Kerry and Billy Townsend, some of the lead characters back in the Clinton days. So it was a pretty big disappointment. But you know, that was manageable. I didn't realize that's the way Washington works. If people understood the way our federal government really, really works, it's pretty ugly. It's kinda like visiting a sausage factory. It may taste good, may look good, but it's a pretty ugly process. And it's not a right process. It's completely wrong.

What do you think would happen if all the 'makers' went out on strike?

KO: Strikes are usually done by workers - organized labor. And most inventors, most people that make things, they don't do it for the money, they do it cause they love it. So the fact that they would turn away from something that they love, to go on strike, I've always wrestled with that one. I didn't quite understand it. Until maybe this year where going on strike, maybe it's a real possibility. I'm not sure "strike"'s the right word, it's just sort of a fed up.

We're hearing a lot about 'class warfare.' Is that what this boils down to?

KO: *They* turned it into class warfare. They sort of pit the rich against everyone else. The top 1%. Whatever you wanna call it. The millionaires, against everybody else. But it's not about class warfare. There are a lot of people that want freedom in every form. Freedom to pursue the businesses that they want. Freedom to pursue whatever sexual preferences they want. Freedom to just live their life, to find happiness. And so... you know, it's kind of interesting, I think, the Tea Party came out as one of the most popular political groups. What's the one commonality? It's sort of their disdain, their mistrust of government. That you just keep taxing everybody more and more. I think people understand now, when you tax the wealthy, it doesn't even make sense. The wealthy are investing their dollars in productive businesses. It's self-defeating.

How do you put a stop to rapidly growing government?

KO: In order to stop big government, you gotta strangle it. And the way you strangle it is you cut off the money. You cut off the blood, and the blood is the money. And you just shrink it down dramatically. And you push government back to local - as local as you can. This whole concept of a powerful central government is just... you know, the founders are spinning in their graves. Along with Rand. This country was founded by folks that were trying to escape that very situation.

The whole concept of having this tyrannical government - people abhorred it. The whole Constitution is geared so that we would never get back to that situation. So I think it's getting back to the individual. And I think that's what *Atlas Shrugged* was all about, and what Rand really celebrated, was the individual. Whatever that individual is, doesn't necessarily matter. As long as that individual is not coercing something out of somebody else, then it's fine.

Are the kind of heroes we find in Atlas Shrugged possible, or are they strictly ideals?

KO: You know, *Atlas Shrugged* characters are fascinating, you know, cause in some ways they're caricatures. They're sort of an extreme, idealistic view of strong, individual characteristics. So, have I ever met anybody like the characters in Ayn Rand? No. I can definitely see pieces of ... you know, there's a little bit of Rearden, there's a little bit of Dagny, there's a little bit of John in there, Francisco, so there's pieces of it. But, I'm not sure the characters in the book were ever meant to be real.

But they represent something?

KO: Absolutely. The characters represent, sort of, fundamental truths of our instincts. And our instincts are to pursue our happiness, to pursue our talents, to pursue the things that we love.

What is it about Atlas Shrugged that so appeals to young people?

KO: It just seems like Rand's philosophies appeal to the young because the young want to be individuals. They don't want to be told what to do. They're escaping parental control. I can't think of a single person that I've ever met who said: "Yeah, I read *Atlas*

Shrugged, but it didn't really have much of an influence." It's quite the opposite. It seems like everyone that's read her books, it's made a mark on their lives. My kid's middle name is Rand. Great friend of mine was like: "My kid's middle name is Rand too!" I was talking to someone this morning. He had done a company. His first company's name was Anthem. You know, in reference to one of her novels. Short of Jesus, I'm not sure I've seen any individual have such an impact on people's lives.

The people you meet who most disparage Atlas usually haven't read it.
KO: That's right – never read it.

Do you find that some people are predisposed to discount or belittle Rand's ideas?
KO: Well, you know, her base concept is a paradox. Which is: self-ishness somehow leads to a better world. It contradicts everything we've ever been taught. You know, if you're selfish, you're taking away from somebody. She said: "No, no, no, it's completely the opposite. You're pursuing what interests you. You're not taking anything away from anybody. In fact, she abhorred that. I mean, that was one of the few reasons government should exist, is to stop people taking away from others. So, this whole concept that: "you know what, if we all pursue what interests us, and what makes living interesting, and worth pursuing, then the whole world would be a better place." And I think that's one of the reasons capitalism… capitalism seems like a really sort of evil. You know, if everyone's competing, and competing means, you know, winners and losers. I mean, it seems really, really mean. But it works. It works beautifully, because that's the way we are.

So, in that sense, 'selfishness' equates with the Golden Rule?
KO: Yeah, completely. I mean you can almost boil the Ten Commandments down - and a lot of what our laws should be - to "thou

shalt not steal." You know, thou shalt not take value away from somebody through coercion. Whether it's at the point of a gun. Or whether it's because they turned their back. That's the Golden Rule.

You say the heroes don't exist per se, just characteristics of them, because they're highly drawn romantic characters. What about the villains? Do you see the villains today?

KO: Who are the moochers, and the looters? At the top of the list goes the government. You look at the federal government today, the Obama administration is filled with people that have never held a job. I mean, they've held jobs, but it's always been in a university setting, or in a government setting. They've never worked in an industry that actually produced something. That had to be, you know, a competitive industry.

The other looters are quite frankly the unions. You know, our public school system is a disaster in my mind, for one primary reason. Well, two reasons. There's just no competition. It's government control, government run. But it's the unions. The unions will do everything they can to suck money out of a situation until it becomes unworkable. They don't want to go by performance, you can't get rid of bad teachers. I'm from Detroit, Michigan. One of the reasons I left Michigan is I just couldn't stand it. Everything was on strike all the time. Michigan is a great experiment gone awry. The auto industry is in complete disarray. They kept sucking money out of it - auto workers making 75 bucks an hour, completely uncompetitive, and now, where are they? They're all out of a job. You know, who won in that scenario? Who controls the State of Michigan today? It's the unions. The government employees. People are completely held captive... you know the number one voting block? It's the unions. The city of Detroit? Dominated by the unions. Well, what's going to happen? Everyone's going to leave. Michigan is going to be, I believe, like in *Atlas Shrugged*: "Oh my God, look at the mess we created. And there's no one here... there's no one else we can extort any money from."

And you've already mentioned the trial lawyers.

KO: Really, really bad, bad group of people. Okay, I'm sure there's a few good ones out there, that really do care for the common man. But everything I've experienced, and we've seen a lot of them gone to jail recently, is because they're just doing it for themselves. It's completely random who they go after. They go after you if your stock goes up, your stock goes down, your stock goes sideways. You know, no matter what happens, they're going after you. And the ones that pay is everyone in society. You know, the trial lawyers have exercised a tax on everyone in this country. And they've amassed a huge amount of money, and they're using it to buy political parties. You know, go look at: Who was John Kerry's biggest supporter when he was running for president? Who was the democratic party's biggest supporter? It's the trial lawyers, as a group of people.

It sounds like you might be speaking from experience. Have you had any run-ins with trial lawyers or class actions?

KO: I've got kind of a funny story. When I was raising - and ultimately *did* raise money for John Kerry. Not that I believed in his policies but because he ran a very important committee that controlled the internet. Something I've never been proud of. But you know in business sometimes you gotta do the lesser of two evils. And I was at a kind of an interesting party. It was at Paul Newman and Joanna Woodward's house. It was kinda cool. And he went around the room asking people for their opinion. And I was pretty apolitical. I didn't know much about it. He asked me: "What was an important topic that wasn't raised." And I thought about it, I said: "What can I say that is... that everyone would agree with. And couldn't possibly disagree with. And I said: tort reform. You know, we gotta fix the trial lawyers." And the whole room was quiet. Dead silence. And everyone busted out laughing. They all started laughing. And one guy goes to the balcony, and said, you know, "If there's ever tort reform, I'd kill myself!" Turned out 75% of the room were trial lawyers. They were all trial lawyers. They thought I was one of the funniest guys they've ever seen. They thought it was just a big joke.

That is funny. Okay, so we've got the government, the unions and the trial lawyers. Anybody else?

KO: I can tell you one other moocher-looter - something that needs to be fixed - this whole attorney-generals-running-for-governor. I happened to be in New York when Elliott Spitzer went on his spree of terror. You know, where he launched all these campaigns at the point of the government gun - totally laid out in *Atlas Shrugged*. Whether it was through public embarrassment or whether it was actually threatening to put them in jail, just did it time and time again. And I'm so happy to see, you know, sometimes justice *does* get paid. And justice was paid there. But it was allowed to go too long.

You see it all the time. Jennifer Granholm became governor of Michigan being an attorney general. No one says "no" to an attorney general. When attorney general comes up to your business, looking for donations, you give it to them. Why? Cause they can ruin you. Look at how many times the government has ruined Arthur Anderson. Destroyed Arthur Anderson. Really, completely, years later, ten years later, unfounded claims. It's just story after story.

Can you name any other victims?

KO: Well, Elliott Spitzer had a long line of victims. I mean, let's take a look at AIG. You know, Greenberg was one of the greatest CEOs of all time. The guy was phenomenal. They forced him out, and now AIG is a government-run industry. Who would have ever thunk that we'd have all these government run... you know, the government have nationalized our auto industry. They have virtually nationalized our financial industry. It's just shocking. They're setting wage controls. They're setting, you know, price controls.

They want to take 17% of our economy in health care, one of the most important things of life, and nationalize it. If people don't think we're a socialist country today, they better be smart enough to know that we're quickly on the path of a socialist country.

How do you see the effects of these moves manifesting themselves?

KO: It teaches kids, it teaches people, that there's always somebody to blame. That somehow life is about fairness. That everything must be fair. And that no one is to blame for anything. You know, whether it's genetics, or the way your parents raised you, and the color of your skin, your religion, your sexual preferences, you know everything, everything must be fair. We've turned into a blame society. We've got this whole nanny-state thing going on. And it just... I don't get it. I used to wash dishes at a Chinese restaurant. And I used to like doing it. Was it a glorified job? No. I can't think of many worse jobs. But I had some money in my pocket and I was good at it. You know, it's something to be proud of. And now I think doing menial jobs is considered menial. And it's not something to be proud of. It's more proud to go on unemployment, or suck on the teet of the government, than it is to work.

We'd imagine you believe capitalism is far and away the best system?

KO: All systems are probably evil. But it's definitely the least evil of all of them. Capitalism is a great system. We're a competitive species. Everything we do is for survival. And capitalism has so many beautiful built in mechanisms, self-correcting mechanisms for everything. A lot of my management techniques were probably very influenced by Rand. At the end of the day people are going to do What's in their self-interest. You know, it's just foolhardy to think that somehow they're going to do what's better for the company. That they're going to sacrifice their self-interest. So, I always try to align the company's interest with self-interest. You end up with better outcomes. Sometimes I think the government - you lay a big piece of meat in front of a starving dog and when the dog eats it you beat it. You know, for doing something that has just been bred in that dog for millions of years. You're not gonna change human interest. You're not going to change millions of years of evolution.

Michael Moore says capitalism is the 'opposite of democracy.' What's your reaction to that?

KO: Democracy in its purest form I don't agree with at all. I would agree with representative democracy. Because three hundred million people aren't going to be knowledgeable to take the time to understand every issue. Not that our 554 Congress people do either but there's at least groups that can focus on issues. Capitalism - people can vote every day. To me, capitalistic companies are representative democracies. You don't like the company? You leave. The company doesn't like you? It fires you.

But in a way, Moore is right, isn't he? Although it's probably not the context he meant. At it's best, capitalism provides for individual choice while democracy in its purest form amounts more or less to mob rule.

KO: To Rand, the government's primary role – and maybe sole role - is to protect people from other people stealing their stuff. Other than that, the government should be pretty small. The reality is we do live in a society and you have to have some level of order and some level of rules. And it should be difficult for the democracy to change those rules. One of the worst situations in capitalism is not knowing what the rules are. Imagine playing a game of football, and the rules change in the middle of the third quarter.

How do you feel about Atlas Shrugged's relevance today? Do you think Rand is gaining acceptance in the mainstream?

KO: I'm always astounded that *Atlas Shrugged* is not required reading. Okay look, study after study has shown that there's a huge liberal bias in colleges and schools – just teachers in general. Ironically – to me - Ayn Rand is incredibly liberal. She's maybe one of the most liberal people I've ever come across. People get confused. They think that somehow conservatism means small government and liberals want big government. I'm extremely social liberal and I don't see how you can have big government and be socially liberal. Because when government gets big, they just want to control things. They want to make laws to control your life.

What has reading Atlas Shrugged as a young man meant for you?

KO: I guess that I don't have to apologize for making something, inventing something, and having it become successful. If anything, it should be celebrated. I shouldn't have to apologize for making a lot of money. It's nothing to be ashamed of. And I won't be ashamed of it. I take that money and I invest it in great things and we give it to schools and invest in the future. And that there's nothing wrong with it.

Santa Barbara, October 2009

CHAPTER FOURTEEN

MICHAEL MIGNOGNA

Michael Mignogna is a young, New York-based entrepreneur. The internet software he's developing for restaurants was the subject of a recent Wall Street Journal article.

What was your first connection with Atlas Shrugged?
MICHAEL MIGNOGNA: Well, when I was 20 I was living in an apartment in college. One of my best friends came over. We were gonna do our normal afternoon of watching stupid TV shows and probably getting high. And he comes over with this gigantic book and he said it's called *Atlas Shrugged.* I said, well why are you reading it? He said, because my father told me that I can't take over the family business unless I read this book. So I bought the book.

I mean had to read the book at that point and then about at – I think about 150 pages in I had decided it was the best book I've ever read. So and from there I read everything she wrote, fiction, non-fiction.

What did you see in that first 150 pages that hooked you?
MM: What got me was that it I could understand it. It wasn't this abstract – well – that's not even the right word to use. It wasn't this deep, like whoa philosophy kinda feeling that philosophy where you have a guy sitting on a hill smoking a pipe, you know trying to tell everyone what life was about in sort of a way that no one could understand. This was totally intelligible. I was able to read it and learn something as I read and it just felt really good to not keep having to say what does that mean.

Do you think it grounded you in a sense?
MM: Yes. It gave you principles. And I think, yeah, that, that's a good point because when I – when, when you learn things sometimes you learn them by accident. You see 10 things happen and then you notice things that are similar in those 10 things and you're able to say, well, these similar things must mean something. You could, you could learn something from that.

How did that contrast with your previous reading experience?
MM: Well, with the news you read about someone supporting one policy and then not supporting another, but principally they're the same. So, to not support or reject both doesn't make any sense. And it's impossible to learn why they are choosing one way or another unless you realize that they just live a contradictory life in general. And I think reading a book that is so principled and that teaches you that principles exist and you can have these absolute beliefs on something really narrows it down for you.

Do you think Rand's ideas were more accessible because she illustrated them in the form of fiction?

MM: I think the fact that it wasn't just a textbook explaining what objectivism meant. And that instead it was a story that showed it in real life or what could be in real life helped 'cause I got to see examples of what she meant by a man that is exalted or a man that has a rational pride for something and why pride is not bad and why selfishness isn't bad. And to *see* why - as opposed to just being *told* why. It helps.

What did you think of the characters? Did any of them have specific appeal for you?

MM: The characters were amazing. I wanted to marry Dagny Taggart and I wanted to be Francisco d'Anconia. I wanted to be *all* the heroes, you know, Rearden and Ragnar and all of them. But I think that's a good thing. If I wanted to be one of the devils in the book, it probably wouldn't be a good sign. (laughs)

They get their just desserts.

MM: Yes, they do. The villains were incredible. There's something super scary about someone that knows what they're doing is wrong but intentionally just evades that reality and then apologizes for it. I think that's hilarious. (laughs) *'We didn't know! We didn't mean it.'* It was so pathetic, I mean I was actually laughing 'cause it's not that, it's not that far off. I mean, I feel like every time I turn on the news there's someone apologizing for something.

So you connected Rand's villains with characters in real life?

MM: I can't honestly say I remember what I was thinking with regards to what was going on in the world when I was 20. It feels like so long ago for some reason. But I do know that when I started reading *Atlas Shrugged*, I knew I needed to learn more about what was going on in the world. 'Cause I didn't follow politics at all. And then I re-read *Atlas Shrugged* after getting more in tune with just news and politics. And, and then I was able to really apply what the book taught me to the world and sort of make those connections.

Where do you see them?

MM: Sometimes I swear people are quoting the book and they don't even realize it. There's a specific columnist in the New York Times that I can't stand - Paul Krugman. He writes columns that seem like they're literally taken from *Atlas Shrugged* - the villain's speeches. And it's very bizarre.

What about any of your friends? Have you recommended Atlas to them?

MM: Most of my friends said "Atlas what?" I said, "Atlas Shrugged, and you should read it." And they're like, okay, how many pages. Why? I mean like we're 25, why are you asking how many pages the book is now? Are you gonna ask me if there's pictures next, 'cause there isn't. I couldn't find anyone really that read it. But then I started asking more and more. And then the common answer from some older people was, oh I read that, you know, to like some older family members, Oh, I read that when I was really young, I used to love it when I was young. Well what happened? You know, did you like give up on your dreams or something?

Why do you imagine it's so often and vehemently criticized?

MM: Well, often times people hate the good simply for the fact that it's good. So that might be a reason. Jealousy, you know, envy, I don't know. I think philosophers hated it because they had or up until that point had this sort of monopoly on total confusion. That's how I think of it. They've got this guy on a hill teaching the world what ideas are and it's like this out of this world stuff that no one can understand. And then I think people are trained to say to themselves, well if I don't understand, it must be because this is too brilliant for me, they're too smart for me. And then Rand comes along with this intelligible philosophy that I think people can understand. I'm not saying it's not difficult, it's very complex.

But it, it does start at one point and it progresses nicely and eloquently and beautifully into the next corollary principle and it makes sense. And I think philosophers were really scared of that.

It's philosophy with a practical application.

MM: It applies to man's life on earth. Whereas I think these philosophers that hated her, their philosophies don't apply to men on earth. I mean, you look at, you look at Plato and, and Plato's Republic, and his idea for how to create this utopia. And sure, it would work great if we were machines. But we're not. We have free will and we have desires to achieve things for ourselves. So, I think they were afraid of her for that.

Rand often acknowledged her philosophical debt to Aristotle citing his defense of reason, logic, reality and the importance of life on earth.

MM: Yes. She liked Aristotle's metaphysics. The philosopher she most despised was Immanuel Kant. Kant basically was well you can't know anything for sure. And I think her response was, *are you positive?* (laughs) You'd be surprised how often you can back someone into that corner. You can say well are you implying that you can't know anything for sure? Please say yes. Please say yes. And they go, yes, you can't know anything for sure. Are you positive? And then they're like, f–k. (laughs) You know. Am I standing here? I don't know. Well then who am I talking to? I think that, that's why people hated Ayn Rand because she said I'm right here, you're talking to me.

In Atlas Shrugged, Rand depicted politicians and crony capitalists as 'moochers' and 'looters.' Who do you see currently as fitting that description.

MM: Well, the woman that came into the restaurant I work at recently is definitely one of the looters and moochers. She works for the health department. That is an example, I think, of legalized stealing. It's so obvious. It's so blatant. This is how it works. They walk in, okay, and first of all the health code that a restaurant has to live by - if they were to follow it to the T- would literally not be able to run. Everyone would be wrapped in saran wrap in the entire restaurant. That's how bad it is. So they come in, they give you a fine. 'Cause something's gonna be wrong. Someone's gonna be garnishing a drink with their fingers. And instead they have to use like tongs, they have to stand like seven feet away. If they want to breathe, they have to go outside first. It's absolutely crazy. So they come in and they fine you. You pay them the money. And then they give you a second chance. Thank you. And then hopefully you get an A on your grade so you can display it on the window. Or you get a C and you owe them more money. They'll come back as many times as you want them to. They have no problem fining you 20 times. They take this self-righteous high ground by saying that what they're doing is for the, the good of society. Because if we didn't control the health of your restaurant, people could die. But find me a government official you can't pay off to say your restaurant got an A.

How vital do you think free enterprise is toward America's success and future?

MM: I think that if you want to see how important capitalism is for this country, you just have to look out the window at the buildings and people going to work and that is because they're free enough - enough to do so still.

Do you think government can and should create jobs?

MM: Sure. We could have 100 percent employment right now. We could. We could have government officials show up at your house every morning, make sure you eat your breakfast, and then take you to the factory. That happened in Soviet Russia for a while. That was 100 percent employment they had. So yeah, actually the government could definitely create jobs.

As a young entrepreneur in New York City, where do you place blame for the 'financial crisis'?

MM: I think that if you're gonna argue that it was greed that caused the financial crisis, you'd have to then say 'whose greed?' I think it was the greed of government officials and the people that made a lot of money and who gave the incentive to banks to make loans that they wouldn't have otherwise made. I mean, it boggles my mind. If you're a bank and your job is to make loans to people that you can charge interest to, then if you're not good at determining who can pay you the money back, you're really bad at your job. Right? I feel like I might be going crazy if it's any more difficult than that. And then if you give them an incentive to make loans to people that can't pay the money back, and they agree to it as if they had a choice. They didn't have a choice. That is just a little bit weird that that actually happened. It's like someone giving you the incentive if you're an ice cream salesman to sell ice cream with bugs in it, and you decide to do that until everyone starts hating ice cream and then no one wants to buy ice cream anymore.

What should the government's role be?

MM: To protect people from the force of other individuals. And to protect contracts that individuals make with each other voluntarily.

To protect me from you punching me, basically. Any act of force from one individual to another is what the government's there to stop. And it doesn't just go for physical force. It includes fraud -

upholding contracts between two people. The government's there to protect the country from foreign invaders and people that want to knock down our buildings.

How long has it been since you read Atlas?
MM: When I was 20, the first time. I'm 28 now.

Have you read it since?
MM: Yeah. I've read it twice since. I learn something each time that I read Atlas. I think it helps to read *Atlas Shrugged* and then one of her non-fiction books. And then sort of go back and forth between the two. Even at the same time - spend a day reading some non-fiction and then the next day reading *Atlas Shrugged*. It's really cool to, to see her philosophy applied to current issues. She wrote a lot of articles on the issues of her time in politics, and then to read *Atlas Shrugged*.

How do you describe Atlas to your friends?
MM: I just tell people it's a great story. *Atlas Shrugged* is just a great novel. It's a suspense thriller love story. There's science fiction in it. There's action and adventure. I don't know how you couldn't enjoy reading it just for the story's sake. Forgetting the philosophy mumbo jumbo that turn people off to it because of their precon- ceived notions about philosophy as a whole. It's just a good book, it's just a good story. It's just a lot of fun.

Do you find yourself using Atlas Shrugged as a litmus test for people?
MM: I do. If they have read the book and they liked it, we're prob- ably gonna get along 'cause at least we have that one thing to talk about, if nothing else. If they've read it and they hate it, we're gonna probably talk a lot more than I would talk to the one that liked it because now I really need to figure out why they hated it. But I ask everybody that I meet if they've read the book, just 'cause

I'm curious. It tells me a lot about the person based on if they like it or, or not.

Do you think we're close to living in the world of Atlas Shrugged?

MM: (laughs) On a scale of one to ten, how close are we to dystopia? I'd say right now we're at a two. You know, as far as a dystopia like that. But you don't have to actually have people dying in the streets to have people dying. And I think that just 'cause your heart's beating doesn't mean you're alive.

'Cause if you can't live the life that you would otherwise be free to live if there weren't people telling you what to do and how to do it - what's the point?

-New York City, February 2010

CHAPTER FIFTEEN

MIKE BERLINER

Michael S. Berliner holds a Ph.D. in philosophy from Boston University. He taught philosophy and philosophy of education for 15 years at California State University Northridge, then was the executive director of the Ayn Rand Institute for its first 15 years (1985-2000). His publications include Letters of Ayn Rand (Dutton, 1995) and newspaper editorials on Columbus Day, environmentalism and the Hollywood Ten.

Dr. Berliner sat down for our interview in his Los Angeles home in the fall of 2009.

What is the significance of Atlas Shrugged?
MICHAEL BERLINER: *Atlas Shrugged* is probably the most profound philosophic novel ever written. When you read it, you don't read philosophy, you read *dramatized* philosophy. You see characters

embodying certain ideas. And I think that's the power of it. Because if you don't like philosophy, didn't do well in philosophy class, never took a philosophy class, what you'll get out of reading any one of Ayn Rand's novels, not just *Atlas Shrugged*, but The Fountainhead, We The Living, is a "concretization" she called it. A philosophy embodied in human beings.

Can you give an example?

MB: When I read The Fountainhead, which is the first book of Ayn Rand's that I read when I was in college, I thought I was an individualist. And I read that book and I saw the main character Howard Roark, how he was living his life and I said: "Oh my God, *that's* what it means to be an individualist!" But you don't have to figure it out. You don't have to infer it from a philosophic treatise. You see it as acted and as embodied in actual human... well, fictional human beings. But a complete human being living his life.

Why did Ayn Rand dramatize her philosophy in a novel?

MB: It fits in with Ayn Rand's aesthetic theory – a theory of art that human beings need to see a view of the world in an ideal and concrete form because the abstractions in philosophy (one's view of the world, and how you use your mind, and what's the right way to behave, and how you should treat others) are awfully abstract, and you can't hold it in your mind that way. But if you see it in a person, as described in fiction, then you can get it.

Like the existentialists did?

MB: The existentialists generally did the same thing. It's stretching calling existentialism a philosophy. Sartre wrote philosophic treatises, but he also wrote fiction, as did Camus, and you get a very direct sense of what that philosophy means. If you wanted to be like that kind of person, how would you behave? What would be the proper way to behave?

How was Ayn Rand different?

MB: She was the only writer I know that wrote both technical philosophy and best-selling wonderful fiction. It's an amazing achievement, which is all the more astounding the extent to which she has historically been ignored, and in the older days vilified, especially by women, because here's a woman who was an accomplished high level technical philosopher and also a great novelist.

But it fits into her whole approach to things. She never wanted to be an abstract, technical philosopher. Her view was always: ideas in the world. And she once described her philosophy, Objectivism, as a philosophy for living on earth. So it's always that connection. It was always the connection between the ideas in your mind, your most abstract ideas and what they mean in reality.

The idea that her philosophy was a primer for living makes her unique. Because it's so much in contrast to what you get in philosophy class. At least when I was in school, and I was in philosophy departments. They don't think philosophy has got anything to do with the world.

How do they view philosophy?

MB: That abstract ideas are intellectual games disconnected from the real world.

I remember in grad school, going to a – a class in contemporary ethics, and the professor starts out by saying: "Don't make the mistake of thinking that what you're going to be learning in this ethics class has anything to do with living."

And I think: "What? Ethics has got nothing to do with living? What are you teaching it for?" But it's all just an end of itself. It's all just playing around with ideas, and that's one of the reasons that for many years she had absolutely no respect in philosophy departments.

And still doesn't have a great deal. But they think that if you're dealing with the world, that's kind of low down, and grubby, and we're dealing with the higher things that don't have anything to do with reality. So if it's going to be any help to you in your actual life then it can't be serious. It's just pop philosophy, or whatever.

How was Atlas Shrugged received generally?

MB: The reception to *Atlas Shrugged* was almost entirely negative. And much, much more so than her previous books. She wrote *We The Living* in 1936 and then *Anthem* in '37, and *The Fountainhead* in '43. And they were all received pretty well. I mean, not completely, but for example, *We The Living* was written during the Red Decade and it's an anti-Soviet book. Of course it was actually anti-all collectivist states, fascist as well as communist. But the reception even from England was pretty positive, very surprisingly so.

The Fountainhead was not widely reviewed. It hit the best-seller list two years after it came out, because it was all word of mouth, not because of the reviewers, who generally ignored it. When they did review it, they treated it as a novel about architecture or a love story, but they weren't particularly negative.

Atlas Shrugged was a different story. *Atlas Shrugged* hit you in the face with ideas. There was no hiding the fact that she was in favor of capitalism, self-interest, reason, individualism, and as a result, everybody practically came out against it. The left, the right, the middle, they were all against it. The left hated it because it was pro-capitalist. The right, or the conservatives, hated it because it was not religious, or even anti- religious, and they were the most anti-, and still are.

And everybody was completely befuddled by the fact that she had answers to things. And she said there are answers. There's a right and a wrong and a good and a bad. It's a moral book. And they did not like the fact that she believed in moral absolutes.

Did they not like the specific morality, or the presence of morality at all?

MB: The left didn't like it because, you know, there are relativists and skeptics and what's good for you isn't necessarily good for me.

There's no right and wrong for everybody. And everybody has his own morality and everybody has his own reality.

The conservatives didn't like it because it was not a religious dogmatic morality. And she said you can determine what's right and wrong for a human being. What's in your self-interest. And life is the standard, and what furthers life is the good. And what inhibits life is the bad.

So they were all turned off by the fact that there were black and whites, and that it was rationally based, not religiously based.

What were the reviews like?

MB: The level of the reviews of *Atlas Shrugged* was just abysmal. I mean they were not respectful. They were snide. They were sarcastic. They distorted her ideas. They just... they just ripped it to shreds. She didn't expect it. As she said, she expected it to be smeared, but not at that level. She said in the older days, especially, the left would have been more intellectual, but by the late 50's it wasn't so. It was a... it was a real blast.

Did that affect her?

MB: Yeah, it affected her. The reviews were so bad and misunderstood her work so much that... that it was one of the things that pushed her into becoming a philosopher.

People thought, and I would have thought at the time, that: well, here's *Atlas Shrugged* – it's so clear, it's so obvious, and it connects everything. It connects metaphysics, you know, your view of the nature of reality, and epistemology, your view of your mind and how you know, and morality and economics, and sex, because it's a systematic philosophy. It's all integrated.

And I think: "Well, people are going to read this book and they are going to see pretty clearly that it's true." That was far from the case. And she was really unprepared for the extent to which people didn't understand. She was talking about it, and she was convinced that she really had to go out and defend the book philosophically.

How did they attack the book?

MB: They labeled the book, and this came from both the left and the right, as a book that promoted Nietzschean supermen who were beyond good and evil.

And she was actually somewhat influenced by Nietzsche in college, or thought that she had something in common with him, and learned very quickly that it was not the case. In fact, it turned out to be the exact opposite of her own philosophy.

But their view was: "if you had heroes, they must be superheroes because we don't believe in heroes anymore." So, you know, once you get past the man on the street, they are all the same. Heroes and superheroes, human beings and super-human-beings. So they dismissed her heroes, and she viewed them as ideals, human ideals, actual human ideals that one could aspire to.

And, as a side, I would say that's why her books are so popular. Because they provide that. Really, no other books do. They really provide an ideal, a moral ideal that people say: "I can be like that. I don't want to copy that person, but that's the kind of person I could and ought to be."

So she was vilified for being a Nazi, a Nietzschean. She's attacked for, by the right, for being a Marxist of all things, because she rejected religion. I mean, it ran the gamut. Every possible contradictory charge you can make against somebody, they made against her and that book.

Why was the response so vehement?

MB: Oh boy, they were afraid – and they're still afraid that people are going to take these ideas seriously, because, I think, it just blasts them to pieces, because they have no foundation altruism, is one example. No one has ever come out with a justification for altruism, for giving up your life.

With centuries of altruism, no one has come up with a justification?

MB: I mean, how could you have a justification for what, as she described it, is a morality of death? Because the good is to give up more and more and more. And so, they're afraid of that. And the religious people are especially afraid of what's happening. People, at least a certain segment, are turning away from religion and starting to think: "Hey, I can use reason. I can guide my life by my mind."

Is there a fear of people 'going Galt?'

MB: Yeah, going on strike. You see, I don't think people are afraid that anybody is going to go on strike. It's not going to work that way in reality. And Ayn Rand didn't think so either. It's going to be more subtle. People are going to say, like doctors have been saying for quite a while: "I'm not willing to live under all those controls. I'm spending two thirds of my life filling out forms. And trying to match what the government wants me to do. That's no way to live – I wanted to be a doctor." So people are both getting out of medicine and not going into it for that reason.

So that's kind of how the strike works right there. But there, she challenged the prevalent ideas at their root. That's why she's proudly called a radical. And that's what's frightening to people.

To what extent are the characters in Atlas Shrugged symbols?

MB: Her characters stand for something, but they are people too. They're not just excuses to spew out ideas, which is another one of the criticisms that was made of her. And you look at these people as ideals, or the opposite. And they capture the essence of certain types of people.

So when you're thinking about: "Oh that guy – he's just like Ellsworth Toohey in *The Fountainhead*." Or James Taggart in *Atlas Shrugged*. It brings together all these different aspects of that kind of a person. And she nails them really perfectly.

Were her characters based on real people?

MB: Some of her characters she based on a little bit, or derived from people that she knew, or she had had some sort of connection to. Not so much in *Atlas Shrugged*. More in the earlier novels, but *Atlas Shrugged* was really her ideal novel.

She found that *The Fountainhead* was a little too journalistic. Because it dealt with a particular period in American history. And it dealt with modern architecture versus traditional architecture. *We The Living* was a very specific time period in Soviet Russia. You know, during the time that she had lived there and afterward.

But *Atlas Shrugged* was her world that she created. And it was a – you know her goal in writing was to create the ideal man and the ideal woman in fiction, and she really didn't do that completely until she got to *Atlas Shrugged*.

Is that part of the appeal?

MB: I mean, I've always thought I just wanted to be in that world. Somebody once asked a fan of hers: "Did you find anything about *Atlas Shrugged* that you didn't like?" And here's a book that's over a thousand pages, and he said, "Yeah it was too short." It's a world that you want to be in. And I feel that way about all of her novels. And you don't want to be in it to escape the world. You want to be in it to experience the world as it could and ought to be.

Why did a lot of reviewers not share this response?

MB: In *Atlas Shrugged*, particularly, there are the producers and the looters. The sort of parallel in *The Fountainhead* was the independent people and the second handers. The mistake that people and reviewers often make is thinking that you're born that way. You're born either a producer or a looter. Or an individualist or a second hander. Or that the producers and the individualists are somehow genetically superior. And to be an ideal... one reviewer of *Atlas Shrugged* said you have to be the inventor of a new metal.

Well, that's ridiculous. She was talking about a character trait and a mindset, and a moral issue, and it applied to anybody at any level of productivity. The issue is whether or not you live by your own effort, and by your own judgment. And it makes no moral difference whether you're working on an assembly line or the highest levels of the computer industry.

Morally, it doesn't make any difference. You're morally equal. But the point was (and this is why the theme of *Atlas Shrugged* was the role of the mind in human existence): if you take the mind out at any level, you'll have collapse. And as a human being, the extent to which you don't use your mind, to that extent, you won't be in control of your life. And it applies on a wider scale to a culture or a society. You remove the mind, i.e. you remove thinking and reason from the equation and, you'll eventually collapse.

Like our economy has collapsed today?

MB: And that's why people have jumped on *Atlas Shrugged* after the economic downturn. She predicted that. She didn't really. I mean, it was not a journalistic novel. It's not a sociologic novel, but it was a philosophic novel, which said that there will be consequences, and they will be bad if you don't follow reason – if you don't respect people's rights.

And how it's going to fall apart, she made no attempt to explain that. But eventually it's going to happen. She actually telescoped the collapse in *Atlas Shrugged* quite a bit. She didn't think it would happen the way – she didn't think that in reality what happened the way that it did in the novel. It would take a much longer time. She was not a financial analyst, so she wouldn't have dared to predict how it would happen. But if you put the shackles on the producers, then what's going to happen? You know, you can't have your cake and eat it too. And that's one of her basic philosophic principles, in popular terms, and that's what people try to do. They try to have their cake and eat it too.

In what way do they attempt that?

MB: They try to get production and put the producers in shackles – and, you know, you can kind of get by for a while, as long as you've got somebody to give you a loan, but ultimately it's going to fall apart. And that's what happened.

If you have a vibrant economy, and they can keep going on what was produced and kind of... inertia, in the good sense. But eventually, they're going to die out, and that's what events have born out. Well, if your philosophy is derived from reality, then that's going to happen. As she says, you really need to live by this philosophy. You need to accept this philosophy if you're going to lead a successful life as an individual and as a society. And if you don't, you're not going to survive. And if she's right about that, and people don't follow that philosophy, then you're not going to survive.

And that's what I think is happening, and that's why people are so excited. Word gets around. "Hey, there's a book that predicted that, you know, fifty years ago." They don't know exactly why it's working that way, why it was predicted. But people are looking for answers. And, you know, where are they going to get answers these days? Not from the intellectuals that say there aren't any answers.

What about politicians?

MB: Oh, I think that if you look around at political life, and that's been the case for many, many years, some walk right out of the pages of *Atlas Shrugged* and... and it's scary. People write to me that "so and so is going on in my country," and I say, "This is right out of *Atlas Shrugged.*"

They're taxing in England at a fifty percent rate all bonuses over... I think it's 25,000 pounds or something, or, I mean, the equivalent of 25,000 dollars. And I wrote to the person who told me that, and I said: "Oh, what happened? Did they read *Atlas Shrugged* and get mixed up about who were the good guys and who were the bad guys?"

But all through her novels you see it. In *The Fountainhead* people in architecture who are advocating the view that all good building is by committee. And I said, you know, "Didn't they ever read *The Fountainhead,* or they read it and got confused?"

But you also see, if you look around you, people who embody the heroes in *Atlas Shrugged* and her other novels who are independent. Who won't take anything from the government, and who insist on their freedom, and the right to live their lives, and run their businesses the way they see fit. It's difficult, if not, impossible to do that given the amount of controls that we have in this country, but you see both sides. You see the good guys and the bad guys.

What would be an example of one of the good guys today?

MB: An example of a heroic person in today's world would be John Allison of BB&T Bank in North Carolina, who has made it a policy of his bank not to loan money to any company that was using eminent domain to take the property in which they were going to build their business.

Isn't eminent domain covered in the Constitution?

MB: Eminent domain is the taking of private property and is allowed in the Constitution for "a public purpose," but it's been reinterpreted to mean for "the public good," which again is right out of *Atlas Shrugged.* Anything is okay if it's for the "public good." And never mind the fact that nobody could ever identify and define what the public good is, but the Supreme Court, in the famous Kelo decision a few years ago, decided that they would not prevent the states from stopping companies that grabbed property to use for private gain. So companies were making deals with city governments to take property from one homeowner, or one business owner, and give it to somebody that they decided was going to provide more tax money.

So that's been rampant. And there were suits against them, and the Supreme Court said that it was permissible within the U.S. constitution. Subsequently, more than forty states have passed laws or done something to put the clamps on that.

But John Allison, at the beginning, said that we will not loan money to *any* company that was going to use eminent domain. I mean, eminent domain is really the theft of somebody's property. There's a huge amount of that going on in this country, and has been for the last, you know, seventy, eighty, ninety years.

How is Rand's view of selfishness different from the kind of moral delinquency we're seeing today – and is that a by-product of the 'me decade/generation'?

MB: Well, the 'Me' decade was a total misnomer, because the people that were supposedly representative of the 'Me' generation were not at all in the mold of Ayn Rand's rational, self-interested person.

They were the opposite. They were people acting on whim. "I want it." That's all it takes. "I'm going to go after it. I'm going to get it. I don't care what the cost. I don't care what it does to anybody else."

And that's not a characterization of Ayn Rand's view?

MB: It's the *opposite* of her view. It's closer to the Nietzchean view that whatever you feel like, it's good. And that was the 'Me' generation. But it was a package deal, because at the same time they were attacking the wrong view of egoism, they were attacking the right view. The term was used in a snide way.

Was Ayn Rand not a proponent of 'Me' first?

MB: Well, she was a proponent of individualism mainly. I mean this: the essence of Ayn Rand's view of individualism is what philosophers would call epistemological – how you use your mind. And individualism for Ayn Rand, for her philosophy, means acting on your own judgment.

And the moral, the ethical consequence of that is that you are acting for your own rational self-interest. You do what promotes your life. And, by the same token, you grant that principle to everybody else. So I don't live for you, but by the same token, you don't live for me. Each person seeks his own good, and we trade, we bargain, and we both benefit as a consequence.

Is that what Francisco's 'money speech' in Atlas is about? The trader principle?

MB: The money speech is really heresy in modern times. You would come out in favor of money and making money, but she understood what it meant. That it was a form of value. It wasn't just accumulating dollars like... not Donald Duck... who was the...?

Scrooge McDuck.

MB: For Ayn Rand, making money is not accumulating piles of dollar bills like Scrooge McDuck. Remember he's sitting in his room there, with this towers of dollars around him. Didn't do anything with it! His whole idea was to *accumulate* it.

But for her, money was a means of achieving value and is also, in certain businesses, the sign of success, because it's measured that way.

Did she pursue wealth herself?

MB: She herself was pretty much disinterested in money and becoming wealthy. She wanted to write, and she didn't live lavishly. She didn't flaunt it. Self-interest is manifested in different ways in different people.

But the attack on money is, as she saw, an attack on ambition. It's an attack on success. And that is horribly what has dominated American culture for a long time. It didn't use to be the case. It wasn't the case in the industrial revolution. It wasn't the case when the founding fathers were dominant in the country.

But it's become that, mostly as the result, I think, of the spread of religion and Christianity. The hatred of money and the hatred of what it means. It means personal, private success and achievement.

How is Atlas Shrugged viewed today?

MB: Whereas in 1957 *Atlas Shrugged* was met with vicious response and vilification, that has changed considerably and fairly gradually, but it's remarkably different now. And I think there are obvious reasons for it. One is that in 1957 nobody had read the book. But now fifty plus years later, millions of people have read that book and her other books. So, it's more difficult for a reviewer or any writer to get away with distorting the ideas, because so many people have read those books and they know that those distortions aren't true.

Also, it's affected so many people. The phrase, *"Atlas Shrugged* changed my life." There was a survey by the library of Congress a number of years ago, "what are the most influential books" and *Atlas Shrugged* came in second to the Bible. And it's changed people's lives. Some of those people have gone into journalism, and some of those people are writing columns. Some of them have TV shows, and radio shows, and so on.

In fifty plus years, there are a lot of people around who love the books, who admire the books – maybe don't agree with them completely, but respect them, think it's important, serious work. And so there's a cultural change because of that.

It is more respected because more people have read it?

MB: And I think another factor is that the culture in the 50's was such that – people were afraid to say that they agreed with those ideas. But there's been a snowball effect. It takes a few people to cut through that and stand up and say "yeah, I think those ideas are right." And other people who kind of agreed with that, but were afraid, have come out of the philosophic closet.

And so there are people who, before, wouldn't have admitted that they liked those books, or wouldn't have stood up publicly and said so. Now, because other people are doing it, I mean, it's not a very courageous thing to do, but nevertheless they are doing it. So a lot more people are talking about it. Not just journalists, but businessmen.

You see it fairly often for major business figures to say "it's my favorite novel," you know, "it's what inspired me, I read it regularly." And I don't think that would have happened a few years ago. It certainly wouldn't have happened in the 50's.

Why were they afraid before?

MB: I think the fear was of not being accepted, not being liked. It goes right back to *The Fountainhead* in that sense. A lot of people have a second handedness in them that they don't want to offend.

Isn't that part of being an individualist?

MB: Yeah, people are mixed. They admire individualism but as far as acting on it and applying it to themselves, they need a little push. They're not quite ready to do it. And sometimes they're so unready to do it, they just give up entirely.

It's too much to fight the social disapproval. And that's so much a part of our upbringing. You have to be liked. The little kid going to school, it's important that people like them.

So everybody's trying to be liked by everybody else and that's what a mass is. There are no souls there – there's no minds there – no individuals there.

Part of the difficulty of growing up?

MB: Growing up is difficult. I think we can all agree on that. And it's particularly difficult at the teenage years because that's when you have these huge conflicts between yourself and your parents, yourself and your peers. What does it mean to be a person? What does it mean to be an individual? And that's the critical time in life.

And it's interesting and somewhat depressing the number of people who are excited by Ayn Rand's ideas when they're young, and then stop being so. Their excuse is that they grew up. My interpretation would be not that they grew up, but that they gave up. They gave up on themselves.

Why are Ayn Rand's books so popular with young people?

MB: Ayn Rand's books are particularly good for people at that stage of life, particularly *The Fountainhead*. The theme of *The Fountainhead*, she said, was: "individualism versus collectivism, not in politics, but in a man's soul." What does it mean to be a person? What does it mean to be a human being?

And the teenage years are when you are becoming an adult. You're no longer even legally under your parents' sway. So you're dealing with all of those issues, and that's the critical time. That's when you're going to say to yourself: "yeah, I don't have to be part of the group, and it's *right* that I don't have to be part of the group."

You have to really understand why, and you have a really solid acceptance of that, because you're going to be so bombarded later on with: "Oh you shouldn't offend other people, and don't think you're so smart, and don't think that you know what's best." And you get enough of that in the culture, and if you don't have the foundation to fight it off, you're finished. Ayn Rand was well aware of that phenomenon.

How did Ayn Rand invent her characters?

MB: When Ayn Rand created a character, she wasn't inventing science fiction characters. She was inventing "real people" in the "real world" in that sense. They're not impossible people. But you can do that only if essentially you're like that. You couldn't conceive of it any other way.

I find it very interesting reading the correspondence that her parents and sisters wrote to her from Leningrad in the 1920's and the 1930's. She had sent them a manuscript of a play she wrote called *Night of January 16th*, which was certainly the least philosophic thing that she ever wrote. It had some implicit philosophy in it, but it was kind of a mystery story and a legal drama.

But it had admirable characters in there. And her younger sister wrote back to her: "You couldn't have come up with those heroes if you weren't like that yourself." And that's why, when she said that I'm proof that those characters exist, it wasn't false bravado or arrogance, it was just that point. How could you possibly conceive of that kind of a person if you didn't have that in you?

Where does Objectivism fit into today's world?

MB: There's such an intellectual bankruptcy in the culture. There aren't any ideas out there anymore. I mean, religion... those are kind of non-ideas saying that we can't explain anything, and we'll give that lack of explanation a name, and that's God. So it's saying I can't figure anything out. It must be supernatural. It's like an admission. There's no explanation, no answers. So there's very little anybody can turn to anymore in the intellectual world, and that's become increasingly the case. And Objectivism is a real philosophy in the old sense. It's an integrated view of existence. Something that people need.

Who is John Galt?

MB: John Galt is the ideal man. The same way that Howard Roark was the ideal man. They're fictional ideals who represent what any person can be and ought to be. And Ayn Rand said the purpose of art is to portray things as they ought and might be. And that is what John Galt is. He is a hero. Not a superhero. Not a non- human science fiction hero, but a hero in the sense that he's merely "human." He's what a human being ought to be, and which anybody can be.

Los Angeles, October 2009

CHAPTER SIXTEEN
RICHARD RALSTON

*Richard E. Ralston is the former publisher of the Christian Science Monitor
and today, as Publishing Manager of the Ayn Rand Institute, Mr. Ralston
is the person most familiar with the numerous editions of Rand's work. He
is also the editor of* Communism: Its Rise and Fall in the 20th Century
and co-editor of Why Businessmen Need Philosophy. *Mr. Ralston is
also currently Executive Director of Americans for Free Choice in Medicine.*

*Mr. Ralston sat for his interview outside his home in Marina Del Rey,
California.*

Why did Ayn Rand the novelist become a philosopher?
RICHARD RALSTON: Because she had a unique view of what an
ideal fictional hero should be, she developed ideas on what kind

of society would be necessary for a hero or for a great character to survive. So she became something of a philosopher in addition to being a novelist.

Why did she decide to write Atlas Shrugged?

RR: By the time she started *Atlas Shrugged*, she was a bestselling novelist. The Fountainhead was successful.

The idea began with a telephone conversation with a conservative priest and telling her it was her duty to write a book of nonfiction or philosophy or essays. At the time she didn't particularly want to do what he was asking. She said well, what if I went on strike? What if all the great writers and intellectuals went on strike against that kind of a demand on their time?

When she hung up the phone she said: well that would be a good plot for a novel. So one thing led to another and then in September of 1946, she started writing *Atlas Shrugged* whose provisional first title was 'the Strike' about what the consequences would be if the great men of the mind, the great industrialists, the great businessmen, the great independent intellectuals and scientists of all sorts withdrew their services from the society—and then the society would learn who was exploiting whom.

What was her purpose for writing Atlas Shrugged?

RR: Her fundamental purpose was what she called man worship. It began very early when she was a nine-year-old girl and read popular magazines for children from the west. The first hero she admired when she was nine years old was a character named Cyrus who was in a serialization in a French children's magazine. She was reading it in French. But he was a Kiplingesque figure in the British India, the British Raj and there are line drawings that we have today. She fell in love with the guy and that kind of man worship, hero worship was her first motivation for what she wanted to do.

Was she inspired by Nietzsche?

RR: Nietzsche's idea of the übermensch, she thought was degrading, that a man would see greatness through power over others, she thought was disgusting. His conception was essentially misanthropic and aggressive and negative and about power over other people rather than individual achievement which she thought would motivate a true heroic character rather than dominance over others.

But she did see man as master of his own fate, right?

RR: That people should rely on their own talents and their own abilities and their own intellect to design and guide and lead and achieve the accomplishments of their own life rather than seek to derive that from others.

It is the self-fulfilled achievement of an individual who establishes his own goals independent of what other people are doing rather than as leeches drawing on other people whether psychologically or literally in terms of materials and just a system of political pull—like the Roman government in the dying stages of the Republic, the Mafia today or the way the federal government works. Ayn Rand called it "the aristocracy of pull".

How was Atlas Shrugged received?

RR: *Atlas Shrugged*, published by Random House in the fall of 1957, was the first novel that she wrote that went immediately to the best seller list. It was actively solicited by probably the most prominent publisher in the country. All of her previous novels gradually caught on. The Fountainhead did not get on the best seller list until two years after it was first published. She always felt and continued to feel that word of mouth was primarily responsible for the sale of her books.

Atlas Shrugged almost immediately went on the New York Times best seller list. I don't think it ever got higher than four but it stayed on the best seller list for four or five months. Two years later when the first paperback edition was published it went back on the NY times best seller list for a couple of years.

How is it doing now?

RR: She achieved what you would call a very steady and consistent sale over the next twenty or thirty years. Probably higher into the mid-sixties than later. By the 1980's when we have very accurate sales numbers, the paperback edition of *Atlas Shrugged* was selling on average 77,000 copies a year. In the 1990's that rose to 95,000 copies paper back a year on average and in this decade it has exceeded 135,000 copies a year

Very unusual for an old novel in its 50th anniversary year 2007 it achieved an all-time high: 185,000 copies of just the paperback edition which we thought was a peak. We were pleasantly surprised when the following year it went up further, in 2008 it sold 200 thousand copies in English paperback alone. So far this year, we only have figures for the first half of 2009, something more is going on. In all English editions it sold 314,000 copies in the first six months of 2009. I don't know what the total today is with a few weeks left to go in the year but if the half year is better than the previous record entire year then obviously 2009 will be a record year so something is going on that is drawing a new audience to *Atlas Shrugged* that is unprecedented for a novel that is over half a century in print. [NOTE: A new annual record sale of 520,000 copies of all editions was reached in 2009.]

Why is it growing in popularity?

RR: No one is a more effective promoter of reading *Atlas Shrugged* than the readers of *Atlas Shrugged*. The more those people read it, the more they talk about it to others.

The plot of *Atlas Shrugged* resonates with what's going on today. When they see the news it calls to mind the plot of *Atlas Shrugged* which is a devastated economy whose devastation was caused by government intervention leading to more and more and more government intervention which makes things worse and worse and worse.

I once had a reporter from the Washington Post ask me why Americans are anti-intellectual and I said that's easy. Americans are anti-intellectual because intellectuals are anti-American. It's as simple as that. They ultimately detect this disdain for American values, and that disdain for individual achievement. When they read something like *Atlas Shrugged* they see the articulation which they come to understand and they say... yes.

Do you see Ayn Rand's villains in the world today?

RR: Not many people are consciously deliberately evil. Everyone in politics thinks that they're a saint. All of the town hall meetings politicians that always presented themselves as the defender of the little guy showed their contempt for the little guy when the little guy confronted them at a town hall meeting. They're political elite. They're snobs. The Hollywood liberal left. The Washington political left: when Bill Maher talked about the stupidity of the American people. He's a big defender of the little guy, supposedly, against the elites, when he showed his contempt for stupid Americans, the little guy. If you're not a collectivist, if you don't buy into the collectivist mode, then you're stupid so you need the dictatorship of the proletariat to guide you on the way. So that's a long term trend that started in the late 19th century dividing the intellectuals to abandon reason and rationality and American values and conflict with the American sense of life and the common man.

How is Atlas Shrugged viewed in academia?

RR: Right now there are a fair number of tenured openly Objective professors in American universities. Fifteen years ago there weren't any. So it's not as closed a world in academia as it used to be. The coherence of the left wing position is deteriorating. And they're all at each other's throats somewhat.

What about businessmen?

RR: There's more businessmen today willing to take a principled stand to defend their own interest and to articulate their own interests—their right to make a profit. So that's a positive sign in the culture in terms of change in status quo.

How is freedom under attack today?

RR: The main way people destroy freedom is either destroy reason or destroy self interest. They destroy reason by – it's the oldest trick on the planet – they say that God [or any arbitrary source] has spoken to me and he's told me what *you* have to do. And by the way I can kill you if you don't. Reason can't be trusted: therefore do whatever I say.

Then the other attack on freedom is: it's selfish. Life, liberty and the pursuit of happiness, pursuit of your own happiness is selfish. It's immoral.

She didn't back off in attacking that. She said unless you maintain your rights to moral values, to self interest, you will be destroyed.

The government that has the power to give you everything you want has the power to take everything you've got. Without capitalism, democratic forms of government or republican forms of government are impossible.

What about the future of Atlas Shrugged?

RR: I have no idea where sales are going to go.

In some sense, sales are so high at the moment because things are getting so bad. And obviously there's a limited trajectory there in terms of how bad do things have to get, we have to persevere and make it clear to people what they need to understand and what they're responding to in the book, in their own lives.

She was always confident that if she reached enough of "my kind of readers," they in turn would reach even more. No one promoted *Atlas Shrugged* to new readers more effectively than readers of *Atlas Shrugged*. That is the most enduring of all sales trends.

Who is John Galt?

RR: John Galt is the ideal, perfect and heroic portrait of man. He's a man as he could be and ought to be.

-Marina Del Rey, December 2009

CHAPTER SEVENTEEN
LISA WOLF

Lisa Bjornson Wolf is an Executive Director at JP Morgan in NY. Previously she was CEO of Jaqua Beauty, an international luxury bath and body brand based in Santa Barbara, California. In the late 1990s, Wolf was a Director at Smith Barney in NY in the International Equities Group. Prior to Smith Barney, Wolf spent 8 years in J.P. Morgan's Investment Banking Division and in the firm's Institutional Equity business in NY, Paris, and London offices.

Mrs. Wolf holds a Master of Science degree in International Economics and Japan Studies from Johns Hopkins University's School for Advanced International Studies (SAIS), and is a graduate cum laude of Cornell University's College of Arts and Sciences.

In the winter of 2010, Ms. Wolf sat outdoors for her interview at a friend's home in Santa Barbara, California.

Why are we talking about Atlas Shrugged?

LISA WOLF: I think people are talking about *Atlas Shrugged* again today even though it was written in 1957 because there is an uncanny resemblance between the government depicted in that book and where a lot of people, Libertarians and Republicans, feel we're heading right now. And they remember reading that book in their youth and they pulled it out and they're reading it again and they're ordering it from Amazon. And they're saying, wow, there are a lot of parallels.

What about younger people?

LW: Discovering it for the first time? I don't know. Are younger people discovering it for the first time? Good.

Maybe from their parents.

LW: Now that I think about it, I got the book from somebody who got it from an older sibling or a parent. It was written in 1957 and I didn't read it until the 80s. So the idea that it continues to have a life and relevancy is interesting. And since it did for me, and it was a book for an earlier generation, it makes sense to reason that it would appeal to younger people now.

Why would it appeal to young minds?

LW: Maybe it appeals to young minds because they see around them among their teachers, among the administrators in their schools, the kind of weak minded followers that that book is so against. And they're strong enough to want to be independent and declare themselves, and stake out new ground. And so they understand the dynamic between the independent free thinker and the Mouch. Maybe better than people who have been in the world of work for a long time and have learned to keep their head down and don't seek originality or independence, just trying to get along.

Everybody has dreams.
LW: Everybody thinks they're gonna make a difference and then they get... there's that great d'Anconia quote about selling out, it's so easy to sell out.

What is it?
LW: I would need to look up the reference. But, you know, it's easy to sell your soul, the hard thing is to stay the course. Then Dagny gets so angry with him because she thinks he has sold out. Only of course he hasn't, he's living between two worlds. But, you know, she's gonna stay and fight to the bitter end and not sell out no matter what, because to sell out makes them win. Whereas everybody else is saying there's no point in fighting this battle of taxation.

What could she say 'I told you so' about?
LW: If Ayn Rand were here today, she would smile bitterly and point out that there are fewer people with private sector experience in this administration than in any administration in the history of this country. When nobody but academics and think tank dreamers is running the country, then the wiser interests that represent capitalism, which made this country great, are eliminated from the discussion. Their point of view is not even taken into account.

They've never had a job?
LW: Most members of the current administration have been academics their whole life.

These people don't have jobs?
LW: They have academic jobs, and they think they're real jobs. It's just that they're operating in a world of theory, not in a real

world context. So what they're trying to do and what they're talking about defies economic gravity. You can't tax non-existent corporate profits. And everyone in New York City for example, the government of New York City is scratching its head going, wow, how are we gonna pay for all this stuff without Goldman Sachs making a ton of money because they were the number one contributor to the city's coffers.

So it's fine to talk about the evil investment banks, the greedy terrible people on Wall Street, but those people are paying the firemen's salaries. And the firemen can't get paid unless Goldman Sachs gets paid. And the idea that people don't understand that drives me crazy.

Why are the best people seldom drawn into public life?

LW: Nobody is attracted to public life if they have a brain in their head. It's too thankless. Here's Meg Whitman running for office. I mean, she does not need to do this at all. This is truly a gift for the public good. And she's being vilified because she voted absentee in Ohio for a couple years, while she was swamped creating more jobs and more value than almost anybody in the history of the state of California? Why bother. Who would ever want to touch it with a 10 foot pole?

I have friends on the school board who are like I'll never do this again. I will never run for any other office. This is a nightmare.

You've got to be a pretty thick-skinned careerist to survive in politics these days.

LW: Our founding fathers wanted regular people to take a quick break and go to Washington to represent the greater good, and then go back to their farming or their company or their law practice. And somewhere along the way, we lost that. And we developed a cadre of professional politicians who, by the way after they serve their term in congress, get paid that congress salary for the rest of their lives. That was not at all the intention behind the creation of this country or its government. Nobody wanted a government of functionaries. They wanted a government of people representing their constituents.

What is Atlas Shrugged about?

LW: *Atlas Shrugged* is about the struggle between the value of the individual and the importance of the collective. And if the individual feels the collective is worth his time and energy, he will lend his talent to it. Once it crosses a line and ceases to serve the individual in any way, it has lost its moral framework. And *Atlas Shrugged* tells an amazing story of what happens when the good people, the contributors, go on strike.

Individual versus the government.

LW: *Atlas Shrugged* is about the delicate balance between the government, which is supposed to serve the people, and the people it serves. And the author said to herself one day, what if all the brilliant creative people, the brilliant engineers, the brilliant inventors, decided to stop showing up for work and they all disappeared? And what was left was all the tax collectors and the guys who say, I should have more? And they're left with nobody wanting to create any value for them?

And the entire economy collapses. And it sort of makes you think. Gosh, if we tax these people too heavily and they go elsewhere, things will really fall apart. Gosh, the individual really matters. And the government better be morally legitimate, or eventually people will give up.

Why do you think people are so polarized on the subject of Ayn Rand?

LW: She wrote this as a philosophical treatise. And just as Karl Marx, you know, wanted no part of the free market, didn't trust or believe in the free market, all socialists hate this. The minute you say money is neutral, it is simply a utility, not it is evil and should be mine, then you alienate socialists. So to me it's the perfect litmus test. I had a friend who carried around a copy of an Ayn Rand book everywhere she went. And if people looked at her askew, she knew that those were not people she would ever talk to.

Other people would come up to her going, oh my God, you're reading that, isn't that the best, I just finished it for the 19th time. And those were her friends.

What kind of person do you think is most apt to appreciate Rand's ideas?

LW: Oh, there's your delicate $100,000 question. Who loves Ayn Rand and who hates Ayn Rand? So people like Mouch in *Atlas Shrugged* can't stand seeing themselves depicted for the parasites that they are. And people who fancy themselves being like Francisco d'Anconio, bold creators, leaders of industry, creative thinkers and problem solvers with inexhaustible energy, they identify with these heroes, and they recognize the villains. And they're excited by the idea that she's created true heroes who really do serve the greater good with their human potential.

These are intellectual heroes.

LW: Completely. And most literary types, a couple people chimed in on my Facebook page saying, you know, her characters aren't well-rounded. They're not in three dimensions. Dagny is a paper cutout, she's a paper doll. And her point was not to create... her point was to create a philosophical debate and personalize it. Not to really create true characters in true situations. They're heroes and villains. They're not well-rounded human beings. Right, what was James Bond? He was never a, a real person.

They represent values.

LW: Right, they're human passions and abilities to the power of three, and human foibles and weakness to the power of three.

Which is what makes it so compelling. The ultimate man versus man sort of conflict. Or man versus society.

Would you classify yourself as an objectivist?

LW: I'm a fan. I'm a fan of objectivism. I'm not ashamed to admit that I'm a fan of objectivism. Even though the free market is getting a very bad rap right now by this populist uprising that we're having in Washington, at the end of the day the free market has served us better than any alternative means of allocating resources in the history of humanity.

How would you define objectivism?

LW: Objectivism, very simply put, defends the central importance of individual freedom over the government or the good of all or society. What makes society work is individual freedom and individual responsibility. And it must be upheld over the good of society or the government or, you know, when individual rights or individual freedoms or independent thinking and creativity are diminished by society or the government, then eventually society will spiral downward.

That the best societies, the most just societies, the most successful societies, are the ones that place the rights of the individual to pursue happiness at the front and center of their doctrine. The liberals poke holes in Ayn Rand because there isn't a whole lot of room for the little guy. Except to the extent that he's free to pursue his happiness and maybe his son or his son's son ends up able to contribute.

My dad ran away from Norway because the tax rate, his boss was taxed at 350 percent of his annual income. And eventually he just said, I'm not playing anymore and left Norway. Ayn Rand, as you know, did the same thing in the Soviet Union which was the ultimate modern example of a not just society, completely confiscating human rights and values to the collective, to the greater good.

And the whole Marxian notion of from each according to his ability, to each according to his need, is just fundamentally flawed in terms of what happens long term when you keep priming the system that way.

How has Rand affected your life?

LW: Yes. I went to Wall Street because of *Atlas Shrugged.* I decided I wanted to be in an environment where everybody saw the world the same way I did. I did not want to have to apologize to anybody for having more talent and more drive and more ambition than everybody else did. And I paid millions of dollars in taxes in New York City and to the federal government as a result of my very high earnings. And it was a magical place to work because we were all on the same page.

Serve your client well, do everything with dignity and honor, and make sure people are making money. Because without that, the system falls apart. By 2000, things had gotten a little out of hand and even Alan Greenspan was saying, hey, irrational exuberance. And nobody was listening, and to me it was clear that it couldn't last too much longer. And I wanted to have kids, so I moved out here with my husband.

What happened?

LW: Wall Street went to hell because Alan Greenspan ran out of ways to prop up the equity markets, which he was ordered to do by the Bush White House. And the Bush White House knew that it was gonna lose its Republican edge unless they could find a way to make Americans better off. So they tasked Greenspan with figuring out how to make Americans better off. And he said, all right, home ownership. And they radically shifted all of the underlying ratios required by Fannie and Freddie, and thereby made more homes more affordable to more people.

And that was what brought Wall Street down. It was a policy decision in Washington. It was the government, not the private sector, that caused Wall Street to collapse.

Why did they do that?
LW: The second Bush administration... So, if you're the Fed chair, and interest rates are at historic lows, so the bond market isn't paying anything to investors, you have to do what you can to make sure that low interest rates translate into high corporate earnings. Because then what the bond market can't deliver to investors, the stock market can deliver through earnings. So once low interest rates had been such a given, that they weren't juicing up earnings anymore, then they had to find a new way to create instruments that were gonna satisfy investor demand for paper that had a chance of going up.

So they began doing jumbo collateralized mortgages and all sorts of derivatives off those collateralized mortgage obligation bonds. And the only way to make those underlying mortgages work was to change the regulatory environment and allow lenders to lend higher percentages of net... give people the money to buy houses they couldn't afford.

How does something like this get started?
LW: Because we have a two party system, the party in power has everything to lose, and so needs to protect itself from the other power coming in saying, you haven't done enough for the American people. And so in order to try to head that off, and to try to head off negative public sentiment, most people will support a government that makes them better off. And there was a fear in Bush 2 that Americans weren't better off.

You're saying it all came down to politics?
LW: The Fed is supposed to be totally independent of the politician environment. And sadly that isn't the case now. My friends

who are still on Wall Street are appalled by how little independence any of the regulatory bodies have. The White House is running our economy right now, which is what's so scary. It's not supposed to be that way. It's supposed to be the free market and wise regulators ensuring that any little minor short term problems with the free market are smoothed out.

How much of this was forseen?

LW: In 1999, when IPOs would get presented to the Street, we all had total judgment and total independence in determining what deals fit what investors. That was the sacred pact. You never had to sell something to somebody for whom it wasn't a fit. By 2000, 2001, there was a lot more pressure coming down to take the really bad deals we had decided to do, and cram them down the throats of investors. And I had to fight hard for the right not to sell bad paper to good investors.

Where was the pressure coming from?

LW: The pressure was coming from senior management who was saying, you know, take one for the team, do it for the sake of the team. We'd lost our sense of individual judgment on what was the right thing for the right guy, which was what we'd been paid to do and how we thought of ourselves, and we were told that for the greater good we should do X, Y or Z. Whenever I hear the greater good, I run. And so, I left.

That was the dot com thing?

LW: Right. Wasn't just the dot com bubble that I was working on. There were a lot of bad telecom deals, there was Global Crossing, a cable under the Atlantic, that was just a badly designed mess. There was WorldCom, there were a lot of really questionable deals that never would have gotten done five years earlier, just as people who couldn't afford a house wouldn't have been given a loan by the bank five years earlier. But when companies need to find a way to make profits and the government's handing it to them free.

Why was the bond market dead?

LW: The interest rates were too low.

No one's making money.

LW: No returns. So if you can't get any return out of the bond market, you gotta go up the risk curve looking for alpha, looking for something. And the same thing happened once equities got too toppy by 2002 or so, you know, they paused at 2000 and then they went back up again. By 2003, there was no juice left in equities, and that's when everybody started looking at CMOs, derivatives, things to do with mortgage linked securities that were a total house of cards, because they were based on mortgages that never should have been written.

Why were interest rates set so low?

LW: Yeah, that's totally managed by the government. The Fed determines where interest rates are. If the Fed is wise, as it was under Greenspan, Ayn Rand's disciple, then he sees, he knows how to read the economy, he knows exactly where it is, and he adjusts rates based on how much economic growth and what the engine is like in a real economy. So the engine wasn't too perky. And therefore they had to leave rates low, they had to leave the price of money low to encourage people to invest.

And by encouraging that investment, they were priming the machine and keeping it moving. The minute the market began to actually really start to have some juice to it, they had to raise rates. And by raising rates, they put every floating rate mortgage in America in peril. Because suddenly people's rates were going way up, and their monthly payment which they couldn't afford when they wrote the mortgage, went to hell. And the mortgage is in foreclosure. And then the underlying bond that it's in defaults.

And then the investor loses money. And then the bank defaults because it doesn't have assets and liabilities matching up. And this whole house of cards built by borrowing from the Fed window, goes south.

Where was Greenspan in all this?

LW: Under Greenspan, for most of his tenure, it was absolutely impeccably managed, with the independence that it needed. Late in Bush 2 was when they started to whisper in his ear, and that's when he quit. And most smart people said the day Alan Greenspan quits is the day you short every market in the world, because no one can manage this as brilliantly as he can.

He totally went the other direction.

LW: Alan Greenspan was a disciple and took the best of Ayn Rand into his working life and created the biggest bull market in the history of the world. I mean, Ayn Rand is to thank for a 10 year bull run. When Alan quit, when the pressure from Washington got ridiculous, and because he's a man of integrity, he's prepared to admit every wrong call he ever made. And nobody right now wants to give him credit for the 20 right calls a day he made. But to work on a trading floor where he was running the Federal Reserve, was a joy.

It was like having a wise, benevolent teacher standing there saying, you can do more, you can do better, be wiser. I mean, what kind of Fed chair talks about rational exuberance, except the most moral, righteous, decent person who says, I'm calling it like I see it. Which was Ayn Rand's lesson to us. Have the courage of your convictions.

Once Bernanke came in, who's an academic, and who didn't have his hands... I mean here's a man who was racing an incredibly precise car at 1,000 miles an hour around a track where one misstep has this huge impact on the economy. And he was perfect. Then you bring in a guy who's a very good driver, he stays at 65 and he goes around that track. And it all exploded because the market couldn't trust his ability to read reality and translate it into the right rate adjustments.

How does this relate to Atlas Shrugged?

LW: To me the tie is that it was the book that caused Greenspan to understand that delicate play between the collective, the government, the greater good, and the ability and the need of individual players in a marketplace to have the freedom to move.

I mean, there were a lot of ways where Rand was off… And her whole thing where she dumped her husband for the guy who… you know, that put a lot of people off because she was such a moralist. That, you know, failing to make good on your own promise, you know, wigged a lot of people out.

Non-contradiction right?

LW: Right. And she had no romantic thing going with Greenspan. But I think he, to some extent, outgrew her. But his entire world view is predicated on her understanding of reality.

Is it possible to outgrow her?

LW: She was making a point that was incredibly linked to the Cold War zeitgeist at the time. She was basically saying, you know, I left the Soviet Union. That's what, the Soviet Union's economy, that's what you'll get if you suppress the individual in favor of the collective, the government, the society, the greater good. And here in America, what you have is at its best, is a land where everything is possible.

And, you know, cherish that and make sure to protect that, was kind of her underlying message. Now that there is no big socialist machine out there to refer to, because the socialists all capitulated and decided that it didn't work, that she was right. She sort of won that battle, and then there's nothing left in a post

Randian world, except capitalism, until socialism rears its ugly head again.

And we come back around and I think that's where we are now, where a lot of Americans who really are free marketeers even if they're just running a little eBay shop on Main Street. They get it, that when they do good business, good things happen. When they pay taxes, the greater good is served. But they've gotta have the means to do that. They need help from the government to do that. They need a regulatory framework that will help them grow their business. And we seem to have lost touch with that because we've got academics in Washington now, who don't understand that if the pie doesn't get any bigger, you can't have more.

Why do you think it took fifty years to make a movie out of Atlas?

LW: I always wondered why they didn't make a movie out of *Atlas Shrugged*. It has all the elements for a great movie. Maybe there just never was a script anybody was excited enough to do.

Maybe because the heroes aren't victims?

LW: Hollywood loves a victim. Hollywood loves a downtrodden down on his luck guy who gets rehabilitated. Ayn Rand is the antithesis of that. *Atlas Shrugged* doesn't have an anti-hero hero. It's all about a political, moral and economic world view that Hollywood hates.

They like anti-heroes.

LW: They want victims. Underdogs. It's tragic. They don't want big superheroes. They want the fatally flawed and the weak and the downtrodden to somehow reign victorious over the man. And Ayn Rand posits that the man is actually the solution to our problem, not the problem.

In a perfect world, who really is the man?

LW: Absolutely. Every one of us is the man. And we need to take that responsibility. But it's a heavy responsibility to shoulder. It's so much easier to say, someone else should pay for my health care. Someone else owes me a job. I want a nice house and so I should have one. And in a world of shoulds, individual responsibility and individual contribution gets lost.

So let's say you're the casting director...
LW: Oh, I'm dying to make this movie.

Who's gonna be in it?
LW: Well, not Angelina Jolie. Because she's a Mouch. No, it needs to be someone who... really it should have been Ingrid Bergman and... the Casablanca cast, would've made it beautifully. But sadly it was not to be. Humphrey Bogart, that's what I was trying to think of. You know, you need a larger than life, I mean, who's your Francisco D'Anconio? I mean, not Antonio Banderas. That doesn't work.

Javier Bardem.
LW: Javier Bardem. Would that work? Okay, Javier Bardem, I'm good with that. And, Angelina Jolie is very beautiful. And it certainly can't be Julia Roberts. I mean, you need somebody titanic though. You need a young Meryl Streep maybe. But we don't have one. And then who is John Galt? Cannot be Brad Pitt with his wussy little face. It's gotta be someone titanic.

How about Christian Bale?
LW: That's who they're talking about, isn't it? Somebody said that on some website I saw. They wanted Christian Bale. Is that you? Did you write that?

No.
LW: Someone on some website wrote that.

John Hamm?

LW: No, I never watch Mad Men.

Hank Rearden?

LW: Oh, Rearden. Rearden. So fabulous.

Maybe Russell Crowe?

LW: What? Oh Russell Crowe as Rearden. It's perfect. I love it.

Are we headed for the same end as the characters in the book?

LW: We can use our brains and survive. And if we could get everyone in America to agree that we're not entitled to anything, we just need government regulations to get fixed. If they fixed Medicare and Medicaid, we wouldn't need this new health care plan that's gonna spend billions of dollars in taxpayer money.

If everybody were willing to say, wait, 545 people control Washington. Let's just get 'em in a room and agree. And let's stop with the noise. 70 percent of Americans believe the government is dysfunctional. That's enough to build a consensus and get us to think our way out of this.

-Santa Barbara, January 2010

"Don't you believe in the operation of the moral law, madame?" Francisco asked gravely. "I do."

Rearden heard Bertram Scudder, outside the group, say to a girl who made some sound of indignation, "Don't let him disturb you. You know, money is the root of all evil—and he's the typical product of money."

Rearden did not think that Francisco could have heard it, but he saw Francisco turning to them with a gravely courteous smile.

"So you think that money is the root of all evil?" said Francisco d'Anconia. "Have you ever asked what is the root of money? Money is a tool of exchange, which can't exist unless there are goods produced and men able to produce them. Money is the material shape of the principle that men who wish to deal with one another must deal by trade and give value for value. Money is not the tool of the moochers, who claim your product by tears, or of the looters, who take it from you by force. Money is made possible only by the men who produce. Is this what you consider evil?

"When you accept money in payment for your effort, you do so only on the conviction that you will exchange it for the product of the effort of others. It is not the moochers or the looters who give value to money. Not an ocean of tears nor all the guns in the world can trans-

CHAPTER EIGHTEEN
NICOLE GELINAS

Nicole Gelinas is the Searle Freedom Trust Fellow at the Manhattan Institute and a contributing editor of City Journal. Gelinas writes on urban economics and finance, municipal and corporate finance, and business issues. She is a Chartered Financial Analyst (CFA) charterholder and a member of the New York Society of Securities Analysts. Her most recent book, After the Fall: Saving Capitalism from Wall Street—and Washington *was published on November 2009 by Encounter Books.*

Gelinas has published analysis and opinion pieces on the op-ed pages of The New York Times, The Wall Street Journal, the Los Angeles Times, the San Diego Union Tribune, the New York Sun, the New York Daily News, the New York Post, the Dallas Morning News, the New Orleans Times-

Picayune, and the Boston Herald. She has also written for Crain's New York Business and National Review Online.

Before coming to City Journal, Gelinas was a business journalist for Thomson Financial in New York, where she covered the international syndicated-loan and private-debt markets. She also wrote a regular op-ed column for the New York Post.

Gelinas graduated from the Newcomb College of Tulane University with a B.A. in English literature.

We interviewed Ms. Gelinas in the winter of 2011 at the Manhattan Institute where she is a fellow.

Why is Atlas Shrugged gaining popularity today?

NICOLE GELINAS: There may be a generational issue here. Because, certainly growing up in the 1980s, you had things like Alex P. Keaton on Family Ties where people knew it was okay to embrace capitalism even if they didn't know all of the details. I mean, certainly Reagan was not an exemplar of Ayn Rand capitalism to say the least. But people knew it was okay to want to make money, that this wasn't something to be ashamed of. So going into reading these books with that perspective rather than 1960s perspective may have made kids less embarrassed to say, oh, they had read this book even if they did not agree with every part of it and did not consider themselves to be Ayn Rand's acolyte or extremists. They weren't embarrassed to say that they read it and liked it at parties.

Alex is a good example.

NG: Yeah, I mean, it kinda goes back to the whole thing of, even the Wall Street movie, Oliver Stone made the first movie to show that this was a terrible evil and this greed is good. And he just ended up encouraging a generation of kids who embraced this and say, I want to go on Wall Street and be like Gordon Gecko.

Same thing with Family Ties. I mean, this was a show written by people who came from the baby boom generation. They were supposed to be embarrassed by their son who had the poster of Nixon up on the wall and was a follower of Reagan and wore the suit and tie. But kids embraced it.

What did Ayn Rand know and when did she know it?
NG: Well, I mean, let's think about it for a minute. You had Ike who warned about the military industrial complex. And so just speculating she may have been worried about crony capitalism from that perspective where you had prosperity and people were working, were doing well. But yet you did have this undercurrent of crony capitalism at the same time, which was starting to build up.

You think she saw that?
NG: Yeah, it is hard to know exactly what she was thinking about. Unless, you know, I don't know enough about her personally to know what she was responding to, if anything.

Is there a way to have capitalism without crony capitalism?
NG: Well, there's always a tension between – especially in developed modern society, like we have. You know, clearly successful companies are going to have resources to lobby. They will do so with, it's a free country, we can't or shouldn't circumscribe people's free speech, freedom to associate and so forth. And of course successful large companies, their goal at some point becomes to create barriers to entry and not have upstart competitors. And so they use their resources in Washington to do that, whether it's to encourage regulations because they know that they have enough resources to work around the regulations. If you are a big bank, you are in favor of regulations because you know that gives you an advantage over smaller banks that can't spend the same amount of money going through all of the hoops. And it's certainly not just the power of lobbying. People in Washington, the staffers who

really write these bills, people in office looking to what they're going to do when they get out of office. They want jobs, they want well-paying jobs. And, and these companies can offer that. So you do have this build up of that dynamic. And it is certainly not avoidable. But the more people understand it and push back against it, the more that they can help. For example, an example from this week, President Obama naming the General Electric Chief, Jeff Immelt, to his panel on creating jobs. GE is a fine company in many respects. But this is not pure free market capitalism. This is a company that depends on government contracts. It depends on what the government thinks is the direction of the country in terms of wind power. And it depends on crony capitalism, not just here but in Asia as well. They want to do business with the Chinese government. And also in Europe with the renewable energy pushes and so forth. So certainly not their fault. They are working in the world as it was, as it is and being entrepreneurial in this world. But this is not competitive, fair, free market capitalism.

What's the difference between capitalism and crony capitalism?

NG: I'll give you a short answer, and then hopefully you can tease out more details about how it fits into finance and so forth.

The ideal of capitalism would be that government just sets out some rules of the road, where of course you can't steal people's technology, so you need patent rules. You can't threaten people's personal safety, so you need policing power, national defense. Those types of things would be the government's job. And once the government has done that, perhaps put down some basic infrastructure. Roads, bridges and the like, although hardcore libertarians would say that even that is not the government's job. Then people could just go about their business, creating jobs, creating businesses, doing what they see fit as the profit motive and the government stays out of this. Crony capitalism would be more the government setting out what are its goals for the economy and the society, and business work within those constructions.

Wouldn't that start with the businessmen?

NG: Well, yeah, it would be both. It's hard to say, what is the chicken and what is the egg. If you have businesses that become very successful, then yes, they amass power in Washington. They get Washington to do what they want. And on the other side if you have a situation more like in China, where you have the government that is more powerful than the businesses at first. The government sets out what kind of economy it wants to build. And to be successful in this economy, businesses have to do what the government wants. So they learn to work very well with the government. If, I mean, you could have examples of this almost anywhere in the world. For example, farm subsidies, government clearly says its policy is to subsidize mass scale farming and export farm products. If you want to be successful in that business, you become very politically connected, very large company like some of the farm companies we have. And you learn to deal in that environment. That happens here. That happens in Asia. And that's all an example of closer to government directed capitalism than pure free market capitalism.

Using political capital to get ahead.

NG: Sure. And vice versa. Politicians using business to further concentrate their own power and get ahead themselves.

Securing political donations?

NG: Right. Political donations, jobs, not just for themselves but for family members.

How closely did that reflect the actual relationship between government and business in the 1950's?

NG: Mmm, I would be better at it doing it from the '80s until now...

When did reality start catching up to the book?

NG: Hmm. I wouldn't go so far as to say that reality has caught up with the book. I would say that she did a very good job of concentrating timeless problems and threats. And arguably going too far with them for narrative entertainment purposes, which is fine. But we can see the reality of some of those threats today where you do have financial regulators or regulations that do not ensure a free fair playing field for financial firms and for the rest of the economy which depends on these financial firms. Instead you have regulators who use their discretion to keep a certain group of firms in business. The too big to fail banks. I don't think that Ayn Rand would have liked this idea of too big to fail financial system very much.

Her father lost his business.

NG: Yes. And the extremes of property seizure, lack of property rights in other countries and other parts of the world today and in the past, can make these threats even more obvious today even when they're not on the same scale. We have eminent domain problems in this country. We had a big case in Brooklyn where you've got the City of New York, the borough president of Brooklyn, many law makers, legislatures saying, we are going to take one group of people's private property and give it to another group because we have found what we think is a better use for the land. We want to redistribute the wealth from these people to people who need affordable housing, jobs and so forth. Clearly this is a threat to property rights, and also a threat to a free economy. So we have these problems here as well.

Do you see a prophecy coming true in the novel?

NG: I think the novel is more of.... not so much a prediction as it is an object lesson in what happens when we surrender to these extremes. And we don't live in a world of extremes. We're always going to live in an imperfect world. But we can certainly see relating to what goes on today to the novel. We want to be careful not to have a world that is made up of too big to fail financial firms, where the companies that are responsible for allocating financial capital to the rest of the economy are permanently protected by government subsidy. And that is effectively what we have. And so it's useful for people to go and look at nightmarish unrealistic versions of this, including Ayn Rand's novels, to get an idea of why it is that we have to make sure to enforce free, fair, efficient markets, even if we don't do it perfectly. You know, we don't want to govern through apocalyptic pronouncements and predictions and terms. But it is good for people to understand philosophical history, narrative history and so forth, and keep this in their heads as they're trying to get through the practical problems. So I wouldn't say that she was some sort of soothsayer in understanding what was going to happen with the economy. It is more like you're writing a novel about love and then the same things happen in real life. It's not a prediction, it is just a useful narrative of human behavior that you can relate to your real life even if your real life is not as extreme and dramatic as this.

Why was it so negatively received?

NG: It is interesting that it's a very long book. I mean, there's certainly parts of it that people skip, speech goes on for too long in many places. The characterization... certainly, it is not an example of a literarily perfect book. But it has been in print for half a century, which is more than most authors can say about their works. And it is interesting that people go to this book on their own. No one makes them read these –no one makes students read Ayn Rand in high school or college. People find these books when teachers are trying to get them to read other types of books. And so when conservatives say, well we need to teach these books in school so that people get another perspective of capitalism, that's not really true. People find these things on their own. So it is a success from that point of view.

So you don't think we're living the events of the book?

NG: No. I mean, I think that the book is not real life. So it is just like any dramatic literary representation of real life. I would not take it literally. I would take it more as a very concentrated object lesson in certain extremes. So I would not be one of these people who says, oh my goodness, if we don't watch out we're going to turn into some kind of dystopian fantasy. I think that it is useful to look at extremes so that we have a good idea of where we should be going in the middle. That we are not going to have one extreme or the other, but there is a danger that when you have a government that is not… or a populace that is not worried enough about crony capitalism, about a financial industry that is not beholden to free market forces, but beholden to the government. You are not optimally allocating capital in the economy. You don't have an economy that could be as free as it should be.

It's supposed to be representational.

NG: Yeah. I mean, there's a lot of people that take everything too literally, no matter what it is. I mean, there's kids that read Wuthering Heights and think that their life should be like this. These are dramatic illustrations of what happens when you don't do things right.

Who are the moochers and looters today?

NG: Yeah. I think moochers and looters is an example of the kind of language that gets people's attention. And we do have this problem today, and it is not the fault of the moochers and looters. It is the fault of the government that has created a system where you are rewarded for looking for government favors rather than having the best business model. And we see this in the financial industry. We've got companies, AIG of course, looking at naming names, you can list through the companies that got the biggest bailouts. AIG, Citigroup, Goldman Sachs, in being the counterparty to AIG that should have lost all of its money, that it had been promised from AIG in 2008. These are companies that were not subject to the free market effects of their decisions. They were cushioned by the government. And so without a government system that enforces market discipline, they have become permanent wards of the government because investors expect that the same thing will happen in the future. And it's not so much, does this benefit these companies? It's more that it hurts the rest of the economy because other businesses are competing on an uneven playing field.

Special interest groups?

NG: Yeah. I mean, there's many groups that depend on government favors, not on free market failure or success. Financial industry is the number one obvious example right now because it's hard for people to see it. People think, well they've paid back their TARP money. So the problem has gone away. The government made a profit on TARP, or will make a profit on TARP. That is not the problem. The problem is that the financial markets will expect that these firms will be bailed out in the future. And so you have permanent government subsidy of financial industry debt. If you wonder how the country ended up so indebted and with consumers owing so much money. It is because the government made a conscious decision to subsidize financial industry debt over 25 years since we first started having too big to fail banks. Financial industry turned around and lent that money right back to regular people. So it was not a failure of free markets. It was a failure of government directed use of capital. And I think that is important for people to understand. In some ways language like looters and moochers, it makes it into more of... who are the bad people and who are the good people? And I don't think that's true. I mean, people get what they can get out of society. So that's fine for them. It's the government's job to set up a fair system of regulation so that companies can fail.

We're talking about patronage – machine politics.

NG: Yeah. It's not capitalism that runs amok. It is the government that runs amok in setting certain goals for capitalism. And capitalism tries to achieve these goals in pursuit of the profit motive. If the government says that everyone should have a blue house, you will have the nation's economy working toward painting everyone's house blue because there was a profit in it for them. That is not irrational capitalism. That is an irrational government mandate. So you name it, whether it's government saying that everybody gets a house even if they can't afford it. It's government saying that we're going to build wind power plants. We're going to subsidize oil industry, special interests. I mean, anything can be a special interest. And if the government decrees that that is a goal, businesses will work in pursuit of that goal.

How can we disabuse people of this mentality – or morality?

NG: Yeah. The first thing we have to do is create a financial system that is subject to free market discipline. Without that, the rest of the economy can't be subject to free market discipline because you've got financial firms that are directing capital to where the government wants it to go. The way you do that is not easy. It does not happen on its own because you can't have financial firms that fail and take the rest of the economy down with them. The social cost is too great. We live in a democracy and people have said since the 1930s, we won't accept that social cost of unfettered failure. So you have to work in the world that you have. We have FDIC insurance, which I think is good. It should allow banks to fail without hurting regular people. You should have limits on speculative borrowing so that firms like AIG can go under without causing a panic throughout the financial system enforcing these large scale bailouts. You have some certain simple regulations set out beforehand. Limits on borrowing, rules governing disclosure of stock market trading and what have you. And then these firms can fail without unduly harming the rest of the economy. And then you've got imperfect financial market discipline, but better than what we have.

Regulating not to manipulate markets but to preserve them?

NG: Well, yeah. I mean, what we did starting in the early '80s was make it very clear to bondholders to large banks that we would not let them take losses on their investments. This was a change from what we had done for 50 years. Before this we let the bondholders take losses. And so they helped discipline the banks. That's market regulation which is good. We took away this market regulation by saying we're gonna protect these bondholders to these too big to fail banks. And so you deregulated a market discipline, which is not good.

That's right out of Atlas Shrugged.

NG: Yeah. I mean, I wouldn't say it's right out of *Atlas Shrugged* only because it's, you know, again, I think books are good in that it is good that people are paying attention to what happens when you have extremes in the economy. And if they pay attention to it through reading *Atlas Shrugged,* that's terrific. But I wouldn't say… I certainly respect other people who would say it, but I would not be a person going around saying, oh my goodness, it's right out of *Atlas Shrugged.* I mean, these things are useful, but separate. If people are worried that we don't have a free market system and they got to that worry from reading the book, I am here to explain some of the details that if you want a system that is closer to free markets, here are some of the rules that we can put in place.

How much can capitalism be held responsible for the financial crisis?

NG: No, I don't think that capitalism is responsible for the financial crisis because the financial crisis came about because of certain government decisions made over 25 years. 1984, Washington under the Reagan administration made an overt decision to start protecting the bondholders to large banks. After that, money went into the financial system. The government invited it there. So when people say, capitalism caused debt to triple as a percentage of the GDP, capitalism caused people to borrow too much, capitalism caused the housing bubble, that is not true. It was the government's decision to protect a certain segment of the economy, which is the financial sector that is behind all of this.

And this is important for people to understand, very important. I would say it's one of the most important things. Because if you blame capitalism, you don't have any solution. And we haven't gotten any solution from either political party in five years. Since the crisis started to people who were paying attention, in 2006, not 2008.

It doesn't appear we're gonna get one.

NG: No. Because you have democrats that say, this was unbridled capitalism, when capitalism was very bridled. And you have republicans that have kind of absorbed this lesson that it was capitalism's fault, but they don't really know how to argue against it. So they just kind of say stupid things or be quiet, which hasn't helped either.

Isn't banking one of the most regulated industries?

NG: Yeah. But you need the right regulations, really rules. Limit borrowing consistently. The reason we got into a mortgage crisis is because we unlearned the lesson that we had learned in the '30s. In the '20s people could borrow 100 percent against their stock portfolio. So you have a right to lose your own money, you don't have a right to lose all of the bank's money so that the bank is bankrupt. We limited borrowing against stock portfolios in the '30s. You should have had limits in the housing market where you've got to put a 20 percent downpayment down. You have that rule and you would have avoided all the fraud. You couldn't lie your way into a mortgage if you didn't have 20 percent. Rich people could not have afforded five houses. Middle class people could not have afforded a giant McMansion. And a lot of poor people would have had to rent. It would have been much better that way and saved a lot of problems. Simple rule that applies to everyone is better than a lot of rules that apply willy nilly and that people with the most money can find their way out of.

Government seems unable to grasp the less-is-more concept.
NG: Yeah. And I'm glad, you know, you understand what a lot of financial experts haven't been able to understand over three years of talking about this. That if you think about it at the level of the financial system, bundling all of these mortgages, they did that because they got triple A ratings. Why do you get triple ratings? 'Cause you can get out of a lot of limits on borrowing with a triple A rating. If the government said, limit on borrowing is the same no matter what rating you have, you wouldn't have had them go through all these hoops to get the triple A rating.

Triple A in this case meaning 'worthless'.
NG: Yeah. I mean, it's just like my example of the blue house. If the government decrees that everyone should have a blue house, I don't blame the painter that's painting the house blue. The government decreed that having a triple A rating was the be all and end all. And so I don't blame the people who got them there. They were doing what was the cleverest thing to do under the crazy rules that were set up. If they didn't do these things, they would be even crazier. Because bucking the conventional wisdom does not get you anywhere.

What is the proper role of government?
NG: Right. That's a good question. The government's job is to create a system where any type of business can fail without tak-

ing down the rest of the economy. That's the only way you have a free market system. So in finance, it's limiting borrowing, having disclosure rules so that people can see where the risks lie. You do these things and you're 80 percent of the way there. And you don't do them and you have this constant cycle of bailouts and the expectation of bailouts.

Secure and maintain a level playing field?

NG: Yeah. It's similar to traffic rules. Even the most hardcore libertarians I think would say it's fine for the government to say everyone goes at a green light, stops at a red light. These are the rules that allow us to get to our jobs and create private sector profits. It would not be fine for the government to sit in your car and tell you where to go and when to stop and when to go on a discretionary basis. That is closer to what we have now, which is not good.

So who's most to blame here – greedy capitalists or meddling politicians?

NG: Certainly improper government interference is the bigger culprit than greedy capitalists. People are greedy. I mean, if money falls on your head you take it. That is what happened in the financial system. The government made a conscious decision to throw money at finance over a quarter of a century. And so people took the money. Why anyone is surprised is not clear to me. It's not a mystery. If you don't want bankers to be taking multi-million dollar bonuses, don't subsidize money that goes into the financial system that is what makes these bonuses possible.

Why would they do that?

NG: How did the government end up with a system of creating large financial firms as national champions? Some of it is just panic, where you've got a bank failing in 1984. You've got the FDIC, the Fed, Treasury, telling the Reagan administration, you can't let the bank fail, it will take down the rest of the economy. No one ever wants to take that chance. So in the crisis they bail out the bank. And people like Paul Volcker at the time said, oh, it doesn't set a precedent. They think that what they say matters. To the financial markets it only matters what they did. Because the financial markets know there'll be a new panic in the future. Same thing will happen, and that each time it happens it will be on a bigger and bigger scale.

So part of it is just confusion in a panic, not a conscious decision. And the other part of it is that as the financial sector grows because you have this expectation of bailouts, they have more power in Washington. And so Washington listens to what they say.

What regulations are necessary?

NG: Any regulation that is in service of creating a level playing field is good. Regulations that favor large firms over small firms, agricultural firms over technology firms, oil over wind or vice versa, these are bad. For example, BP. A lot of people don't realize this, but the government bailed out BP. You've got punishment by words, not by allowing the free market to punish firms for bad deeds. Back in summer right after the BP oil spill happened, you had David Cameron come from Britain and say, this is an important company, it is integral to the British economy.

And he said this while standing right next to President Obama on the stage. That's a clear diplomatic signal to the financial markets that neither government would let BP fail. You can say all you want about weaning the country off of energy. The better way to wean the economy off of fossil fuels would be to say, a company like BP can fail if the market has determined that.

Then drilling costs for these projects will go up. It will be harder for these firms to get insurance. The price of oil would be higher set by market forces, not by government forces. And people would use less oil. The free market can fix these problems better than carbon tax or other government efforts can. And it would. But we have signaled over and over that we will yell at these firms, but we will not let them fail.

Would that be the end of the world?

NG: If they cannot drill for oil without making unacceptable catastrophic errors, the market will tell them that this is not a good business model. Government can't do that.

How vital is a vibrant capitalistic system?

NG: Certainly it is, it's important to Americans to have a vibrant capitalistic system. We need this to figure out what types of technologies work, what don't work, what types of business work, what don't work, what creates jobs, what doesn't create jobs. You need a financial sector that supports the rest of the economy and doesn't compete with it in order to have this. Financial firms that buy companies, get rid of jobs, move jobs overseas, that's all fine if this is happening under a free market system. It is not fine if the only way these financial firms can do this is because they've got permanent government subsidies. And that's the way it is now.

Do you see America slipping?

NG: Yeah. We'll slip as an economic superpower if we insist on subsidizing certain parts of the economy to the detriment of other parts, which may be able to stand on their own two feet better.

Can you give me an example?

NG: Sure. You go back to the financial sector. We are clearly subsidizing finance. Other businesses have a harder time competing. And so we are subsidizing weaker businesses at the expense of businesses that could be stronger. Not good for the nation over time.

Because of the pull that they have?

NG: Yeah. That's partly because of it. And also because it's hard to wean the American economy off of borrowing. It's a lot of short term pain and no politicians want to suffer that pain.

Two million copies of Atlas Shrugged have sold in the last five years.

NG: Yeah. And I think it's a heartening sign, a lot of people buying Ayn Rand's book are young people. And older people too. It's a heartening sign that anyone wants to learn what happens if you completely dispense with free market capitalism in a dystopian environment. Obviously we are not anywhere near there. But it is good for people to see the extremes so that they can say why is it important to make sure that we have a system where free market capitalism can thrive.

But the fact that so many people are reading it, you take as a positive sign?

NG: I think it's a positive sign that more people are reading Ayn Rand's, I mean, I think it's great that people want to read anything and learn more about capitalism, certainly not be slavish adherents to literal interpretations of the book. But understand that this is part of the pull of what is out there. I think it's a great book. I don't think people should take it as... and I respect people who want to be hard core libertarians, who are very clear about their philosophy and don't let any rules and regulations muddle that philosophy. I think that's fine. But I live in the practical world, and so to me it's a story, it's entertainment. And I think Mr. Greenspan eventually came up with the same conclusion. So, I'm not out there saying, this is an illustration of what happens if we don't do the right things. And that is not true. But I respect people who believe that and who may come to wanting to learn more about free market capitalism because they're worried about this. I think that's great.

At least people are thinking.

NG: Yeah. But honestly, I mean what I say. I'm glad people are reading *Atlas Shrugged*. I'd be glad if they're reading Karl Marx. I think people should read and people should make up their own decisions about things.

So you don't see Atlas as a cautionary tale?

NG: No. I think, I'm too optimistic about Americans to think that that would happen. People come here because they want to make a living. And people still come from all over the world because they want to try out their ideas in America. So, I mean, we have problems, we have more problems today than we've had in a long time. But people will fix these problems even if they don't come up with the perfect solutions.

Should they teach Ayn Rand in schools?

NG: No. I don't think they have to teach Ayn Rand in schools. I think that's probably a bad idea. People come to this because they wonder exactly about what they do learn in schools. People teaching Ayn Rand and making them buy the novel is not responsible for selling half a million copies last year. People read the book because their friends read it and they think it was interesting. That's good. So don't make it a punishment.

Anything else?

NG: More people would read Charles Dickens if they didn't make you read it in school.

How old were you when you read it?

NG: I was younger than college, 'cause I had to have... I know I had read these things going into college, maybe a couple summers, during high school.

Which Rand book did you read first?

NG: Fountainhead.

Did you get the philosophy?

NG: I understood the philosophy. I thought it was a good story. And it does show you that ideas matter and you should respect people who – who believe in their own ideas, and who take them to fruition.

What did you think about Atlas Shrugged?

NG: I liked The Fountainhead better than *Atlas Shrugged.* But I think Atlas is an important book. It gives you, it gives you a good philosophical grounding in the extremes of certain ideas. And you have to understand the extremes before you can understand the middle.

Do you believe in objectivism?

NG: Yeah. I mean, I'm familiar with it. I am not a philosopher. You'll have to get other people who say, oh, this is the philosophy of the future or something like that. I take what I take out of everything.

Speaking of the future, are you optimistic?

NG: I'm optimistic, but it is good that people can be worried about certain extremes. And so maybe they will be more willing to listen to the details of what we have to do permanently. A lot of people may think the financial crisis is over and so why should I care about financial regulation? But it's not over. And if we don't put the right rules in place, we'll just have this happen over and over again and get worse each time. You see what happens in Ireland when the financial system outgrows the government's ability to bail it out. So it would be better if the political process worked rather than the market process.

Are we living in a dystopia?

NG: Oh no. I don't think we live in a dystopia. I mean, we have our problems, but in a lot of ways they're good problems.

-New York, February 2011

CHAPTER NINETEEN

NORTHRUP BUECHNER

Dr. M. Northrup Buechner is an Associate Professor of Economics at St. John's University. He received an A.B. in economics from Lawrence University in 1965, and a Ph.D. in economics from The University of Virginia in 1971. His fields of specialization are microeconomics and methodology. He has published articles in The New York Times, The Objectivist Forum, The Southern Economic Journal, and other scholarly and popular publications. He regularly contributes papers to meetings of professional economists. He was awarded the Teaching Merit Award of St. John's University in 1974. The 2010-11 academic year marks his forty-first year of teaching at St. John's University.

His recent book, Objective Economics: How Ayn Rand's Philosophy Changes Everything about Economics, is available on Amazon.com.

We conducted Dr. Buechner's interview in a Manhattan hotel room in the winter of 2011.

How did you first discover Atlas Shrugged and Ayn Rand?

NORTHRUP BUECHNER: Between my sophomore and junior years in college, I was hitchhiking around the country and a young lady I was very interested in told me to read The Fountainhead. I found a paperback version of The Fountainhead. And then I went on and read *Atlas Shrugged.*

What did you think?

NB: Reading *Atlas Shrugged* was like being hit by lightning. It was like, holy cow. What amazing ideas that contradicted everything I had held as my own personal philosophy up to that point. It just turned me upside down.

Rand's philosophy appealed to you?

NB: The effect on me was to change my life, and to change all my fundamental ideas. My mother was virtually a socialist. I was raised in that ideology and service to others as the primary value of a human being. And I had accepted that. And I was gone after I read *Atlas Shrugged.*

What year is this?

NB: 1962.

You were a teenager?

NB: I think I was 20.

What was going on in the world?

NB: That's a good question. I wondered how come I haven't heard of this book. It's been in existence five years. You know, this should have changed the world. Where is it? And actually that was the year that Ayn Rand started publishing the Objectivist Newsletter, which I started subscribing to. I mean, at that point, I guess the interest had grown sufficiently to support her own publication.

The 60's social revolution hadn't begun?
NB: No, they weren't radicalized at all actually. It's the mid-60s (during) the Goldwater campaign when the free speech movement started in Berkeley.

How did reading Atlas change you?
NB: Well, I quit the job I had in Scottsdale, Arizona and went out to Shell Beach, California, just sat on the beach and read it a couple of times. And I had planned to spend the year hitchhiking around the country. And I felt I didn't need to go on with that. I had found what I was looking for. I didn't know that's what I was looking for, but in fact it was.

And I went home, and worked that summer, and went back to college, and finished college. Changed my major from political science to economics. And went on to get a PhD in economics at Virginia.

And I was struck reading her that everything she said on economics contradicted completely what I had been taught. And it took me a long time to see where what I had been taught was wrong.

What was wrong?
NB: Well, the economics in the early '60s, and actually for [the nation's] whole history pretty much, has been directed at setting up some ideal system which is called pure or perfect competition. Setting this up as an ideal, and then showing how the economy as we deal with, the real world economy, does not measure up to the ideal, and therefore the government should intervene in order to move us at least in the direction of the ideal. The whole system was, in effect, a justification for government involvement in the economy. And you asked me what was wrong with that?

(laughs) 'Cause I just spent 20 years writing a book that's coming out in June that is my answer to that question. (Objective Economics)

But basically, that methodology of creating a fantasy and then showing how the world does not measure up, that's just completely invalid.

How does this idea relate to Atlas Shrugged?

NB: Well, the bombshell in *Atlas Shrugged* is the attack on altruism and the proof of selfishness as a virtue, and the means of life. The big revelation is the blowing up of altruism as a moral ideal and establishing rational self interest as a moral code for life on earth. And then, not just that it would be nice, but that it's not optional - that is, if you want to live on earth. That's how you have to live. That's what flew in the face of my mother's teachings. She didn't teach me anything about economics. What she taught me was the ideal of selflessness and self-sacrifice. So I knew that stuff inside out. It's puzzling to me how some people read *Atlas Shrugged*, and they don't see that there's a revolution there. I think it depends on their background. I teach my students these ideas more or less. And it's only rarely that I have a student say, professor, are you advocating self interest? Most of 'em just sit there and take it in. See, for me, I knew this. I had that as an ideal. And I knew it was that culture was shot through with it. And everybody believes that really, consciously or not they believe it.

Does altruism remain the dominant philosophy in America today?

NB: Altruism is still the moral code. I think we have a president really who is consciously, avowedly, an altruist. And I think he's the first one we've had. I mean, everybody believes it more or less, but they have other influences. But the way he went after health care, that was clearly a moral imperative for him. It had very little to do with taking care of people. It had to do with what's required by that moral code.

How was Rand regarded in the 60's?

NB: She was a public figure. She spoke on campuses. And then in the mid '60s she started limiting her speaking to the Ford Hall Forum. And that became an annual event. Everybody in New York who was interested in her went to Boston and stood in line over night, in the freezing cold, in order to hear her. That was quite a phenomenon. And then there was the famous division between her and her most prominent follower. [Nathaniel Branden] And after that she was limited strictly to the Ford Hall Forum.

How was the book regarded in those days?

NB: Well, there were people like me who thought it was wonderful. But I think mostly she was regarded as a kook by the intellectuals. And particularly, it was the liberal intellectuals that were in control. How scared they were by the Goldwater campaign, because they thought that was just totally outside their frame of reference, the kind of things he was saying. And he said some very good things, although he ran a terrible campaign. But the idea that those ideas... that he would say something like that into the public mind. They were beside themselves. And they loathed Ayn Rand. I would say essentially no support or recognition in academia. That has changed dramatically.

Has it?

NB: Oh, a lot of people still hate her. But she's gotten respect now.

Why now?

NB: Because the ideas have spread. The Ayn Rand Institute has done a lot. But people are reading the books, they continue to read the books. And the ideas are spreading. Selfishness is not such a damning idea anymore. I mean, it's a slow process. It's 50 years since Atlas Shrugged was published. The historical record shows it takes about 100 years for new ideas to actually begin to affect the culture in which they appear. But, we can see the change happening. The question is whether it'll happen in time.

Do you see the emergence of the Tea Party as a backlash? And if so, is it a backlash against big government or the altruism that perpetuates it?

NB: Oh, that's a really interesting question. Is the Tea Party a rebellion against statism, or collectivism, or just large government? I think it's a rebellion against all three. I don't think that the Tea Party people see yet that altruism is the motive power behind statism. And they certainly don't see that, even on the political level, the answer is man's rights and the whole concept of individual rights as it was believed by the founding fathers. That has not entered anybody's consciousness yet at a general level. And that's the idea they need. They really need that idea desperately if they're gonna have any long run effect.

Do you think most people are familiar with the concept of altruism – or even the word?

NB: They don't know the word. They know self-sacrifice. They know selflessness. And I think, judging by the people I've talked to and my students, you can show them that if they're gonna be consistent with that morality, they really need to give away everything they have, and follow the path of Albert Schweitzer or Mother Teresa. And then of course they get very frustrated and say, well, no, you can't live that way. Well, you know, that's actually a very profound answer. You cannot live that way. You need a different moral code.

Morality then is...what?

NB: Well, Aristotle, the Greeks, thought morality was to show you how to live a happy, successful life. They took for granted that the individual wanted to be happy and successful, and that that was appropriate. That's a much more uncontroversial and unchallenging idea, to say: why should you care about yourself? Then to say what's good about selfishness? If you're not selfish - if you don't want to live, if you don't want to support your life, if you don't want to be happy, if you don't want to get the things that make you happy, then why are you alive?

With collectivism your life is not your own?

NB: The collectivist ideal is that the individual exists to serve others and the collective can sacrifice him in that cause any time and any way it wishes. The individual has no rights. His purpose is to serve the group.

How does that contrast with democracy?

NB: Democracy is a form of collectivism. It holds that whatever the majority wants should happen. Whatever the majority wants is good and right. And the view that dominates our time. It's impossible with that view to say why 51 percent of the people shouldn't get together and kill the other 49 percent. Now, a *limited* democracy says that you can vote democratically to do things, but it has to be limited. And the only concept that can limit democracy is the concept of man's rights. And if that's what governs the society, as it did in the early years of this country, then you can have a democracy to elect your leaders who figure out what is required to protect those rights.

That's a republic – isn't it?

NB: Is that a republic? The word has just gotten totally lost. I mean, it was the Union of Soviet Socialist Republics. And people took that as, okay, if the Soviet Union was a union of republics, what the hell was the United States? I don't know what to call this - I think that the system we're looking for is freedom, liberty, capitalism.

Why are more people reading Atlas Shrugged?

NB: Because they have heard, and it is true, that there are elements in *Atlas Shrugged* which parallel what's happening to us now. The same pattern of instituting some regulation which then makes things worse; And then you institute another regulation to mitigate the effects of the first; All that is in *Atlas Shrugged*. And it's really quite remarkable that a book written 53 years ago when people who reviewed it said, you know, she's describing this cataclysm. I do not see a single thing in today's culture that would justify that. And 50 years later, there it is. I think that's the attraction of the book to people now. They can see, she predicted these things. And if they're smart, they can see that there's more than prediction involved here. She's identifying the cause. How widely people get that, it's impossible to know.

Do you think that most readers connect the story to current events?

NB: I think, probably, there's a fair number who got maybe 10 pages into Galt's speech and said, well this is not anything I really wanna know, and went on to finish the story. If you don't read Galt's speech, you don't get the philosophy, the basic causes and the fundamental things that have to be changed if we're gonna reverse this process.

Who is making the connection?

NB: People who read it when they were in their 20s and who liked it and remember they liked it, re-read it and say, holy cow, and then tell their friends and neighbors about it. I think that's part of it. I think also that it's because the ideas have spread.

Her name is more widely recognized now than it was when she was alive. And we've had 50 years for that process to be in motion.

Are Rand's ideas considered as radical today?

NB: Well, she said radical means fundamental. And you can't get more fundamental in terms of... I mean, she took things back to the basic starting point of knowledge and identified what that starting point is, and why that's the starting point. And how everything depends on that. So that is fundamental. I don't know what could be more fundamental.

What was that starting point?

NB: Well it's the starting point, the basic axioms of knowledge. Existence exists. Consciousness is conscious. And things are what they are. And on that basis, you can know something. And without that, you can't know anything.

How crazy is it?

NB: It is crazy. I mean, that's the point actually, it is crazy. These are people that have no concept of reason, no concept of identity, no concept of anything except the wild swirlies of their minds. And this idea that I don't want to live, but I'm willing to die in order to kill you. That's the bottom. That's the bottom. And most people are all over the place. The suicide bombers, they're everywhere. And you can't get more evil, but also you can't get more crazy than that. I don't wanna live, but I'm willing to die in order to kill you. That's the bottom.

They believe the purpose of life is to die?

NB: Well, it's medieval philosophy, what was believed in the dark and middle ages, was that we are here to serve God. And that is our purpose and our goal, and what do we get out of it?

We hope when we die we'll spend eternity with God in heaven, but they didn't even believe that you could be sure of that. Now the Muslim fanatics at the time of 9/11, when there was a lot of back and forth about it, and some Imam was quoted in the Times, I saw this and it's been widely quoted. He said Americans want to be happy and live. We want to serve Allah and die. And that's the difference.

That's the extreme.
NB: That is the extreme.

But not necessarily the norm?
NB: Well, you know, basic absence of self in the sense that these people never had an original thought in their brain. And they're raised in these schools. And they're taught this stuff from the time they can understand anything. But, you know, actually it's a pretty small fraction of the Muslim population, as far as it seems to be, that believes this extreme selflessness.

It's a matter of degree.
NB: Yeah, a little bit of poison will ruin your life.

How does objectivism affect you and what you teach?
NB: Interesting question. I have two answers to that. Actually I've struggled with this problem over my teaching career. You know, what do the students have a right to expect from me when I teach them. They cannot judge what I teach. They cannot tell whether the law of supply and demand is true or false. They don't have any means of refuting it or of proving it to themselves, except what I show them. So I think what they have the right to expect, fundamentally, is that what I teach them is in some sense the accepted viewpoint in the profession. I can't teach them what's in my book. Because that is nowhere in the profession. And they're not interested, you know,

they can't judge that any more than they can judge the traditional material. So I have to teach them the things that is basically part of modern economics. Now, within that context, I present it in a way, mostly to show them how the economy works. And it does work. And most economists think it works. I mean, they do think for the most part it works, but they've got all these areas where there's market failure that they want to fix.

What parallels do you see with the book?

NB: Well, unfortunately all the villains in *Atlas Shrugged* are everywhere. You know, but they're not defined in the dramatic terms of a novel. But they are there. Their ideas are there. The government functions as a looter in the sense, you know, they are constantly scheming on some way to get more of our money and just use it to distribute to the people who will keep them in power. There are no independent businessmen. All of them go to Washington looking for help.

Most businessmen.

NB: Most businessmen behave like the villains in the novel. They go to Washington when they get in trouble and their businesses get into trouble, they go to Washington for help. I mean, Washington has taken giant leaps in the direction of establishing the principle that they will help. I mean, the government still owns General Motors. And that was the biggest bailout of this past crisis. But they're setting us up for more, because they're establishing this principle that they will bail out and the Republicans, or at least most of them, are saying, we got to get over this principle. We've gotta pass a law that we can't, we won't, and never will bail out anybody ever again. And the problem with that is, if they pass the law, but then, when the next candidate comes along, they can go ahead and bail 'em out anyway. You know, 'cause they are the law. I mean, unless you put a constitutional amendment that made it against the Constitution for the government to provide funds for private business purposes. But, you know, that's just way too small. You can't put that in the Constitution. What you need in the constitution is something to the effect that the government shall make no laws that interfere with private trade and exchange.

But doesn't the Constitution already provide for that? Congress may pass no bill that benefits one group and penalizes another?

NB: I know, but they do it. I mean, it seems like all of the wealth, you know, all the stuff that they distribute in all the different programs, to college students, to small businesses, to the lame and the blind. I mean, all that is certainly using funds that are collected from one portion of the population to benefit another portion.

There were fifty thousand federal regulations issued during the Bush administration alone.

NB: 50,000. John Stossel had it on his program. The other night, he stood there surrounded by piles of paper this high. And he said, these are the regulations that were issued by the federal government, the bureaucracies over the last year. It's impossible. You know, and Ayn Rand identified that principle in *Atlas Shrugged*. You have to create a situation where you cannot live without breaking the law. And then, everybody's a law breaker and nobody's innocent, everybody's guilty. And the politicians can do whatever they want to with us. That's shocking.

How similar is this situation to what was going on in the novel?

NB: On a scale of one to ten, how close are we to the complete obliteration of the economy that appeared in *Atlas Shrugged*. I would say five. I think we still have a great chance to win out over the long run. I think we'll see some bad times. We may have, you know, armed conflict. But the human race does come back from these things. And it's gonna come back with, Ayn Rand's philosophy, you know, widespread and clear. And at some point that will dictate what kind of a society is established.

We've got a fifty-fifty chance?
NB: I wouldn't say, we're just… I think we're half way to the end. Of course, she saw all this. She saw the ideas. If you ask where are the ideas, all the ideas are there to destroy us. But in terms of the economy and, and where we are in terms of government controls. I mean, the economy is still mostly free. And as long as it is mostly free, it will recover and will progress, and we will survive.

Despite the grip altruism has on our society?
NB: Well, you know, altruism was a dominant moral code in 1776. Adam Smith did not, you know, talk about the morality of selflessness to the self interest of the businessman. But The Wealth of Nations, you know, led to the age of free trade in the 19th century. He thought he didn't have a chance. All the entrenched interests were against what he thought was needed. And again, it was, could not succeed. And it took about 50 years, and it did succeed.

What mistakes did the founding fathers make?
NB: Well, if they knew objectivism, they could have eliminated the commerce clause. You know –

They were confounded by religious –
NB: The founding fathers were deists. They didn't have an answer to the question: when are man's rights violated? They held up the ideal of individual rights in the Declaration of Independence. They set up the government to protect man's rights. But they did not have a definition of when are his rights violated. That's the philosophical thing that's missing. It opened the door to all kinds of declarations. Well, I have a right to this and you have a right to that. And the people on the east side of Manhattan are claiming they have a right not to have a shadow

fall on their neighborhood. Ayn Rand has the answer to that. Physical force is the only way that rights are violated. But, you know, that's a little late. You know, she didn't name that principle 'til '57. 1957, not 1757.

Anything else?

NB: I'm in favor of *Atlas Shrugged*. I hope your documentary succeeds. And I hope it greatly increases the readership for the novel.

New York City, February 2011

CHAPTER TWENTY

YARON BROOK

Yaron Brook is president of the Ayn Rand Center for Individual Rights. He is a columnist at Forbes.com, and his articles have been featured in major publications such as the Wall Street Journal, USA Today, and Investor's Business Daily. Dr. Brook is often interviewed on radio and is a frequent guest on a variety of national TV programs. He is co-author of Neoconservatism: An Obituary for an Idea and a contributor to Winning the Unwinnable War: America's Self-Crippled Response to Islamic Totalitarianism. Dr. Brook, a former finance professor, is an internationally sought after speaker on such topics as the causes of the financial crisis, the morality of capitalism, and U.S. foreign policy.

Dr. Brook was born and raised in Israel. He served as a first sergeant in Israeli military intelligence and earned a BSc in civil engineering from

Technion-Israel Institute of Technology in Haifa, Israel. In 1987 he moved to the United States, where he received his MBA and Ph.D. in finance from the University of Texas at Austin; he became an American citizen in 2003. For seven years he was an award-winning finance professor at Santa Clara University, and in 1998 he co-founded a financial advisory firm, BH Equity Research, of which he is presently managing director and chairman.

Dr. Brook sat for his interview in his Irvine, California office at the Ayn Rand Institute in the fall of 2009.

Why are we seeing so much interest in Atlas Shrugged today?

YARON BROOK: A lot of people are reading *Atlas Shrugged* in really much larger numbers today than ever before. This last year saw *Atlas Shrugged* sales double its best year ever. And of course when it first came out it was a best seller. So I don't know what that makes it fifty-two years later.

Did it take this long for her ideas to be appreciated?

YB: I think the book represents fundamental truths that are being born out by events. So she wrote the book in 1957. The fundamental philosophy of America in 1957 was the same as it is today. It is just more so today.

How did Rand know back in the post-war period, a relatively benign era in American history, that all this was going to happen?

YB: All the negative trends – philosophical, ideological and ultimately economic trends existed in 1957. They were just more under the surface. There was still just more of the spirit of capitalism, the spirit of individualism kind of surviving from the nineteenth century.

So over the last fifty-two years the negative elements – negative philosophical elements have come up through the culture – have become much more prevalent in the culture. And the positive element – the individualism, pro-capitalism has faded more as we've distanced ourselves more from the century where they were in their height – during the nineteenth century. So that the logic of where those philosophical ideas would lead – we've seen it in the history of the last fifty years. She understood that if nothing changed – this is where we would be. And in that sense she predicted the future, but only in the sense that she could see – if you hold these ideas this has to be the outcome. She also said she wrote the book to prevent it from coming true.

So the whole idea was to write the book to convince Americans to turn away from these philosophical ideas – to turn back in a more substantial way towards the ideas of capitalism and individualism. And one could argue that that failed. That America hasn't listened to *Atlas Shrugged*, and as a consequence is going to have to live through *Atlas Shrugged*.

But it appears people are listening now. That wasn't always the case.
YB: For many, many years people said well *Atlas Shrugged* is a nice story. It is fiction. It's theory. And this is just Ayn Rand's view of how that theory plays itself out in reality. I think what's happening right now in America over the last two or three years is that people are seeing that story playing out in reality. Now they are listening. What they have to learn is – that it is that theory that is driving that story.

Most are looking for somewhere to place blame. Usually in the wrong places.
YB: There still is that disconnect. People are seeing what's going on and they are saying – Why is government behaving this way? Why is the economy collapsing? Why did bankers(get) to do what they did? Why did all of this happen? They still are not looking for those abstract ideas that explain it. *Atlas Shrugged* provided those abstract ideas.

How many readers do you think totally get what Rand was saying in the novel?

YB: Unfortunately a lot of people even that read *Atlas Shrugged* only get it at a very superficial level – they only get the plot. They don't get the ideas – the theoretical ideas driving the plot – the theoretical ideas driving reality.

You can have somebody casually reading the book and just getting a great plot, a great story, an exciting story, a mystery really. And you can get somebody's who's interested in philosophy reading the book and getting a whole new world opening up to them in terms of philosophical ideas and philosophical theories, and developing those, and articulating those. And the story becomes a sub issue. The real exciting thing about the book is the philosophy.

Which aspect do you think attracts most readers?

YB: I think for most of us – it's both. You get a great story. You know you can't put the book down. But at the same time those ideas are having a profound impact on you. And it changes lives. It changes so many lives.

How would you describe Atlas from a literary perspective?

YB: *Atlas Shrugged* is very much a romantic novel. Ayn Rand described romanticism in literature as projecting life as it could and ought to be. You know larger than life characters – larger than life stories. But heroes that can exist and have existed in human history.

We don't see heroes like that much today – outside of the pulp realm.

YB: It's very rare to see them projected particularly today in literature. And Hugo did that. Hugo projected those grander than life. And really that idea of romantic art being a projection of life as it should and could be – is really an idea coming from Aristotle. Aristotle – that's how he defined drama originally. Coming out of life, but being as life should be – as life could be, not as just life. So much of the movies we see today – so much of the literature we read today is naturalism.

It's just describing life that each – every individual lives – nothing special – no real bigger than life heroes – no dramatic stories. And that really has dominated most of the twentieth century literature and a lot of cinema.

Maybe not movies so much.

YB: No, not all, I think one of the reasons movies are more popular than any art form today is because some of them retain some element of the romanticism – of the drama – of the larger than life. They are romantic characters and they are real people. People like this can and do exist. Not in the exact form and they don't speak in exactly that way. But they do those kind of things.

I mean this country wouldn't be where it is today if there weren't giants of industry who do exactly what Dagny and Reardon do in *Atlas Shrugged*. In essential terms there are plenty of people like them – like them out there and it's possible to be somebody like them.

And that's what Ayn Rand's philosophy is all about – is being the kind of person in your own personal lives – in whatever career you choose – and whatever level of ability you might have – being a heroic character like those in the books is realistic.

Some critics viewed them as caricature.

YB: Yes. She was always criticized for having these unrealistic heroes – but also unrealistic villains. You know the villains were viewed as caricatures and so on. And lots of criticism – and yet –

unfolding before our eyes right now are villains in Washington that make the villains of the book seem like moderates.

You know like the stuff happening in Washington today is so crazy and ludicrous and corrupt that if she had written that into the book people would have said – now that – that is ridiculous – even more so than she did. The reality of the last few years in Washington and in our political system has really vindicated – at least the villains of *Atlas Shrugged* as being very scarily realistic.

How was Atlas received at the time?

YB: When the book first came out in 1957 it was a best seller. A lot of people read it and it was reviewed extensively. But almost all the reviews were negative. Both the right wing establishment and the left wing establishment – both liberals and conservatives attacked the book. Maybe the most vicious attack was from William Buckley's magazine – they wrote a horrible review of the book. And that represented the kind of the religious conservative attitude towards *Atlas Shrugged*. And of course The New York Times – from the left – slammed the book. The reviews were very negative.

But readers liked it.

YB: The book sold and many many people read the book. But very very few people stood up. Particularly influential people – well-known people – stood up and declared their sympathies or their agreement with the book.

And Ayn Rand I think was disappointed by the fact that almost no businessmen – almost no leading businessmen stood up and said – yes this is exactly it. So that was a huge – I think – disappointment at the time.

Was it realistic to think businessmen would stand up?

YB: This book makes businessmen as heroes – it presents them as heroes for the first time in history and yet very few businessmen stood up at the time. That's changed. I mean, people are much more open today about liking the book.

Many, many more CEOs, movie stars, sports figures are open and public about the fact that *Atlas Shrugged* had an enormous influence on them. That they loved some of the characters. They like the book.

I think in academia even – you know in 1957 there were no professors really who sympathized with the philosophy, agreed with the philosophy, talked the philosophy. Today there are several dozen who do. There are sixty programs at least where Ayn Rand is being taught at major universities in the country.

So I think a lot has changed. There's much more openness and the viciousness with regard to attacking the book, which was expressed by again both the right and the left, a lot of the edge has gone from that. So you see the attacks are softer and yet a lot more people have positive things to say about the book than ever before. And I think it's just accumulated.

I mean millions of people now have read *Atlas Shrugged* – a significant number of them view that experience as very positive. And a significant number of those people – the book actually – they will say the book has changed their lives – had a profound impact on them.

And some of them take the ideas presented in the book – the philosophical ideas seriously enough to call themselves objectivists or sympathizers with objectivism.

One of our other interviewees said that it takes a minimum of fifty years to effect social change. Do you see Atlas and Rand's ideas in general as having reached some kind of 'critical mass' after fifty years in print and now the ideas are beginning to take hold?

YB: Maybe even it had a profound impact on them – maybe even forgot, and went into business, made a lot of money, became successful, maybe reread the book now or five or ten years ago and said – wow, yeah this is the book that really changed my life. Well now they're in a significant position, the book is kind of a thread throughout their life. They don't feel embarrassed about it. They don't feel like they have to apologize for it. They're willing to stand up and speak. And there's millions of people who have read the book as well so there's an audience.

I think in '57 it was so revolutionary – businessmen in the '50s and '60s might have picked up the book and read it and said – yeah I agree with a lot of this, but wow this is kind of scary stuff – and it's philosophical and I don't know if I agree with all of this.

What was Rand's goal in writing Atlas Shrugged?

YB: Ayn Rand was on a quest to portray what she called the ideal man. She wanted to portray these grand heroes. John Galt of course is the culmination of that, but Dagny and Rearden and Francisco and all the lead characters in the book really all serve that purpose of portraying what a heroic life can be. And I think that's the aesthetic purpose of writing *Atlas Shrugged.*

It is an incredibly ambitious project. Because here she is – she's trying to create real heroes, real characters and at the same time present an earth shattering brand new philosophy that over-turns the philosophical ideas common in western civilization for 2,000 years.

Thinking about it, it was quite a tour de force for an author. Wasn't it?

YB: Certainly the morality is a brand new conception. And at the same time make an interesting story and I think she pulls it off. And that is what makes this one of the great novels of all time – is the fact that there is this really interesting – really profound aesthetic experience and at the same time a whole philosophical world opens up. And you read it and you go – wow – what a mind – because the philosophical ideas and the way she integrates – she does such a brilliant job integrating the philosophical ideas into the plot. So that the bad ideas are reflected in bad characters and bad outcomes.

For example?

YB: There's a famous scene where the train is heading towards a tunnel and everybody's heading towards their death – and she puts thoughts in each person on the train's mind – that show some level of responsibility for what's about to happen. There are no innocent victims here. But it's not direct responsibility, it's indirect responsibility through – you know – errors and bad ideas that they're holding that are gonna lead to their death.

And it's kind of a metaphor for all of us. The world is heading towards this cliff – or this country is heading towards this cliff – we're gonna fall off of it. The ideas that drive every individual out there – and they could be the nicest, most pleasant person – but they are being driven by evil ideas – that are gonna drive them and their kids and their grandkids off the cliff – and they're gonna wake up one day and say – what happened. And *Atlas Shrugged* explains – it's the ideas that you held – necessitated this falling off a cliff – this economic, political, cultural disaster that we are heading towards.

We're seeing 'Who is John Galt?' on bumper stickers and tee shirts now too. What has that question come to represent?

YB: Who is John Galt? It's a great literary device and you can see that it's held up by the fact that so many people today are using that phrase in tea parties – there were big signs – you know – who is John Galt? People who don't necessarily even understand completely what the novel is about use that.

It's a term in a sense of frustration of the world is coming to an end – you know – things are falling apart. What do we do about it? How do we – you know – we don't understand it. And John Galt does understand it. It's a slogan out there for those people who are frustrated by what's going on in the world around them and are looking for something better.

Here is a person who lives his life fully for himself – being rationally self-interested – a long-term rational thinker. And yes – all of us can be John Galt.

Without pain or fear or guilt.

YB: Without pain or fear or guilt.

Ayn Rand confirmed your description of Atlas Shrugged as a non-naturalistic romantic novel when she said she'd created an entire world as a backdrop for her novel. The world of Atlas Shrugged seems almost like a parallel universe to this one, doesn't it?

YB: The book was written in '57 and it's very much of its time in the sense of railroads, airplanes, automobiles, what is going on and the kind of world that's being projected in terms of threats. There are no Islamic terrorists in Atlas so it *is* dated in that sense. But on the other hand the basic conflicts, the conflict between collectivism and individualism, between altruism and self-interest, between capitalism and statism, all those conflicts still exist today. The collectivists might not be communists, they might be communist-lites or they might be Islamists. But they're collectivists. You might not have a communist bloc like back then with the socialist countries of Europe but you've got something very similar around the world with the direction the United States is going.

You might not have railroads dominating but you have banks being nationalized. Airlines kind of semi-nationalized after 9/11 bailing out and everything. So a lot of what happens in the book, it doesn't take much to see what's happening today even if the industry isn't exactly the same, even if the type of characters are not exactly the same.

Could Atlas be described as an allegory or morality play?

YB: I don't know if you'd call it a fable or certainly a morality play at some point but the theme as she defined as the role of man's mind in human life, in the necessity of using one's reason to survive, and the virtue of using one's reason to survive, that's all around us. You see the advocates of unreason whether it's faith or emotion, you see them all over the place and you see reason being shunted and as a result you see the world go crazy.

In a sense, Atlas is about 'everything.'

YB: At some level, *Atlas Shrugged is* about everything. It's about every aspect of our life, everything that's happening from politics to sex. It really covers every aspect of human life and that's part of its genius. On the other hand, it's a mystery. The world is falling apart. Somebody is kind of behind it. There's a man in the background causing the leading minds of the country to disappear. And nobody knows why and part of the book is a mystery story about why he's doing it. And it's a mystery story about what's really, what's the underlying cause of the decline of America, of the destruction of the world around them – in the book. But all that is true in reality today. The same causes that cause America to decline in the book are causing America to decline today.

Which characters hold most appeal for you?

YB: I have to say that when I first read the book, the character that most appealed to me was Eddie Willers because I never thought of myself as a John Galt or Dagny or Rearden. I was sixteen when I read the book. I thought I was a pretty good person but nothing exceptional and Eddie Willers just strikes that kind of balance. He's incredibly honest, thoughtful; he's always trying to figure out what's going on around him. He stands up for the heroes. He stands up against the villains. To me he represents kind of the everyday man who is a hero and I still sympathize and identify with Eddie Willers in that book.

But there's so many wonderful characters. I love the pirate, the swashbuckling type who goes out there and fights for justice. That has always appealed to me.

The villains in Atlas are great, aren't they? And memorable.
YB: Even the way they look. The villains look like villains and you – we all have people in the world we associate with the villains and we associate potentially with the heroes.

Whom do you associate with the villains? For example, if you were casting the movie…
YB: I would love to have Barney Frank play Wesley Mouch. (laughs) Barney Frank is the ideal representation in my mind for—or James Taggart. He can pick and choose between the two.

If you were casting the heroes, whom would you pick? For Dagny?
YB: Oh, I don't know (laughs- thinks) I don't know, Barbara Stanwyck. It needs to be a powerful woman. It needs to be a woman who has real charisma on stage. She needs to be sexy but in a muted way. For example as much as I like the way that Angelina Jolie looks, I don't see Angelina as Dagny. She doesn't have that strength and that power. She doesn't look like a businesswoman. She looks like a sexy woman on stage who can play a lot of characters but I'm not sure that Dagny is the right one. So it needs – it needs to be someone with real presence and real character and strength.

What about Galt?
YB: Ideally John Galt will be played by an unknown actor, by somebody we don't associate in my mind with a lot of other characters. If it was Brad Pitt, let's say, and there was talk about that at one point, Brad Pitt is associated in my mind with so many other characters. You want somebody clean, fresh, a new character with that kind of face that she describes in the novel.

Rearden?

YB: Russell Crowe. He's powerful, strong, torn, he can portray those kind of emotions. People criticize Ayn Rand for having cardboard characters, which boggles my mind. Rearden is so torn internally and it's expressed externally. He feels duty bound to his wife but he really deep down hates her and he doesn't know that. He thinks sex is a bad thing but he's such a passionate lover. And Dagny is so torn. You need an actor who can pull that off and I think Russell Crowe can probably do it.

Francisco?

YB: Francisco's a tough one because he has to have a Latin flare to it. You need someone who has that joie de vie – the love of life that Francisco just projects and again it might have to be somebody young or new and he has to have this grander than life presence on screen.

If Ayn Rand were here today, what events or circumstances do you think would most prompt her to say 'I told you so?'

YB: The novel *Atlas Shrugged* is so predictive of what's going on today. I think one of the things she told us in the novel but then she told us in the non-fiction that she wrote is that regulation breeds regulation. Controls breed controls. When a government program fails, when a government regulation fails the answer is not to do away with that regulation but to load up new regulations on top of it. And we've seen that over the decades, really the decades.

Bank regulations caused the S&L crisis. The solution is more regulations which caused another crisis and of course now the solution is let's just nationalize them all. Why bother with the regulations?

Student loans, there are not enough of them so the government gets involved so it distorts the whole market for student loans. Now Obama wants to do away with the middleman, the government's just going to give the student loans directly. Which raises the cost of tuition which is going to cause ultimately who knows what? You know, caps on universities.

Even more fundamental is the idea of altruism, the idea that self-sacrifice is the virtue – it's the essence of morality – has to lead to statism. For decades, libertarians and conservatives have pretended that morality doesn't matter. As long as we argue that capitalism works, that capitalism creates the most growth, the most prosperity – which it does – and there's been plenty of proof.

What Ayn Rand told us is it doesn't matter and she wrote about this extensively all the way back in the 1930's. It doesn't matter. People don't learn from experience. They don't learn from what happened in the past. People are shaped by their ideas, by their philosophy and libertarians and conservatives want to ignore that philosophy. Conservatives in particular actually believe in the morality of self-sacrifice and the morality of altruism. She said as long as you believe in those ideas, it doesn't matter what you advocate in economics, we will get more and more and more statism. And it could manifest itself in a variety of different ways but governments will grow and freedoms will shrink.

And that has all come true. You see it now with the health care debate – need – the fact that I need something like health care is now perceived as a right. And that comes directly from the morality of altruism, the morality of need, the morality of self-sacrifice. We're all expected to sacrifice our gold-plated insurance policies and healthcare for the sake of those who don't have any for whatever reason it is. We're expected to sacrifice our wealth for the sake of businessmen who squandered their wealth away and need to be bailed out.

The idea of self-sacrifice is so much more entrenched today in the culture because nobody's challenged it except Ayn Rand.

Define 'statism' in the context you're using it.

YB: Statism is the broad concept that underlies communism, social-ism and fascism and all the isms that put the state at the center.

The idea is this: who owns your life? Do you own your life? And if you say yes then that's individualism. Individualism is the idea that each individual is - his life belongs to him. He has the right to life, liberty and the pursuit of happiness – his happiness. His own happiness. Statism is the idea that the state owns you in some sense, that you belong to the collective. And the collective under communism could be the proletariat. The collective under Nazi-ism could be the race. The collective under statism is the state. And you saw that in this last campaign: McCain versus Obama. Where McCain said country first…statism. Where Obama said – in a sense -country first…just a different kind of country. But they both shared this in common. They both advocated not for individualism – not individuals pursuing their own life of liberty and happiness, but individuals as part of a group with a duty and responsibility primarily being for that group. Again, this notion of sacrifice for what? For your neighbor, for the state, for some kind of group.

What's behind statism that makes it attractive to so many? Is it fear of having to go it alone?

YB: They impart fear to encourage us to become statists, to abro-gate our rights and they do that by demonizing individualism. By demonizing capitalism, demonizing freedom and you saw this in this financial crisis. 'It's the bankers!' It's always been the bankers, for two thousand years. It's always the bankers whenever there's a crisis. But it's free markets, it's capitalism, they're at fault.

And all you have to do is peel off the layers, just one layer and you can see government everywhere in this financial crisis. You know, from Freddie and Fannie to low interest rates to all the reg-ulations that are involved. But they don't let you peel that off. They want you to believe that businessmen are inherently evil that people left alone do really, really stupid things, they need to be taken care of. And that's true of both Republicans and Democrats. There's no difference there. Democrats are somewhat worse but both share this view.

And it really comes from Original Sin. The original sin is to be selfish. And selfishness we've been taught is evil. It's evil because it leads to Bernie Madoff. It leads to bad things. And what Ayn Rand says is no. True selfishness, true self-interest is about making the most out of your life – living the best, most rational life you can live and that disqualifies the Bernie Madoffs and the crooks and the thieves and the short-term thinkers.

But they want to demonize self-interest. All philosophers, almost all philosophers at least since Aristotle with a few exceptions here and there have demonized the individual, have demonized self-interest. Think of Hobbes – we're wolves, if we're left alone we would tear each other apart. That's the opposite of Galt's Gulch. That's the opposite of Ayn Rand's views of rational, heroic, individuals living life to the fullest and trading with one another. Treating one another with respect as traders, not as enemies, not as opponents.

Are we being extorted philosophically?

YB: Well we *are* being extorted. They're using our morality against us. So they're telling us morality is about self-sacrifice. You can never live up to it.

Think of it this way. Mother Theresa is the moral ideal, right? Abandoning your middle class life, abandoning all your passions, all your views and going to pursue a duty. Not to pursue your happiness. Mother Theresa was very, very clear. She did not want happiness out of what she was doing. She was doing this out of a pure sense of altruism. She was doing this out of a pure sense of duty and she went off to Africa to help the poor. That's the moral idea. How many of us are going to be Mother Teresas – none of us.

So what do we feel? We all go out there, most Americans go out there and pursue a career and try to make as much money as we can, try and feed our family, buy a nice television, buy a nice home, live life as much as we can. But there's this tug, right? We're not Mother Theresa and if we were really noble, really good people, we'd be Mother Teresa.

So what does that inculcate in us? Guilt. And most Americans feel this guilt – they're selfish most of the time. Most Americans live for themselves 90 percent of the time. But they feel guilty about that because they are not living up to their moral ideal. And Ayn Rand rejects that.

Live for yourself, that is the moral ideal. Living for your life, for your happiness, making the most out of what your life is. And that involves people that you love. That is what morality is about and as long as morality is about other people, about self-sacrifice, Americans are going to feel guilty and then politicians are going to use that guilt.

If you know that you should be giving more of your salary to the poor, but you know what, you can't be bothered because you want to buy a big TV so you're not going to do it. When the tax man comes around or the politician comes around and says look we're just going to take a little bit more of your income – which you should be doing anyway out of your own free will. We're just going to take a little bit more to give to them – look at them, they're starving, they're really hurting, how can you say no? You have no moral, ethical foundation to object to higher taxes, to more regulations to more controls because you know deep down that you're guilty of not helping your fellow man enough. That's what altruism and the morality of sacrifice does to people. And that's what makes us so vulnerable to the intellectuals and the politicians that want more and more and more of our lives, more and more and more of our sacrifices.

It's ironic, isn't is that, in places where people are less free, their economic hardship is proportionately greater.

YB: To a large extent, the people who are in trouble, who are poor, who don't have health care, that is a consequence of government intervention. There's always going to be people that are less well off than other people. You're always going to be able to use that guilt argument. And one of the outcomes of that is that the more you redistribute, the more you control, the more you regulate, the bigger that class under poverty is going to become. The more people are going to lack the proper health care and so on.

So instead of reversing the process and saying what we need is freedom, we never do that and why is it we never do that? Why is it we always go in the direction of more and more and more control? Why is it that regulation breeds regulation? It's cause morally we can't come to grips with the idea of just leaving people alone. That is offensive to altruism. And that's the real challenge of *Atlas Shrugged*. *Atlas Shrugged* is a challenge to the morality of altruism that says no. What is moral is to leave people alone and to live for yourself and to make the most out of your life. And if somebody else doesn't make the most out of their life, that's their problem, not yours.

If we're going to become freer in this country, that is the real revolution. It's not a political revolution, it's not replacing Republicans with Democrats or Libertarians, whatever. It's a moral revolution. We need a revolution in this country where people accept as moral living for their own lives and reject as evil the notion that they should sacrifice their lives for others.

In that sense Objectivism is as much a religion as a philosophy, isn't it?

YB: Ayn Rand called her philosophy – she called it Objectivism – but she called it a philosophy for living life on earth. Living life in this reality, in this world. It's a realistic philosophy given what human nature is and given the reality that's around us. It's about living. It's about succeeding. It's about prospering and making the most out of one's life and her whole ethic, her whole ethical theory is saying: given human nature, given the way human beings function, given who we are, what are the principles, what are the moral principles, the principles for action that are best suited for human nature and that's why for her the prime A is reason. It's rationality because everything, every value around us, everything that we as human beings attain, we attain through thought. Through using our minds, through using reason, through understanding the world around us, understanding the reality around us and then applying our mind to solving problems and making our lives better. And to her, therefore, rational self-interest is the essence of morality.

Can this be simplified to a moral choice between life and death?

YB: The core of Ayn Rand's ethics is this alternative that we all face. We all face, like every living being out there, that we can either live and prosper or die. And dying doesn't necessarily mean we literally physically die but we live a half-life, we live a life not lived, we die slowly if you will. And that's basically an alternative we all face. And we face that alternative in every choice that we make. Political choice but also in the choice of a spouse, in the choice of a career. Are we living life fully and...

If you really think about it, most religions are on the death premise. Life sucks – it's just to be lived. Because the real kicker is in the afterlife and you see it most passionately and concretely in Islam now, in the fundamental Islamists who want the 72 virgins and are willing to kill themselves. But really that's true of – if you read Luther or if you read Calvin – to them this life it's horrible, it's scum, it's terrible. You do what you do to get by. The real pay off – and the reason to be good, the reason to be good because you're not going to be paid off in this life, you're not going to be happy in this life, doesn't matter. It's 'cause you get to the after life. And Ayn Rand rejects all of that. Her philosophy is about living in this world and making the most of it. And the whole idea is life can be exciting. Life can be fun. You can achieve happiness and that should be the purpose of life.

It's hard to imagine primitive man who spent every waking moment just trying to survive being torn by a philosophical choice like that, is it? In a life or death situation, he was going to choose life every time, wasn't he?

YB: I don't think there's any difference between the cavemen who faced life or death every single choice – the sabre tooth tiger was right there and they had to make a choice – and the choices we're making right now in modern times. Death for the caveman was faster. Today many people make the wrong decisions and die slower but the consequence is the same.

What a waste. Life can be so fulfilling, so exciting, so rich. And to watch human life wasted and withered away, that is a real tragedy.

How much is capitalism responsible for the world's current financial woes?

YB: It is so ludicrous to blame capitalism. It's as if three years ago we had capitalism and it failed. What does Capitalism mean? It means free markets. Free of what? Well free of regulations. Capitalism means free markets, where the government's not involved. And the question is with the mortgage markets, the banking markets, Wall Street – are they free of government intervention? Is that what happened? That these purely free markets failed?

As soon as you dig a little deeper, you find that there's no real free market in the United States. We have a Federal Reserve that prints money and has a monopoly over the printing of money and determines interest rates. Free markets don't have government prices, government controlled prices. They have free market where prices get set by supply and demand, which is what would happen with interest rates. And when the fed sets interest rates too low which is well below the rate of inflation, what does that encourage people to do? Well that encourages people to borrow money so people borrow money like crazy. And yet now we ask: why were so many people who couldn't afford their homes getting mortgages?

Is that just capitalists gone crazy? Well it turns out there was things like Freddie and Fannnie and the United States has housing policy and they have all kinds of entities that encourage banks like the community reinvestment act, the federal home loan banks, all these things that encourage bankers to lend and potential home owners to borrow money in order to own a home. It's the American dream and it's the role of government to give us that dream.

What about banks? How much are they responsible?

YB: Banks are the most regulated business in the United States. You know you can't start a bank in the US without the regulators approving the management team, approving the business plan, approving who provides the capital and how much capital is provided. All of that is determined by the regulators. It's ludicrous. The thing that I find interesting is here we have this crisis that has occurred in the most regulated space in the economy – and capitalism is blamed for it. It just shows that people don't look at reality. Their concepts are being formed by their ideas. They hate capitalism. They reject capitalism because capitalism is about self-interest and the pursuit of self-interest. They know self-interest is bad therefore capitalism is bad so that when bad things happen, it must be capitalism.

You also saw that after Enron and all those scandals. You know it was interesting. Nobody points this out but all those scandals – Worldcom, Enron, they all happened in specific industries: in the telecom space, in the utility space, in industries that are heavily regulated. You didn't have an Enron or a Worldcom in the software space, the computer industry. You had them in these regulated spaces because the people who are going to be most corrupt are the people who deal the most with politicians and they need to buy these politicians off. So for example, when Enron failed, what was the response? The response wasn't let's put the crooks in jail. When Enron failed the response was all businessmen are crooks. We just happened to catch these ones. So what we need are better mechanisms to catch the crooks and so we passed Sorbanes – Oxley. And I'd like to remind the Republicans that Sorbanes Oxley passed when the Republicans controlled the senate and the house and it passed the senate 97 to 0. Not a single republican voted against it. And it was basically a bill to penalize all CEO's for the crimes of a few CEO's and that is a consequence of this notion that we don't trust self-interest because we don't trust businessmen because what are businessmen after? They're after profits and they're after their own self-interest. And therefore if they're after profits and their own self-interest, they must be crooks.

Have you seen the recent IMF report that showed that corporations with the heaviest lobby presence in Washington were the least profitable and most likely to fail?
YB: If you look at all the bailouts, this isn't new. Citibank is the largest bank in the US – at least before this catastrophe – but Citibank is a bank that's been bailed out every single decade since the 1970's. It went bankrupt in the seventies and got bailed out. In the eighties it was bailed out because of Latin American debt, and we bailed out Mexico in order to bail out Citibank. In 1991, Citibank went bankrupt because of commercial real estate and we bailed them out. And we bailed them out twice now. So every decade. And what do the bailouts do? They perpetuate bailouts because people start behaving like we're going to be bailed out and if we're not going to be bailed out, we better send somebody to Washington – our Mouch, right? – send our man to Washington to make sure next time we're the ones who get bailed out.

So what you get is more and more lobbying and the firms that are going to lobby the most, that are gonna provide the politicians with the most benefit, guess what, they're the ones that are going to be bailed out.

There's a famous story about Microsoft. Microsoft, before the justice dept. went after them, didn't spend a dime on lobbying. They had no lobbyists in Washington. Today Microsoft spends tens if not hundreds of millions a year in lobbying because they saw what happens when they didn't have their man in Washington.

Sounds like a scenario direct from the pages of Atlas Shrugged – 'the Aristocracy of Pull.'

YB: In *Atlas Shrugged*, there's this concept of aristocracy of pull. These are the people who manipulate – they're not aristocrats by birth, they're not aristocrats just because they're wealthy. They're aristocrats because they control the politicians. And the politicians can use rules and force and guns and regulations and laws to benefit these crony businessmen. And you're seeing it today. Look at Jeffrey Immelt at GE. Look at some of the things that Wall Street has done. This clearly what we're seeing today in America is an aristocracy of pull.

Have we lost the concept of 'cause and effect' in this country?

YB: One of the things that Atlas really points out is that there are causes for all the things that we see out there. And today, we pretend that we can wish things into existence. If we want an economy with jobs, we'll just wish it into existence. So we call it a stimulus plan, right? We'll take money from one pocket and put it into another pocket and pretend – as long as everybody's playing along – we pretend that we created….jobs are caused by private investment. Jobs are created through profits, through people making money by values that they create, wealth that they create. That makes it possible to create jobs. Just taking money from some people and giving it to other people doesn't create jobs. You lose here, you gain here, at best you're at the same level you were before and worst you've actually lost some stuff because of the inefficiency.

But we've lost that concept of what cause is. We just want to have the effects and how are we gonna get the effects? Are we gonna pray for them? You know and the whole Obama campaign was like that, right? Hope for change. How? What kind of change? What kind of hope? Why should we hope? It doesn't matter. It's just all emotion. And *Atlas Shrugged* was about the role of reason in human life. We're living through a world where reason has been abandoned. Cause and effect has been abandoned. And where prayer and wishing and emoting are the most powerful tools.

So economic 'tweaks' by politicians or treasury people don't really work, do they?

YB: Yeah, there's this notion that politicians and bureaucrats, a Tim Geithner or Barney Frank can just tweak things and make things better and adjust and the fact is that jobs get created by the Bill Gates of the world, they get created by the Steve Jobs of the world, by the Thomas Edisons of the world. By great inventors, entrepreneurs, wealth creators, by really each one of us going out there and doing our job, creating value as best we can, by being productive. That's how jobs get created.

Is mysticism taking hold in our society?

YB: A lot of this emotionalism is driven by mysticism. What do we get when we reject reason? When we reject reason what are we left with? We're left with emotion but emotions are not quite enough of a guide for action so we need to frame our emotions in nice little packages and some of the packages are religious packages and some of those packages are new age packages. Some of those packages are just Obama, right? This worshipping of an individual. But they're all about some form of mysticism. And mysticism as we know is on the rise. We're seeing declines in certain established religions. The general sense of rejection of science and reason and human rationality – that is prevalent and that is really the source of all our problems and what will lead this country into decline unless we manage to reverse it. It is reason, only reason and rationality that can save us.

Is Objectivism as a philosophy being accepted today in academia?

YB: Objectivism is not getting the respect it should be getting in academia. But it's getting a lot more respect that it did five years ago, ten years ago, certainly twenty years ago. So objectivism is clearly gaining respect, gaining momentum, gaining credibility. We now have for the first time ever a chair in the philosophy of objectivism in a major university, at the University of Texas in Austin. In the philosophy department. So here's a chair in a philosophy department - it's one of the leading philosophy departments in the world. They're studying Ayn Rand. There are fellowships for the study of objectivism at other top philosophy departments, the University of Pittsburg, the University of North Carolina at Chapel Hill. So her ideas are being studied for the first time in serious university settings. In a way that, again, even ten years ago was unimaginable.

Ayn Rand is being taught in high schools today. We believe there are about a million kids reading Ayn Rand in high school, whether it's Anthem, Fountainhead or *Atlas Shrugged,* one of the programs the institute engages in is any teacher out there who wants to teach Ayn Rand, we'll give them a classroom set of books, teacher guides, lesson plans and the books themselves, all for free. We ship about 350,000 books a year to teachers who want to teach Ayn Rand.

So the exposure Ayn Rand has in the culture is unprecedented. It's never been like this, she gets more respect than she ever has, but I think this is just the beginning. Project ten, fifteen years out we will have had 15-20 million kids who will have read Ayn Rand in high school, we'll have two, three, five hundred programs in universities where she's being taught, she will be everywhere in the culture and I think finally she will get the respect that she deserves.

-Irvine, California 2009

Photographs of Ayn Rand courtesy
of Leonard Peikoff and Ayn Rand Institute Archives.

Writer/Director Chris Mortensen is a television producer and documentary filmmaker whose many programs have appeared in the U.S. and Europe. His biographies of Field Marshall Bernard Montgomery, Hermann Goering and John Paul Jones have aired internationally. In the U.S. his documentary subjects have ranged from American Gangsters to the HIV crisis to the Iraq War to Professional Wrestling; from the CIA to Halle Berry to the Suez Canal. His programs have appeared on A&E, History Channel, ESPN, Fox Sports, Lifetime, Discovery, BET, TV One, et al. He lives in Los Angeles.